THE
REPORTER
WHO KNEW TOO MUCH

The Mysterious Death of What's My Line
TV Star and Media Icon Dorothy Kilgallen

MARK SHAW

A POST HILL PRESS BOOK

The Reporter Who Knew Too Much:
The Mysterious Death of *What's My Line*
TV Star and Media Icon Dorothy Kilgallen

Library of Congress Cataloging-in-Publication Data

Shaw, Mark 1945– author.
    The reporter who knew too much : the mysterious death of What's my line
tv star and media icon Dorothy Kilgallen / Mark Shaw.
    Franklin, TN : Post Hill Press, 2016. | Includes bibliographical references
and index.
    LCCN 2016044326 (print) | LCCN 2016051642 (ebook) |
    ISBN 9781682610978 (hardcover) | ISBN 9781682610985 (e-book)
    LCSH: Kilgallen, Dorothy. | Kilgallen, Dorothy—Death and burial. |
Journalists–United States–Biography. | Television personalities–United
States–Biography.
    LCC PN4874.K53 S53 2016 (print) | LCC PN4874.K53 (ebook) |
    DDC 070.92 [B] –dc23
    LC record available at https://lccn.loc.gov/2016044326

Cover Design by Quincy Alivio
Cover Photograph courtesy of Corbis Images
Interior Design and Composition by Greg Johnson/Textbook Perfect

Post Hill
PRESS

Post Hill Press
posthillpress.com

Published in the United States of America

"Wherever Dorothy Kilgallen goes fame precedes her, envy follows her and a crowd looks on. She is one of the communication marvels of the age."

—New York Post Daily Magazine, 1960

"Justice is a big rug. When you pull it out from under one man, a lot of others fall too."

—Dorothy Kilgallen

INTRODUCTION

On the blistering cold, windy day of November 11, 1965, nearly 3,000 mourners gathered inside the St. Vincent Ferrer Roman Catholic Church on New York City's Upper East Side. Another 1,500 huddled outside to pay respects to the famous *What's My Line?* television star, radio personality, celebrated journalist, revered investigative reporter and author Dorothy Kilgallen. Those present and millions across the country were still reeling from her death, an unexpected tragedy.

Honorary pallbearers included publisher William Randolph Hearst, Jr. and *What's My Line?* moderator John Charles Daly. Among the celebrities attending were actress Joan Crawford, Ed Sullivan, jazz pianist Bobby Short, film producer Joseph E. Levine, and actress Betty White. Flower arrangements were present from Bob Hope, Elizabeth Taylor, Richard Burton, and New York City Mayor John Lindsey whose sympathy card included the words, "Dorothy will be missed, not only by those who knew her, but also by the millions whose lives she reached daily." The day before the funeral, *United Press International* reported, "10,000 people walked past Dorothy Kilgallen's covered 'African mahogany' coffin for viewing at the Abbey Funeral Directors at 888 Lexington Avenue."

On November 8, Kilgallen, called by Ernest Hemingway, "One of the greatest women writers in the world," had been discovered dead in her lavish East 68th Street New York City townhouse. The NYC medical examiner issued a report stating Kilgallen, 52 years of age, died of "Acute Ethanol and Barbiturate Intoxication; Circumstances Undetermined." Despite this depiction pointing to accidental death, some believed Kilgallen committed suicide. However, a third possibility remained, that she was murdered, that the woman called "the most powerful female voice in America" was silenced because she was the reporter who knew too much.

The likelihood Kilgallen, one of the most courageous journalists in history, the larger-than-life true Renaissance woman and first female media icon whose accomplishments rival modern day legends like Oprah Winfrey, Barbara Walters, and Diane Sawyer, was the victim of foul play, must be considered. During the 1940s, '50s, and '60s, the college dropout-turned-feisty-journalist with the light-up smile, Irish wit, and high society manners who achieved phenomenal success in a man's world, made enemies ranging from show business celebrities to government officials to those in the underworld. Years of Kilgallen's scathing *Journal-American* "Voice of Broadway" columns, ones that could further or inhibit a career, triggered hatred from television, film and Broadway personalities experiencing her wrath. These columns, focused on the rich and famous, were syndicated by the Hearst chain to more than 200 newspapers across America with Kilgallen's loyal readers glued to every word.

Kilgallen also upset government officials through dogged investigative skills exposing secret documents before their official release. To those in the Mafia, she was a constant threat since Kilgallen wrote poison-pen *Journal-American* stories aimed at those who believed they were above the law including archenemy Frank Sinatra. These dangerous men knew CBS music producer Marlon Swing's statement was true: "[Dorothy] was a very powerful woman—people don't have any idea of the power and contacts she had."

More than anything, it was Kilgallen's strong belief in justice—her determined pursuit of the truth—that triggered condemnation, vows of revenge and death threats. Fellow *What's My Line?* panelist and Random House co-founder Bennett Cerf said, "A lot of people knew Dorothy as a very tough game player; others knew her as a tough newspaper woman. When she went after a story, nothing could get in her way."

By re-visiting the remarkable Kilgallen's trailblazing thirty-five–year journalistic career, it is possible to provide a plausible scenario as to how, and why, she died. The primary questions concern whether the justice Kilgallen demanded for those she wrote about was, in fact, denied her by police, public officials, and journalistic colleagues. In addition, whether there was a diabolical plan conceived to cover up Kilgallen's search for the truth about what arguably is the greatest murder mystery in history, the JFK assassination.

The answers lie in the numerous clues present at Kilgallen's death scene. Such clues should have triggered a full-scale probe since it is apparent based on new evidence uncovered by this author that Dorothy was screaming from the hereafter, "Investigate! Investigate! Investigate!"

CHAPTER 1

Any re-investigation of Dorothy Kilgallen's death begins where a crack detective would start—with a background check of the deceased. Learning about Kilgallen's roots and the part they played in her ascendance to celebrity status is essential to learning the truth about how she died.

Dorothy Mae Kilgallen was born during a violent rainstorm on July 13, 1913 while her family lived in a low-rent apartment at Garfield Boulevard and Morgan Street in Chicago. Her father Jim, a tadpole of a man also called "Jimmy" or "Kil," worked as a Hearst newspaper chain reporter and met her mother Mae, a lovely redhead, when she aspired to become a singer in Denver. The couple chose the name Dorothy since it meant "Gift from Heaven."

Kilgallen was sufficiently precocious that at age 15 months, she appeared in a local Elks Club production of *One Thing After Another*. Billed as "Tootsie," Kilgallen impressed the audience.

Kilgallen's interest in the creative world stirred when Jim and Mae took the youngster to a stage play. It starred an actor named Fred Stone, a circus and minstrel performer who became a vaudevillian and then appeared on Broadway. Kilgallen's enthusiasm for the stage drove her to begin writing, producing and starring in plays with neighborhood friends.

Despite her early interest in the theater, by the time she turned eight, Kilgallen yearned to be a reporter like her father. She admired his growing reputation as a tenacious journalist. Jim's editor said, "When he got hold of a story, Jim was just like a bulldog—he'd get his teeth in it and never let go."

Al Capone and Thomas Edison were among the celebrities Jim interviewed. He also covered the Rosenberg spy case, the McCarthy Hearings, and, as a correspondent during World War II, exposed existence of the Dachau prison camp in Germany.

Kilgallen loved to hear her father talk about his adventures, but she and sister Eleanor, six years younger than Dorothy, were disappointed he traveled so much. However, when Jim returned from one lengthy trip, he put smiles on their faces by giving them shiny dimes millionaire financier John D. Rockefeller had gifted him. Her dad also won Dorothy's heart by bringing a chunk of wood from actor Rudolph Valentino's coffin. Jim had carved the letters, "D.M.K" on it.

When Kilgallen recalled what impressed her most about her father, she noted other fathers in her neighborhood may have had more money, but they worked in mundane jobs whereas her dad led an exciting life by tackling breaking stories of national prominence. No wonder Kilgallen argued with her mother when Dorothy insisted on becoming a reporter instead of obeying Mae's wish that she pursue a career as an English teacher. Mae pushed that career because of the good hours and summer vacation time. Dorothy's stubbornness led to several arguments.

The first significant defining moment in Kilgallen's life happened when Jim moved the family to the Flatbush section of Brooklyn, New York. Kilgallen started school in a red brick building, P.S. 119, located one block from their home. She was an A's and B's student. Nearby St. Elizabeth's Catholic Church provided religious instruction and the family regularly attended St. Thomas Aquinas Church on Sunday mornings.

When instruction could be set aside, Kilgallen spent much of her free time reading. The Elsie Dinsmore series written by Martha Finley between 1867 and 1905 became a favorite. For reasons unclear, Kilgallen bonded with the main character, a young Victorian girl raised by relatives.

Like Elsie, popular in her neighborhood, Kilgallen enjoyed friendships with several schoolmates. However, some were harsh. When she learned one girl called her "stuck up" even though she was not "even good looking," Kilgallen boasted, "I'll show you. Someday I'll be very famous and all of you will read about me."

The "not even good looking" comment may have been true at the time. Those who knew Kilgallen said she was of medium height and skinny like her father. She parted dark hair in the middle. She did not have full, attractive lips. One friend called her a "sweet" girl but another said she was "mousy." While Kilgallen was dealing with schoolmates, Jim continued reporting for the Hearst syndicated International News Service. Kilgallen trailed along, excited about living near New York City.

At her father's urging, the twelve-year-old Kilgallen began writing letters to newspapers. One she wrote to the editor of the *Brooklyn Eagle* was so special it became her first published work. This happened after a reader criticized Ramon Novarro, a Mexican-born silent screen legend at the time. Defending her idol, Kilgallen fired off a letter. The writing was professional enough that an *Eagle* editor thought an adult sent it. Instead of using her own name, Kilgallen signed the letter, "Dorothy Laurington."[1]

When the letter appeared in the newspaper, Kilgallen made copies and gave them to all her friends. Her father passed the newspaper around his office. The next day she visited him and received a round of applause. She liked the attention. She liked being special.

Kilgallen kept sending letters to the editor but despite her predictions of becoming famous, she gave no hint of stardom, at least through academic achievements. Her Erasmus Hall High School marks in English were dismal. She flunked French, Latin, and Physical Education.

Writing was a different matter. She excelled enough to become associate editor of *The Erasmian*, her school's literary magazine. What may be her first lengthy published work told the story of an English flier and his romance with an Italian peasant:

> When he flies away without her she tortures her dog to appease her bitterness. The flier returns later, tarries a while, then tries to sneak off without her again. This time the plane crashes, the flier is killed, and the girl, an evil glint in her eyes, walks off stroking the file with which she had cut the wires in his plane.

---

[1] There appears to be no specific reason Kilgallen chose this pen name. Perhaps she did not want to use "Kilgallen" for fear the editor might connect her with her father.

When writing did not consume her time, Kilgallen took the job as associate editor seriously. Bernard Malamud,[2] later to win both the National Book Award and the Pulitzer Prize for Fiction, submitted a novella to Kilgallen. She rejected his story as being "too depressing."

While dating fellow *Erasmian* editor, Princeton-bound John Woods, Kilgallen gained valuable training by observing her father's reporting skills. She visited his office regularly and enjoyed the daily chatter of reporters sharing stories with her. When she asked Jim, later described by revered writer Damon Runyon as "an editor's dream of a reporter," what the most important characteristic of a journalist should be, he said, "nothing was more important than the truth."

In July 1929, as temperatures sweltered in Brooklyn, Jim and the family weathered the stock market crash. Fortunately, Jim kept his job. His modest salary had not permitted investments. Regardless, Kilgallen witnessed sadness all around her. She commiserated with those families stung by the crash.

When Kilgallen celebrated her 16th birthday with a modest party, she invited friends whose families were suffering hard times. One girlfriend later said Kilgallen was "the best friend I ever had. She gave me a dollar her dad had given her for her birthday."

Meanwhile, Jim's dinner-table talk about his journalism adventures continued to fascinate Kilgallen. She was still an avid reader and peppered her father with questions about the headline stories of the day. In turn, he told Kilgallen and her younger sister Eleanor[3] of his exploits. Two of the stories focused on millionaires J. P. Morgan and John D. Rockefeller.

In 1930, despite an urge to join Jim's world of journalism, Kilgallen entered the College of New Rochelle located 25 miles from Brooklyn. Ursuline nuns were the educators. Kilgallen lived on campus and visited her parents on weekends. George Kuittinen, whom she dated, later described her as having

---

[2] Malamud recalled Kilgallen at the time as a "unique, tall, animated, immaculately dressed woman without a chin, very careful about her physical appearance. Though visibly adorned with rouge and lipstick, it was well-applied. She had a sense of her own importance."

[3] Eleanor Kilgallen became a casting director at *NBC* radio in the 1940s before launching a highly successful talent agency in New York City. Among her clients were Warren Beatty, Jack Klugman, Robert Redford, Jamie Lee Curtis, and Harrison Ford. Eleanor was 95 when she died in December 2014.

"fine and Irish skin—flawless porcelain; her eyes very large and blue. Though she was thin, her breasts were well-developed and her legs excellent."

Although Kilgallen's intentions toward a college education were sound, she became restless and wanted something more. In June 1931, Amater Spiro, the *New York Evening Journal's* city editor, provided the temptation. He agreed, as a favor to Jim, to give his eighteen-year-old daughter a two-week trial as a reporter. "I was still at college [but when] it came time to send a check for the next semester," Kilgallen said later, "I told my parents 'I don't want to go back. I want to be a reporter.'" Her mother objected, Kilgallen recalled, "because her idea of a female reporter was someone who drank whiskey straight, sat on desktops, swore, and had more mannish haircuts and clothes."

That two-week trial run turned into decades at the newspaper. From day one, Kilgallen immersed herself in the world of journalism. When possible, she accompanied reporters covering social and political events. However, the world of law most fascinated her. On a daily basis, she roamed the criminal courts, captivated by the human drama of trials where freedom and even life or death was on the line.

Kilgallen begged for assignments to important stories like her father covered. However, the newsroom was definitely a man's world and women were supposed to stay in the background and let the men undertake the crucial stories. Besides, Kilgallen was still a teenager even though she was more mature than her age indicated.

Undaunted, and to prove her worth, Kilgallen re-wrote an article published by one of her male colleagues without divulging her name. When the editor praised the re-write at a meeting and asked who wrote it, Dorothy proudly raised her hand.

To her good fortune, the newspaper editors became obsessed with front-page murder case headlines. Kilgallen leaped with joy when assigned her first murder trial. It involved the beating death of a girl her own age. When she handed in the story, the editor rejected it. She re-wrote it and submitted it again. He rejected it again. Five re-writes later, the story was published.

Those who underestimated Kilgallen's prowess as a competent reporter paid the price. She was tough-handed despite her young age. Building a

Dorothy Kilgallen wearing her favorite wide-brimmed hat.

reputation, she wrote sharp-edged stories including a headline-maker about a sensational Bronx case. It involved a woman charged with killing her philandering husband by lacing his chocolate pudding with arsenic. At the courtroom entrance, Kilgallen proudly displayed the New York Police Press Card she had earned.

Proof that Kilgallen had arrived as a newspaperwoman of stature despite her young age was an *Evening Journal* three-quarter page promotion:

> To read one of Dorothy Kilgallen's brilliantly written stories—it might be an interview with a famous politician or a gangster, it might be the current day by day reporting of a famous murder trial—one would immediately infer: Here is the writing of a veteran newspaper woman with a lifetime of experience in reporting.
>
> A glance at the picture above will show how far from the facts such an impression can be. For Dorothy Kilgallen is only 20-years-old… She is a modern up-to-the-minute woman reporter. With her versatile, sparkling writing and her far-beyond-her-years perception and power of observation, she can cover everything from a baby shower to a sensational police court trial.

CHAPTER 2

At age 21 in 1934, Dorothy Kilgallen covered the infamous Anna Antonio murder-for-hire trial. Prosecutors said the slight Italian woman paid drug dealers $800 to kill her husband, Salvatore. Motive: a $5,300 life insurance policy.

Kilgallen's front-page story announced the guilty verdict. She included quotes from those upset when the jury pronounced a death sentence for "Little Anna." Last-minute appeals to save her proved fruitless. Kilgallen reported the gory details of the Sing Sing prison electrocution.

Despite her youth and inexperience, *Evening Journal* editors praised Kilgallen's articles. Kilgallen was not only a gifted wordsmith, but more importantly, had a knack for understanding the legal system like a seasoned lawyer. Her storytelling acumen and talent for focusing on critical aspects of trials set her apart from other reporters. It caused those in the newsroom to realize Jim Kilgallen's daughter had a bright future.

As 1935 dawned with a frigid winter storm, Kilgallen got her big break when she was assigned to cover a murder case dubbed by the media, "The Trial of the Century." Prosecutors charged German-born Bruno Hauptmann with kidnapping and killing famed aviator Charles Lindbergh's son. Kilgallen sat directly behind Hauptman during one court session. After prosecutors entered into evidence the ladder used during the kidnapping, the baby-faced Kilgallen tapped Hauptman on the shoulder. She asked him about the ladder. Despite being impressed with her gumption, he told her his lawyers forbid him to talk to the press.

Kilgallen and her sister Eleanor relax at the swanky Beverly Hills, California, Copa Club (circa 1942).

Although pleased with Kilgallen's trial coverage, *Evening Journal* editors decided to head her in an alternative direction. Despite no experience, she began writing a newspaper column, *Hollywood Scene*. It mixed entertainment with serious issues.

While Kilgallen explored a new writing style for the column, she campaigned for a special challenge. After hours of urging, Kilgallen convinced her boss to enter her in the heralded "Race Around the World." Competitors were required to employ methods of transportation only available to the public during the globetrotting excursion.

Kilgallen's competitors for the trip were two New York newspaper reporters: Bud Ekins of the *World Telegram* and Leo Kieran of the *New York Times*. Displaying her resourcefulness, Kilgallen managed to obtain 16 visas and a passport in *two* days. Her only baggage was a converted hatbox and battered typewriter.

During the race, Kilgallen, who finished second to Ekins, was referred to as a "modern day Nellie Bly." Aware of the historical aspects of her

Dorothy Kilgallen, Bud Ekins, and Leo Kieran entering the "The Race Around the World."

adventure, Kilgallen wrote, "Nellie Bly, watch over me. You may be astonished at what you see—but, watch anyway."[1]

Flights on the German dirigible *Hindenburg*,[2] Nazi Swastikas visible on its sides, Pan America's China Clipper, and several other airlines permitted Kilgallen to make the trip in 24 days, 13 hours, and 51 minutes. Among the countries she visited were England, France, Germany, Italy, Greece, Egypt, Iraq, India, the Philippines, and China. When the *Hindenburg*

---

[1] Nellie Bly, the pen name for Elizabeth Cochrane, was a revered writer who invented a new type of investigative journalism and who at one point faked insanity to report on a mental institution from inside its walls. She was famous for an 1889 record-breaking trip around the world in 72 days.

[2] Ekins recalled the scene when Kilgallen arrived to board the *Hindenburg*: "She was in a big black limousine with detectives on both sides of her, and behind her were two or three newspaper trucks filled with bruisers from the circulation department. They made damn sure she got on the ship."

landed in Berlin, "250 Nazis were drawn up in military arrays to jockey it into her huge gray hanger."

Ever the pioneer, the young daredevil had become the first woman to travel around the world on commercial airlines. She was also the first female to fly across the Pacific Ocean. At one point the fearless Kilgallen[3] set a record for the fastest 5,000-mile span ever flown, Hawaii to New York City.

First Lady Eleanor Roosevelt[4] congratulated Kilgallen on her achievement. Women across America including famed aviator Amelia Earhart cheered the young reporter's feat. She was famous at last, just as promised early on with several newspapers lauding her willingness to carry the banner for women's rights by challenging the two men.

Soon after, Kilgallen wrote *Girl Around the World*, chronicling the amazing adventure. It was her first published book. She was only 23 years old.

In the Foreword called "A Tribute from Dorothy's Father," Jim wrote:

> I am proud of you. Not because you were a good newspaperwoman at 18. Not because you have become famous at 23 by flying around the world. I am proud of you because, now that your greatest journalistic achievement is over and the plaudits have died down, you are the same unspoiled girl you have always been. Today your future looms bright. I believe your success is assured…[You have given me] the thrill of a lifetime…[and] you proved you had what Damon Runyon termed 'moxie'—COURAGE.…

In the book, Kilgallen trumpeted her willingness to take chances. She wrote, "I'm a reporter who likes danger and excitement."

---

[3] Marguerite Mooers Marshall, a noted writer at the time, described Kilgallen in an article she wrote: "She is the most daisy-fresh globe-girdler I ever hope to see—and so much prettier than even the best pictures of her printed in the *Evening Journal*. Her little features are cut with cameo delicacy, her skin has the lucent pallor of white lilac, her Irish eyes are not only smiling, but sea-blue and black-lashed, her dark hair, parted in the middle, is arranged in a most artful series of curls and purrs—not a hair out of place."

[4] Mrs. Roosevelt wrote on White House stationery (October 26, 1936), "I have been so interested in your flight around the world with the men and even though I am sure you are disappointed in not being the first to arrive, I wanted to tell you that I was rather pleased to have a woman go! It took a good deal of pluck and it must have held a good many thrills. With congratulations and good wishes, I am. Very sincerely yours, Eleanor Roosevelt" with the signature in her own hand.

Enjoying her new celebrity, Kilgallen visited Hollywood to collect gossip about film and television for her *Evening Journal* column. In a prelude to her ever-widening media exposure, she appeared in the movie, *Sinner Take All.* It starred Bruce Cabot and featured him as a former newspaper reporter turned lawyer representing a family whose members kept "getting bumped off." Apparently, Kilgallen's acting ability was impressive enough that she screen-tested for a film role in *The Reporter.* When no offer came her way, she sulked over the rejection.

At Warner Bros., Kilgallen presented producers with a screenplay based on her around-the-world adventures as chronicled in *Girl Around the World.* It was produced as *Fly Away Baby* in 1937 starring Glenda Farrell as Kilgallen. She did not have a role in the comedy/adventure. The film credits included "Based on an idea by Dorothy Kilgallen."

Not yet 24, Kilgallen's résumé was ever blossoming. She not only was a respected reporter and a columnist for a major metropolitan newspaper but also an author with acting and film credits. To say that she had burst on the scene from virtually nowhere was an understatement. Louis Sobol, a fellow reporter at the *Journal-American*, wrote of Kilgallen's world at the time: "This slender, wide-eyed, deceivingly naïve in attitude and soft-spoken mannerisms female reporter was to herself mingling with a new set of characters—racket guys, grafters, phonies, creep janes, society fops, chorus girls, pimps, overdressed jezebels and their rent payers."

Sobel, commenting on Kilgallen's appearance at a theater opening, wrote, "Out of a streamlined, shiny chariot stepped a fragile, raven-haired honey…A thinnish youth with bat-ears and pop-eyes and a Tenth Avenue subdeb fought each other to be at her side. 'Willya sign this, Miss Kilgallen?' pleaded the boy thrusting out his soiled autograph album…" Sobel added, "She still goes to church on Sundays, blushes when profanity is set loose within her hearing, and walks away from obscene stories."

Meanwhile, the column titled "Hollywood Scene as Seen by Dorothy Kilgallen," (later changed to "As Seen in Hollywood by Dorothy Kilgallen") appeared in the *Evening Journal.* In 1937, that newspaper and the *New York American* merged into the *New York Journal-American*, an afternoon edition. Dipping into the entertainment world, a prize assignment permitted

Kilgallen to cover the wedding of FDR Jr. to Ethel Du Pont. She then traveled to England and attended the coronation of George VI. She also made her debut in London Society at various high-profile events.

During the Christmas holidays, a surprise announcement appeared in Hearst newspapers across the country:

> The first and only Woman Columnist Dorothy Kilgallen's Voice of Broadway Column Starts Monday. A Man's Job. Beginning Monday in the *New York Journal-American*, Dorothy Kilgallen will Report Daily on the Deeds and Misdeeds of Broadway. A Man's Job. But Dorothy has been doing a Man's Job and Doing It Better.

The new *Journal-American* column, "The Voice of Broadway," dealt with the news and gossip of the day, theater, politics, and crime. Kilgallen's main competition were all men—Walter Winchell, Ed Sullivan, Lucius Beebe, and Leonard Lyons.[5]

At the height of its popularity, the column appeared in 200 newspapers nationwide. Kilgallen's prominence as a woman reporter with spunk caused the audience for the column to increase weekly. At twenty-five, she was the only prominent female Broadway columnist. One magazine called her an "authentic celebrity."

The lofty status continued as her "Voice of Broadway" column became even more popular. Of significance was a column item she wrote in late summer 1939: "Richard Kollmar, *Knickerbocker Holiday* [Broadway show] baritone, gave a combination New Year's Eve and birthday party Saturday night, to which guests were asked to come in kiddie costumes."

Who was this man with such a strange sense of humor, Kilgallen wondered? She soon found out.

---

[5] Later, Kilgallen's friend, CBS producer Marlon Swing, said of her, "Dorothy developed her own style and forcefully went into the man's world. Her main focus was crime and heavy duty investigation."

CHAPTER 3

During the days that followed, Dorothy Kilgallen's "Voice of Broadway" columns favorably mentioned Richard Kollmar.

Then Kilgallen met the man who played "Boston Blackie" in the radio crime drama. It happened on a sunlit but chilly November 14, 1939 at Manhattan's Algonquin Hotel. Kilgallen later recalled that Richard, Broadway handsome, remarked about an unusual hat she was wearing. Conversation led to them realizing they both loved jazz bandleader Artie Shaw and his music. On their first date, that night, they went to hear Shaw and his band. Kilgallen swore, "It wasn't love at first sight" but after six dates the engagement was announced.

On April 5, 1940, the twenty-seven-year-old Kilgallen married the thirty-year-old graduate of the Yale Dramatic School turned singer and Broadway producer. After Richard appeared in the musical *Too Many Girls*, *Variety* called him "an exuberant comedian unspoiled by cleverness."

Among the 800 wedding guests were Tyrone Power, Ethel Merman, Walter Huston, and Milton Berle. Thomas Dewey, the 1944 Republican presidential candidate who lost to FDR, also attended. Kilgallen did not become Mrs. Richard Kollmar to the outside world. Instead, she kept her maiden name.

Meanwhile, Kilgallen's "Voice of Broadway" column continued to mix Broadway and Hollywood gossip with politics and crime news. Ed Sullivan, whose CBS variety program had become a big hit, was a constant target of

Richard Kollmar

Kilgallen's. Sullivan said she was jealous because he became a television star and she had not done so. Finally, the two rivals made peace.

Like Sullivan, Kilgallen, who scribbled notes for her column on matchbook covers, had become a true New York City celebrity. She even had a sandwich named after her at Reuben's, a noted delicatessen on East 58th Street. The cost was $1.10. It was 25 cents more than the "Ed Sullivan Sandwich." Nearly two decades later, the sandwich, described as "Tongue, Turkey, Broiled French Roll" cost $2.50. It was listed along with sandwiches named after Ginger Rogers, Jack Benny, Orson Wells, Jackie Gleason, Dean Martin, and Frank Sinatra. Frank's cost $2.15.

While Kilgallen continued to expand her reach, she and Richard lived on Park Avenue. The news-making couple welcomed the arrival of their first child, Richard Tomkins Kollmar II ("Dickie"). The announcement appeared in Maury Paul's "Cholly Knickerbocker" *Journal-American* column on July 11, 1941.

Meanwhile, Kilgallen added to her budding media empire. She hosted a *Voice of Broadway* radio program broadcast nationally. Her distinctive voice and easy manner made her a natural for delivering the entertainment news of the day.

Exposing her patriotic nature during the month when Winston Churchill launched his "V for Victory" campaign, Kilgallen sent FBI Director J. Edgar Hoover subversive material forwarded to her at the *Journal-American*. One note alleged that she played favors to the "Soviet Marxist Jews" through her "daily hate of Hitler." In her FBI file secured by this author through the Freedom of Information Act, Kilgallen was labeled, "flighty and irresponsible." Later, Hoover and the Bureau would learn a valuable lesson. She was neither.

In 1943, amidst the juggling of her various professions, Kilgallen delivered her second child, Jill Ellen Elizabeth Kollmar. Kilgallen's "Voice of Broadway" column was ever popular especially with the addition of a section called "Tops in Town." It recommended theatrical and club performances to readers. Ever-expanding her media presence, she penned an article for *Photoplay Magazine* titled, "The Ten Most Attractive Men in Hollywood." Humphrey Bogart, of whom Kilgallen wrote, "He represents love in bloom in a furnished room with fire escapes," finished first. Ronald Reagan was #3, while Cary Grant and Clark Gable were numbers 5 and 10, respectively.

Since Kilgallen's column appeared during the era without extensive television coverage or internet, people mostly relied on newspapers for their news and opinion. Kilgallen's visibility had made her a powerhouse.[1] From her lofty perch as a giant of the industry, she suddenly had the ability to influence a career in a positive or negative way with her words. All the while Kilgallen continued to be enamored with crime stories.

---

[1] Entertainer Bobby Short said of Kilgallen's influence, "She was tremendously powerful. People would kill to be in her column."

The 1944 trial of Wayne Lonergan fascinated Kilgallen, now 31. Prosecutors said he murdered his high society wife Patricia, heir to a beer fortune. A pair of silver candelabra was the alleged murder weapon.

Focusing on the wealth of the couple, Kilgallen became a daily visitor to the trial. As a preview to a knack for receiving inside information before or during trial, Kilgallen revealed a secretive defense strategy. It focused on the sordid past of Patricia's father, Bill Burton. This exclusive was one of many Kilgallen achieved. Sources knew they could trust her. They chose her instead of more seasoned reporters.

When the trial ended, Kilgallen reported the 35 years-to-life sentence for Lonergan. She wrote that his confession became the main reason for the conviction. Kilgallen added that it was a case "involving love, hate, jealousy, the scandalous behavior of the young 'cafe society'[2] set of New York, and a $7 million fortune."

Within months, Kilgallen was yet again increasing her media exposure. The opportunity arrived on the New York City scene in early April 1945.

To the delight of New Yorkers, "Breakfast with Dorothy and Dick" premiered on WOR radio. Airing Monday through Saturday starting at 8:15 a.m., the show was exactly what a *Variety* ad called it, "Homey as a Front Porch Rocker, Smart as a New Spring Bonnet." Showcased were Dorothy, husband Richard, the Kollmar children, butler Julius and the family's singing canary, Yasha (some reports called the canary Robin). The radio program remained on the air for 18 years, from 1945 until 1963.

Each program, one was hosted from the famous Plaza Hotel, began with the salutations, "Good morning, Darling," from Dorothy, with Richard responding, "Good Morning, Sweetie. Here we are at home in old New York ready to visit with our radio friends." At one point, the show was so popular those mailing the couple merely used the address "Dorothy and Dick, New York." They received the letters.

During the show, the family sat around the dining room table often-times in their pajamas. They chatted about the theater scene, celebrity

---

[2] *Journal-American* columnist Maury Henry Biddle Paul's connotation of the term "Café Society" was intended to describe New Yorkers who frequented tony night clubs and expensive restaurants.

parties, gossip du jour, and trendy Manhattan nightspots. During commercials, they pitched sponsor products. Kilgallen's friend, press agent Jean Bach called the twosome, "The original Mr. and Mrs. Radio."

On many programs, Richard and Dorothy described their exciting nightlife adventures at celebrity hangouts. These included the Copacabana, P. J. Clarke's, and the Stork Club. At the latter, a large photograph of Kilgallen, queen of the fast-paced New York City newspaper scene as well as a heavyweight media star, hung near the entrance.

The radio program was a huge hit even while Kilgallen was receiving hate mail. Those who wrote felt that because of her right-leaning politics she was too strong of an advocate in her "Voice of Broadway" columns. Kilgallen reacted to the critics by increasing the volume of her attacks on anyone she felt deserving of a good verbal spanking.

CHAPTER 4

"Breakfast with Dorothy and Dick" was front-page news in *Broadcasting: The Weekly News* magazine.

Beside a photograph of the cozy couple was the copy: "Kilgallen and Kollmar: They are headed for star heights as WOR's Man and Wife Team in Breakfast with Dorothy and Dick." Under the photograph were the words: "Even Radio's magic can only create them only infrequently, a hit man and wife team is a station's and sponsor's dream…. It stars two people who *make* news on an intimate ad-libbed-from-home that makes *sales*."

The cover story, paid for by WOR radio, insisted that the program had an audience of "300,000 home listeners" and "approximately 1,000,000 employed women." The reason: "Dorothy and Dick are wise in the audience-attracting gimmicks of the radio, newspaper and theatre world."

Extensive coverage of the New York City theatre scene in mid-1946 led to the designation of Kilgallen by *Variety* as "The First Lady of Broadway." Never one to rest on laurels, she hosted a second radio program called "Dorothy Kilgallen's Diary." On the short-lived show, she interviewed Broadway stars.

During the three years that followed, Kilgallen's star continued to shine. She had become a household word. When New Yorkers said, "Dorothy," people knew whom they meant. "Dorothy and Dick" became a daily regimen during the morning hours. In the afternoon, the "Voice of Broadway" column was a must read.

Meanwhile, Richard made his movie debut in the 1948 film *Close Up* starring Alan Baxter and Virginia Gilmore. He played a ruffian in the thriller about a newsreel photographer caught in a web of intrigue when he unwittingly photographs a Nazi fugitive in New York City.

In 1949, Kilgallen, now 36, appeared on the syndicated television show, *Leave it to the Girls*, akin to today's popular ABC television program, "The View." Along with five career-minded women, Kilgallen bantered about female challenges in a man's world. They delved into such touchy subjects as love, relationships, and business. Each connected to "the battle of the sexes." Viewers were impressed with Dorothy's drive toward winning, her need to succeed in every aspect of her life. Some viewed her demeanor and the tone of her newspaper columns as "bitchy." Nevertheless, her popularity rose through the program exposure.

A year later, the national spotlight shone even brighter on Kilgallen. She became a panelist along with actress Arlene Francis, Random House co-founder Bennett Cerf, and a rotating guest panelist on the CBS television game show *What's My Line?*[1] Each week, the panelists questioned contestants in order to determine their occupations.

Former radio personality John Charles Daly moderated as program host. A seven-story theatre on West 54th Street became the production site. Years later, it was the infamous Studio 54.

The program's openings varied from time to time. One show began with a series of question marks on the screen. The announcer then proclaimed, "Time now for everybody's favorite guessing game, *What's My Line?*" At this point, one of the panelists appeared. Then he or she would introduce fellow panelists with a cute quip before Daly made his appearance.

The Emmy-Award winning program featuring Kilgallen aired on CBS for the next 15 years. At its height of popularity, the show had a weekly audience of 25 million people. The women wore fancy gowns, expensive jewelry, and gloves on occasion. The men dressed in dark suits and bow ties. When a celebrity appeared trying to stump the panel, each panelist wore

---

[1] According to producer Gil Fates, *What's My Line?* "evolved from an idea from a program called *Stop the Camera*…the brainchild of Bob Bach with an assist from Martin Stone, the developer of TV's *Howdy Doody*."

What's My Line? stars: Dorothy Kilgallen, Steve Allen (not pictured), Arlene Francis, Bennett Cerf, and moderator John Charles Daly.

a blindfold to keep from indentifying the celebrity. They included Gloria Swanson, Lucille Ball, Joe DiMaggio, Willie Mays, Bob Hope, Donald Duck, Walt Disney, John Wayne, and Elizabeth Taylor, to name a few. Many of the programs are available on YouTube. One, featuring comedian Groucho Marks, has hundreds of thousands of hits.[2]

On the show, Kilgallen often wore a lavish string of pearls to accentuate an expensive dress, one in tune with the latest 5th Avenue boutiques. Her hair was always perfectly coiffed. Most times, her personal hairdresser Marc Sinclaire handled the chore.

Kilgallen's nails were brightly polished. Her make-up was just the right skin tone. It provided a steady glow to her facial features. "*What's My Line?*" she said later, "is almost like a license to steal. I love to play games and its

---

[2] Through the efforts of W. Gary Wetstein and the "*What's My Line?* Facebook Club," episodes of the program are featured on a WML Channel. Wetstein and his colleagues have also been responsible for preserving "lost" episodes of the show. A "Dorothy Kilgallen Facebook Page" also exists as a tribute to her.

all fun. I get to the studio about 9:30 [p.m.] for make-up because my skin is so light they have to put on a darker base and draw some eyebrows or something and I have to use darker lipstick. We all take it seriously though Bennett has his puns and Arlene is very witty and has the personality that goes with it."

As the series continued to terrific reviews, Kilgallen stood out since she was the tough questioner (some said she played "bad cop" to Arlene Francis' "good cop"). She played to win. Viewers recognized her as the panel member with the sharp tongue. Fans across the country, especially women, adored her. They admired Kilgallen's willingness to challenge male panel members and John Charles Daly. Comedian Steve Allen, who often appeared as a guest panelist, said of her, "Dorothy's job on the panel was to ask impertinent questions. She probably guessed more people's jobs than anyone else." Friend and CBS producer Marlon Swing, who knew of Kilgallen's prowess at charades, recalled, "Dorothy played to win but she was also a little girl playing games." A *New York Post Daily Magazine* article stated, "She played the game like a relentless prosecutor."

With Kilgallen's popularity rising by the day, her influence increased and she became more involved in social issues. In July 1950, the right-wing journal *Counterattack* published an anti-Communist book, *Red Channels: The Report of Communist Influence in Radio and Television.* The pamphlet-style book named 151 actors, writers, musicians, broadcast journalists, and others of note. They were listed in the context of purported Communist manipulation of the entertainment industry. Among them were Edward G. Robinson, Burgess Meredith, Lillian Hellman, Orson Welles, and Pete Seeger.

In her "Voice of Broadway" column, Kilgallen denounced the blacklist. She wrote the allegations were not predicated on "evidence of Communist sympathies" but instead "rumor and innuendo." At the same time, while defending the masses, she displayed her equal opportunity bashing skills. She criticized those with Communist leanings who keep saying they did not favor the party.

One column Kilgallen wrote alleged that Radio Free Europe was not "free" but instead influenced by subversive groups. This column triggered the CIA's interest in her. A subsequent dossier documented Kilgallen's less-than-cooperative attitude when contacted by CIA agents in search of a source for her column entry. She flatly refused.

During Kilgallen's meteoric rise to true stardom, husband Richard developed a roving eye with the ladies. This and his reluctance to hit the Broadway social scene caused Dorothy Kilgallen to seek "friend" escorts for her nights on the town. Regardless, the epitome of the modern day woman balanced three professional careers with motherhood when few, if any, professional women were doing so, spending as much time with her children as possible. Without question, Kilgallen, armed with a burning desire to succeed, had cracked the so-called "glass ceiling" before the term was even fashionable by overcoming any, and all, career obstacles a woman faced on a daily basis.

One escort she enjoyed was *WML?* producer Bob Bach, one of the originators of the program. He assisted with finding contestants and "mystery guests." All were celebrities attempting to stump the panel. Bach, raised in high-society Westchester and a schoolmate of Joseph, Jr. and John Kennedy, became a steady "date" for Kilgallen. Within a short time, Bach and his wife joined Dorothy and Richard on a trip to Paris.

Soon after, Kilgallen sought additional male companionship besides Bob Bach. She noted that on Christmas, 1951, singer Johnnie Ray burst on the national scene. His songs "Cry" and "The Little White Cloud that Cried" were smash hits. The double-sided record was the first one in history to occupy the top two spots on the Billboard charts. Only Gene Autrey's "Rudolph the Red Nosed Reindeer" rivaled Ray's success.

With a continuing eye toward the entertainment world as January 1952 dawned, Kilgallen noted that "Please Mr. Sun" became another of Johnnie Ray's hit records.[3] She reacted to her appreciation for his music by mentioning the crooner in her "Voice of Broadway" column writing, "A simply awful thing had happened to me. How am I going to say it? Goodness, it's too frightful really. (Steel yourself, girl. Get it off your bodice once and for all.) All right. Here it is. I've come to just love Johnnie Ray's record

---

[3] "Please Mr. Sun," "Cry," and "Walkin' My Baby Back Home," Ray's biggest hits, led to descriptions of his having what was called a "lachrymose, ranting style." This inspired several nicknames, among them "Prince of Wails," "Nabob of Sob," and "The Atomic Ray."

of 'Please Mr. Sun.' Now will anybody ever speak to me again?" Ray and his manager were thrilled at the endorsement. Any mention in Kilgallen's column was a home run for a celebrity.

While enjoying her continued visibility at NYC hot spots, Kilgallen decided to check Ray's performance herself. In April 1952, Ray appeared at the high-society Copacabana along with the "Famous Copa Girls." The billing also featured ventriloquist Jimmy Nelson, famous for his Nestlé chocolate commercials featuring Farfel the dog. Along with Kilgallen, celebrities who flocked to the Copa included Frank Sinatra, mobster Frank Costello, allegedly the Copa's true owner through a front man, and J. Edgar Hoover.

A month later, Johnnie Ray made another appearance at the Copa. Kilgallen joined an SRO crowd including Tony Bennett, Ed Sullivan, Yul Brynner, Marlene Dietrich, and Ava Gardner, the new Mrs. Frank Sinatra. When Ray performed "Walkin' My Baby Back Home," Kilgallen cheered. In her column the next day, she described Ray as "Endsville. He held the town's toughest audience spellbound (or maybe it was paralyzed with astonishment)."

As September 1953 dawned, Kilgallen, continuing to keep abreast of world events while soaking up the NYC nightclub scene, noted the marriage of John Kennedy to Jacqueline Bouvier and attended Queen Elizabeth's coronation. Wearing a tiara, Kilgallen looked stunning in a silver gown with 10,000 embroidered jewels and pearls encrusted at the scalloped neckline. A white mink cape lined with silver lamé completed an outfit truly fit for a queen. Kilgallen's coverage of the coronation earned her a Pulitzer Prize nomination.

CHAPTER 5

Despite her own roving eye, one pointed in the direction of Johnny Ray, on March 19, 1954, Dorothy Kilgallen birthed her third child, Kerry Ardan Kollmar. The couple named him after a county seat in Ireland. In a column intended to tribute motherhood, she wrote:

> It is sad to think that any woman should regard pregnancy as a dreary interlude rather than a heightening of the adventure of life, because an expectant mother ought to be a happy egotist. She is doing something only she can do…the burden of the miracle is on her. She is a dramatic figure, honored, privileged, blessed…

Two days later, Jill and Dickie appeared on *What's My Line?* Kilgallen was absent. Panel members guessed the children's identity when one of the questions dealt with Kerry's birth.

That same year, with her "Voice on Broadway" column read by millions, Kilgallen was unwilling to restrict her notoriety to her society column and *What's My Line?* appearances. Instead, she continued to write front-page stories featuring her favorite subjects, crime and criminal trials.

The headline-making case Kilgallen tackled involved the Cleveland murder trial of Dr. Sam Sheppard, on trial for killing his wife. He swore he was innocent and that a "bushy-haired man" intruder struck Mrs. Sheppard with a sharp metal object 27 times.

Prior to jury instructions, the judge asked to meet Kilgallen privately. They posed for photos while chatting. Later, Bob Considine, writing for the Hearst Syndicate, described Kilgallen's star power:

Dorothy's daily arrivals at the little courtroom in Cleveland where Sam Sheppard was on trial were not unlike the arrival at home plate of Mickey Mantle with the bases filled. All the girl wanted was to get on with the story, do her job, but the jury, judge, defense attorney, prosecution and warring families of the accused murderer and the deceased all seemed straining to get her autograph.

Kilgallen's articles in the *Journal-American* were incisive as she honed her skills as a true investigative reporter. Listening to the evidence during the nine-week trial, she had doubts about Sheppard's guilt. When the jury voted for conviction, the newspaper headline read, "Dorothy Kilgallen on Sheppard Trial, ASTOUNDED BY VERDICT SEES REVERSAL POSSIBLE."

The accompanying story read:

The prosecutors for the State of Ohio did not prove [Sheppard] was guilty any more than they proved there were pin-headed men on Mars.... I have covered a score and more of murder trials. This was the first time I have ever seen what I believed to be miscarriage of justice in a murder case. It is the first time I have ever been scared by the jury system and I mean scared.

Having blasted the Sheppard verdict, Kilgallen returned to the entertainment world. Sweet on Johnnie Ray despite his being married, Kilgallen appeared puzzled by the star singer's mindset. She wrote in her Spring 1955 column:

Johnnie Ray must be one of the most confused fellows in all Hollywood. During a recent singing engagement there, he spent most of his time in his bungalow at the Garden of Allah crying his eyes out and being just downright miserable.... He finally admitted he hatednightclub work and wanted only to sing at teenage benefits because it gave him a chance to be with kids his own age. Teenagers, his own age?

Meanwhile, Kilgallen's star status earned her an appearance on television's most popular interview show, *Person to Person* with Edward R. Murrow. To indicate the prestige Kilgallen enjoyed, guests on other programs had included then-Senator John F. Kennedy and his wife Jacqueline as well as

Dorothy Kilgallen at the Sam Sheppard Trial, 1954.

Marlon Brando, Humphrey Bogart, and Marilyn Monroe. Fidel Castro, Frank Sinatra, Elizabeth Taylor, and Sammy Davis, Jr. also made appearances.

The interview, aired January 20, 1956, took place at the couple's 22-room Neo-Georgian townhouse. Dorothy wore a low-cut, glittering dress complete with flashy large, rounded earrings. She and Richard showed the viewing audience around the home as Murrow, obviously a Kilgallen admirer, questioned her. He asked which of the circle of careers, television, radio and print, Kilgallen enjoyed the most. She chose the latter, telling Murrow, "I would have to settle for my first love, my true love, the newspaper business."

Highlights of the program, (available at TheReporterWhoKnew-TooMuch.com), aired in black and white, included showing the audience the *Gone With the Wind*-themed drawing room. It featured pale lavender walls and white bridal satin curtains. Above the fireplace was a large portrait of Dorothy.

The Victorian-themed dining room and the "Black Room," one floor up, were also showcased. In the latter, the walls and ceiling were black with white draperies and a large Kelly green rug providing contrast. The "Americana" room was a true conversation piece. It featured Civil War relics including a Battle of Princeton painting, a lady cigar store Indian, and a lavish collection of eagles (17 in all) on walls, a lamp, and a drum table. There was also a collection of antique penny piggy banks (a trick dog, Punch and Judy, and a clown). They were on the mantle above another fireplace. Making appearances were Jill, age 12 and Kerry, 22 months.

To Murrow and the outside world, the family appeared happy and carefree. Unfortunately, unrest smoldered beneath the surface. Despite boasting about his Broadway exploits, Richard was experiencing a downturn driving him to drink excessively. Kilgallen, at the peak of popularity, enjoyed her celebrity status and sought companionship with men other than her husband. The two were married but there was little romance in the relationship as they drifted apart.

While Richard wallowed in self-pity, Kilgallen once again displayed her star status. She covered the fairytale wedding of big screen goddess Grace Kelly to Prince Rainier of Monaco. Meanwhile, *What's My Line?* continued to be a television spectacle. One critic applauded Kilgallen's "prosecutorial" skills.

When Johnnie Ray appeared on *What's My Line?* Kilgallen was upset when she could not guess his mystery identity. Regardless, backstage the two chatted for better than an hour. In an article describing Kilgallen, a *New York Post Daily Magazine* reporter wrote:

> Kilgallen is an attractive woman with a delicate, moon-pale complexion, dark brunette hair, a knock-out hourglass figure and no inconsiderable bustline…she [is] a scrupulously coiffed model of respectable high fashion style, her deportment and appearance bespoke of 400's traditional veil-and-white sensibility with an added twist of enviably tasteful, up-to-date chic. She exudes class, grace and noble distinction. Dorothy is, viewed from the proper angle, quite a dish.

Apparently, Johnnie Ray agreed with the depiction, especially the "dish" part. Like other men pursuing Kilgallen, he must have been infatuated with her power. She was not a beautiful woman, not truly photogenic, but the power she wielded provided the aphrodisiac necessary for romance.

Dorothy Kilgallen and Johnnie Ray photo with unidentified friend. Their love affair was the talk of New York City Society.

Surprising the famed columnist, Ray appeared at daughter Jill's 14th birthday on July 16, 1957. To friends, Kilgallen said she was "impressed as hell" by the singer. To that end, Kilgallen invited him to escort her to the premiere of *An Affair to Remember*. The tearjerker starred Cary Grant and Deborah Kerr. Those that applauded the celebrity couple outside the theater didn't know that the spark between Ray, a known bi-sexual, and Kilgallen, had ignited a torrid love affair that had been ongoing for some time. Johnny Whiteside, Ray's biographer,[1] wrote: "They found themselves in bed—a cascade of violent release and deep passion...."

---

[1] Jonny Whiteside is a noted entertainment writer with award-winning publications continuing to this day including articles in *LA Weekly*. *Cry* was originally intended to be Johnnie Ray's autobiography. The two worked on the book before Ray's death in 1990. Whiteside had access to Ray's diaries as well as family members and friends.

While Kilgallen enjoyed the budding romance, her "Voice of Broadway" column not only dealt with theatre and society news but the national political scene. She wrote, "Top ranking Republicans confidently talk of Thomas E. Dewey as our next Secretary of State succeeding John Foster Dulles when he is later appointed to the Supreme Court." In another column, she pulled in the entertainment readers by writing, "Now that Hollywood has adjusted itself to such streamlined types as Grace Kelly and Audrey Hepburn, a whole new treasure trove of potential star material had developed: the fashion world."

Meanwhile, *What's My Line?* greeted millions of television viewers across America every Sunday night. On November 18, 1956, the mystery guest was Kilgallen's father, Jim. He stumped the panel, which included *Life of Riley* television star William Bendix. At the last minute, Kilgallen finally guessed her father's identity.

Interaction with guests, including her father, on the program symbolized another enviable Kilgallen character trait: a terrific sense of humor. She was lively, she laughed, she poked fun at others, and she enjoyed life to the fullest despite marriage turmoil.

The celebrity status of her *What's My Line?* appearances stretched to *her* being covered when she covered an important event. Always assigned to the headline-making stories, Kilgallen wrote about Queen Elizabeth and Prince Phillip's 1957 visit to the United States. Her *Journal-American* colleague Bill Slocum described the scene: "Everywhere we went the crowds oohed about the Queen, aahed about the Prince and screamed 'Hiya Dorothy' when they saw Miss Kilgallen. Dorothy was only a little less regal than the royal pair, better dressed than any of her colleagues, or the Queen, and writing the best copy being filed on the trip." *The New York Post* agreed with the "Dorothy look," describing her as "tall, slim, unwrinkled, unruffled, fresh-faced, and dressed in a brown suit with a chinchilla beret" while reporting on the queen's visit.

Without doubt, Kilgallen had become as big a celebrity as those she covered. Millions of fans admired her accomplishments. She was a true Renassaance woman in every sense of the word.

CHAPTER 6

In late 1956, Dorothy Kilgallen made a deadly enemy when she began to carry on a public feud with Kennedy family friend and Mafia-connected singer Frank Sinatra. He was inflamed after she wrote a *Journal-American* series titled "The Real Frank Sinatra Story."

In her articles, Kilgallen detailed Sinatra's various romances with, among others, Gloria Vanderbilt, Kim Novak, Lana Turner and Ava Gardner. She added:

> A few of the women, like Ava and Lana, were public idols themselves and priceless examples of feminine beauty. Many more, of course, have been fluffy little struggling dolls of show business, pretty and small-waisted and similar under the standard layer of peach-colored Pan-Cake makeup. [They are] starlets who never got past first base in Hollywood, assorted models and vocalists, and chorus girls now lost in the ghosts of floor shows past. Others belonged to the classification most gently described as tawdry.

In turn, Sinatra derided Kilgallen's "chinless" appearance. She responded by writing about his Mafia connections. This included associating him with Chicago gangster Sam Giancana and L.A. crime boss Mickey Cohen. One evening, Sinatra walked by her at the Stork Club. Noticing that she was wearing sunglasses, he dropped a dollar bill in her coffee cup. Then he said to a friend, "I always figured she was blind."

Sinatra's antics irritated Kilgallen but she disregarded them to celebrate Richard's 46th birthday hosted at New York City's Plaza Hotel. Kilgallen surprised guests by accepting an invitation to dance with entertainer Bobby Short, an African-American cabaret singer and pianist best known for his interpretations of songs by popular composers of the first half of the 20th century.

Onlookers who objected to any interaction between the races were thunderstruck by Kilgallen's audacity. She did not care. Bobby Short was a friend; she was ready to break down barriers; skin color made no difference to her.

During this time, Kilgallen was truly a household favorite. Various commercial opportunities abounded, and she took advantage of them. One involved print ads pitching her as enjoying flights on a particular type of airplane. The ad copy, next to a beaming photograph, read, "For business or pleasure, I fly DC-6."

Kilgallen's star power stretched to family members. Even though he did not bear the magic Kilgallen name, oldest son Richard hit the ad scene as well. Double Bubble bubblegum hired him to pitch its product to the younger set.

Despite Richard's financial downturn, Kilgallen's earnings from the commercials, *What's My Line?*, the "Voice of Broadway" column, the "Dick and Dorothy" radio program, and other endeavors permitted the family to live well. Home was the lavish five-story townhouse located on the upper east side of Manhattan featured on CBS's "Person to Person." It featured an Otis elevator and front and rear staircases. There was a reception area on the ground floor next to a large powder room and a small mailroom. The bottom flight of the main stairwell was nearby. Gazing straight up permitted the view of a roof top skylight.

During the Christmas season giant snowballs, giant snowflakes, and colorful ornaments hung from the top over the staircase. In the room featuring furniture from the *Gone With the Wind* set, French doors, chandeliers, and expensive art completed the décor. There was only one electric light in the room with candles spread throughout.

Despite marital problems, Dorothy and Richard were truly society's darlings. The couple hosted lavish parties. Entertainer Steve Allen said, "Everybody who was anybody was at Dorothy's parties." Guests included Jayne Mansfield and George Harrison of Beatles fame.

During the holiday season, Dorothy and Dick hosted a fancy Christmas tree-trimming extravaganza and New Year's Eve Costume Ball. Separate rooms became decorated nightclubs. When guests dressed as movie stars and other celebrities entered these rooms, they gasped. There Judy Garland, the Count Basie Orchestra and other friends of the Kollmar's performed. One year, Dorothy dressed as Scarlett O'Hara and Richard as Rhett Butler. At these parties, Kilgallen was the champion at word games and charades.

All the while, Kilgallen's love affair blossomed with sandy-haired singer Johnnie Ray, fourteen years her junior. Fellow columnist Liz Smith called the affair "peculiar" while adding, "Here was this white-gloved Catholic making out with a homosexual all over town."

Kilgallen called *An Affair to Remember*, the film she and Ray had watched together, a winner. In her column, she wrote that the movie was a tribute to those "who are getting tired of pictures about dope addicts, alcoholics, unattractive butchers, and men who sleep in their underwear." In contrast to the hard-edged persona Kilgallen was infamous for, Ray said of her, "She was probably the most feminine woman I've ever known. And I always thought she was a pretty lady—the softest thing you ever touched. All those people that made fun of her. That was just plain sick."

Friend Hank Wesinger said of the couple: "[Kilgallen and Ray] were like two little kids…. They would go romping off and do their little silly things…. Together, they were like two children. They were in love."

CHAPTER 7

Upping the stakes, Dorothy Kilgallen continued to use her "Voice of Broadway" column to attack Frank Sinatra. She did so in an unabashed, unforgiving style, writing:

> Success hasn't changed Frank Sinatra. When he was unappreciated and obscure, he was hot-tempered, egotistical, extravagant, and moody. Now that he is rich and famous, with the world on a string and sapphires in his cufflinks, he is still hot-tempered, egotistical, extravagant, and moody.

Striking back, Sinatra featured Kilgallen in his nightclub act. He told audiences she "looks like a chipmunk."

Sinatra must have been jealous of Kilgallen's extended popularity. Johnny Ray's biographer Jonny Whiteside observed: "Rules must be followed. That was how they played it in Gotham. But Dorothy Kilgallen was in a position to change the rules anytime it suited her—everyone from the Mayor on down to [mobster] Frank Costello (who occasionally joined her table at P.J. Clarke's) knew it."

Whether changing the rules or simply disregarding them, Kilgallen had the freedom to do as she wished. Besides being a regular on the Broadway scene and appearing on *What's My Line?*, Kilgallen guest-starred on many hit television programs. They included the popular *Milton Berle* show. She appeared in a funny skit with Berle and actor Mickey Rooney.

In Kilgallen's "Voice of Broadway" column, Elvis Presley became a favored personality. She announced his pending release from the Army.

In the same column, she mentioned another favorite subject, crime. NYC District Attorney Frank Hogan and his grand jury investigation of a harness-racing scandal caught Kilgallen's attention.

During 1958, Kilgallen diverted away from media chores to enjoy special time with Johnny Ray. He hosted what friends called the "63rd Street parties." These happened at his new address located at the corner of 3rd Avenue and 63rd Street. Kilgallen chose the wall paintings in the 2,000 square foot apartment. She gifted Ray a candle-burning crystal chandelier.

Visitors besides Kilgallen included Sophie Tucker, Yul Brynner, Ethel Merman, and Lucille Ball. On Sunday evening, everyone watched *What's My Line?* Then Kilgallen joined the festive group following the program.[1]

In early 1959, Kilgallen used her celebrity status to jump into the deep waters of international politics. She criticized Jack Parr, host of NBC's *Tonight Show*, for his support of Fidel Castro. Kilgallen opposed the Cuban rebel leader and wrote anti-Castro articles. Displaying her investigative reporter skills, and her refusal to back away from controversial issues despite the danger, she interviewed Cuban exiles in Miami. Kilgallen then wrote exclusively about their hatred for the Cuban dictator.

In July of that same year, six years and counting before Kilgallen died, she stunned readers with what observers called "A Kilgallen Exclusive." Becoming the first reporter to allege that the CIA and organized crime were teaming up to eliminate Castro, she wrote:

> If our state department heads in Washington deny they're gravely worried over the explosive situation in Cuba and nearby Latin American countries, they're either giving out false information for reasons of their own or playing ostrich, which might prove to be a dangerous game.
>
> US intelligence is virtually nonexistent if the government isn't aware that Russia already has bases in Cuba, and Russian pilots in uniform are

---

[1] Johnny Ray biographer Jonny Whiteside quoted one party guest regarding Ray and Kilgallen's saucy romance: "It was just part of the routine, that [Kilgallen] drug him out of the living room into the den, in which there happened to be a long leather couch. We would sit in the living room and listen to all the activity that was going on in the den. It was lust out of control. You could hear it. We used to go over to the keyhole and look into the room. It became a joke to us."

strutting openly in Havana. Fidel Castro is the target for so many assassins they're apt to fall over each other in their effortsto get him.

The Mafia want to knock him off. So do the Batista sympathizers, of course, and then there are his own disillusioned rebels, just for starters. He has machine guns and other ammunition mounted on every key rooftop near his base of operations, but the smart money doubts if any amount of precaution can change his status as a clay pigeon.

This Kilgallen scoop must have infuriated those in the State Department, whom she criticized for spreading "false information." Members of the CIA and the Mafia who intended to keep their clandestine, cooperative operation a secret, also were offended. Certainly all three wondered who Kilgallen's source was feeding her the secret information.

True to her credo of protecting sources, Kilgallen never told anyone who the mole was insisting Castro had become a "clay pigeon" ripe for elimination. As time passed, Kilgallen's enemy list was expanding. Besides Frank Sinatra, it now included three dangerous foes: the State Department, the CIA, and those in the underworld who were cooperating with the government to kill Castro.

During this time, Kilgallen rarely visited the *Journal-American* offices. Instead, she used her "office" workspace on the fifth floor of her townhouse. She called it "The Cloop." It featured chartreuse carpeting, embroidered Swiss curtains with tie-backs of taffeta ribbons with bows, floral wallpaper, and a bed. No one could enter "The Cloop," not even family members including youngest son Kerry.

Continuing to expand her power of influence into international affairs, Kilgallen covered Nikita Khrushchev's September 1959 visit to the United States. Familiar with the famous columnist, the Soviet Premier waved at her when he arrived at Andrew's Air Force Base. The Soviet leader met with President Eisenhower but was upset when denied a trip to Disneyland for security concerns.

Exposing her disdain for even the wife of a world leader, Kilgallen became embroiled in a media war. This happened when she described Nina Khrushchev in a *Journal-American* story bearing the headline, "Our Miss K says Mrs. K's Clothes fit like a Slip Cover." The article read:

Dorothy Kilgallen and youngest son Kerry at townhouse.

The grisliness of her attire amounts almost to a demonstration of piety....
It would be difficult to find clothes comparable to hers in the waiting
room of a New York employment agency for domestic help; in this
decadent capitalistic republic, applicants for jobs as laundresses, cham-
bermaids, and cooks usually are far more *a la mode* than Russia's first lady.

Reader comments included one feeling "revolted," and another
"ashamed" of Kilgallen's comments. Worse, now Kilgallen had offended
the Russian government adding them to her enemies list.[2]

Such conduct triggered a later comment from an unidentified journalist: "From the late fifties until her death, [Kilgallen] grew more notorious
than she had ever been popular." Being notorious meant she was a target for
anyone with a grudge to bear.

---

[2] Apparently embarrassed later with what she had written about Mrs. Khrushchev, Kilgallen told a
friend, "Sometimes you sit at a typewriter and the words come out sharper and maybe a bit more unfair
than you would want them to if took more time and thought it over."

CHAPTER 8

In November 1959, thanks to Dorothy Kilgallen, Johnnie Ray remained a free man. She stood by him when Detroit prosecutors charged the popular singer for soliciting sex with men.

Kilgallen was certain her lover was "set up" by police. She did all she could behind the scenes to publicize Ray's innocence. It worked: The all-woman jury acquitted the singer.

CBS producer friend Marlon Swing observed:

[Kilgallen] was a very powerful woman—people don't have any idea of the contacts and power she had.... I was with her when she called the judge. And she put pressure on him—made sure [the case] was expedited and that Johnnie got fair treatment. Dorothy had favors she could call in from people all over the world. She made sure that Johnnie was exonerated.

Having saved Johnnie Ray from prison, Kilgallen was busy with yet another murder trial during the summer of 1960, five years before her death. In Los Angeles, prosecutors charged Dr. Bernard Finch and his mistress Carole Tregoff with the murder of Finch's wife Barbara Jean. One witness against the two defendants was a worthless grafter. He had accepted money to kill Barbara Jean but never did so. Dr. Finch claimed shooting his wife was accidental. A jury, after two mistrials, convicted both Dr. Finch and Tregoff.

During the trial, Kilgallen used her celebrity status to secure an exclusive interview with Dr. Finch. In her *Journal-American* article, she wrote,

"The doctor does not look like putty. He looks more like leather-encased steel but the legend of the siren who can make men strong is old and undying." She added, "The trial is more than a whodunit, it's a who'd believe it."

Compliments for Kilgallen's coverage of the trial abounded. A reporter for *Time* magazine wrote, "In Los Angeles, busy Dorothy Kilgallen sometimes attracted more attention than the trial. She posed for pictures with the defendant, signed scores of autographs for admirers, and received an orchid from an unidentified California Judge. Yet, for all that, her copy, rattled off on an electric typewriter in her hotel room, provided the best coverage of the Finch-Tregoff trial." It was also reported, "Kilgallen posed for pictures with the accused and had dinner at the home of both the prosecutor and the defense attorney."

Fresh off the trial, Kilgallen visited Los Angeles again. There she celebrated her lofty status as a media icon on February 9, 1960 with a ceremony awarding her a Star on the Hollywood Walk of Fame.

Meanwhile, an August 1960 six-page spread in the prestigious magazine *TV Radio Mirror* provided Kilgallen additional media exposure. *The Price is Right* and *I've Got a Secret* popular television host Bill Cullen appeared on the cover. Included were stories on Kilgallen, Frank and Nancy Sinatra, and *American Bandstand's* Dick Clark. A full-page color photograph accompanied the article. Kilgallen looked radiant in a yellow, green and orange striped low cut dress.

The lead-in to the article was "Her line is Headlines—About other celebrities, that is! But Dorothy Kilgallen can't help being a star herself, whether as TV panelist on *What's My Line?* or as hostess in her own fabulous home." Large photographs featured Kilgallen relaxing on a couch in the "Americana" room, in front of a typewriter in her home office, and nestled closely to son Kerry, age six, in the "Victorian" room. Interviewer Martin Cohen described her as wearing "a champagne-colored silk sheath and coral shoes, her only jewelry a multi-colored necklace. Her hair is reddish-brown, her skin delicate and translucent." In a separate photo, Kilgallen wore the ostrich-feather gown displayed at the wedding of England's Princess Margaret.

Kilgallen discussed both her private[1] and business life. She called television, "an altogether different world. It's wonderful. Suddenly, you have literally millions of friends, who recognize you wherever you go and call you by your first name." Regarding *What's My Line?* partners Bennett Cerf and Arlene Francis, Kilgallen said, "Arlene and Bennett and I are there because we're pretty good game players. It's silly to say we aren't—otherwise, they would have cover girls to play the game, and, instead of Bennett, there would be a rock 'n roll singer."

The extensive media exposure proved the relentless Kilgallen was a national personality with stature. She was someone of importance when she made a claim. Her first-rate reputation as an investigative reporter was solidified when she met privately with Cerf, Kilgallen's fellow panel member on *What's My Line?* He was also a co-founder of the publishing company Random House. Cerf hired Kilgallen to write a book about the famous murder cases she had covered.

A researcher assisted Kilgallen's preparation to write the book with the working title, *Murder One.* Meanwhile, Kilgallen kept close tabs on the presidential primaries and countdown to the general election. She and millions of Americans watched the charismatic JFK burn Richard Nixon in the first debate, September 26, 1960. This happened when the Vice-President, pale and underweight from a recent hospitalization, appeared sickly and sweaty. Kennedy, well rested, appeared calm and confident.

The debate became the turning point in the election. Kilgallen decided to make a prediction in her "Voice of Broadway" column. She wrote that JFK would win since:

> [JFK] was adorable on television…his promises and connections would get him the labor vote and the machine Democrats…. Sammy Davis' support would guarantee him the Negro vote…the majority of Jews

---

[1] During the *TV Radio Mirror* interview, Kilgallen mentioned her children stating, "I get so gabby when I talk about the children. So stop me because I know it's bragging." She then lauded Dickie's interest in music stating, "Right now, he's immersed in thirteenth-century choral music and progressive jazz. He's always had flawless taste in music." Of Jill, Kilgallen mentioned her prowess as an artist and noted that Jill "had the Josephine Hill part in 'Arsenic and Old Lace'" where she gave "a grand performance." Regarding young Kerry, Kilgallen described him as a "husky, six-year-old with freckles across his nose who loves Dennis the Menace."

would go to the polls for him, and no true [Frank] Sinatra fan would dare vote for anyone else.

Kigallen's prediction was right. Asked after the election whether she would write about JFK's dalliances with women, Kilgallen said, "No one could." This was an admission that the president's personal life was off base, for the time being.

All the while, Kilgallen continued to perpetuate the myth she had a solid marriage.[2] She hosted a lavish surprise birthday party for Richard at their townhouse. Celebrity guests included Jayne Mansfield, Betty White and husband Allen Ludden (*Password*). Richard continued to drink heavily, a cause of concern for his wife and friends.

At the same time the marriage struggles continued, Kilgallen had to deal with an exposé in the *New York Post Daily Magazine*. The editors called it, "The Dorothy Kilgallen Story: A Post Portrait." Released in unprecedented TEN full-page editions worthy of a woman at the height of a remarkable career unmatched by anyone of her era or perhaps any era, the stories alternated between dirt and devotion regarding the Kilgallen mystique. It also touched on her immense popularity in the entertainment world and beyond.

Furious with the series, Kilgallen struck back. She wrote a rebuttal including the following statement: "Newspapermen all over town were laughing over the fact that it takes five alleged reporters to set the facts wrong in the first sentence of a series running in New York's most inaccurate gazette. And every paragraph that followed compounded the joke."

Abandoning her crusade to dissuade the *Post* stories from being taken seriously, on January, 20, 1961, four-plus years removed from her death, Kilgallen covered the JFK inauguration ceremonies. She traveled to the nation's capital on a cold, windy day in the style her fame required: a Silver Wraith Rolls Royce. During the swearing-in, Kilgallen sat in a position of respect, the fifth row beside columnist Bob Considine and a *Life* magazine representative with a clear view of JFK.

---

[2] Kilgallen's friend Jean Bach said, "That marriage was a little fishy. Dick's roving eye, his getting drunk and squeezing someone on the dance floor. Dorothy acted as if it never happened."

During the gala event for the 35th president of the United States, white-haired Robert Frost read his poem, "The Gift Outright." JFK, coatless despite the cold weather, uttered his famous line, "And so, my fellow Americans: ask not what your country can do for you—ask what you can do for your country." Despite a blizzard threatening the five inaugural balls, Kilgallen attended the "Rat Pack" gala. It headlined Frank Sinatra and his celebrity pals. Whether the mortal enemies exchanged insults was unknown.

Continuing to play by her own rules while blasting Sinatra whenever possible, in early June, Kilgallen flaunted her romance with Johnnie Ray as they frolicked at various New York hotspots including the infamous Copacabana. Husband Richard fumed. Regardless, he could not cool the affair.

Richard did attend a few social functions with Kilgallen but he missed Ernest Hemingway stopping by her table at the Stork Club. After his wife Mary left, Hemingway called Kilgallen "daughter" and told her she was "one of the greatest women writers in the world," a compliment yet one she probably disapproved of since Kilgallen felt like she should be judged as a writer not a female writer. Regardless, she later wrote, "If I couldn't be me, I would want to be Mrs. Ernest Hemingway more than anyone I [can] think of. It strikes me as a fine thing to live in a cool house, in a sunny place like Cuba, with a gentle and virile man, listening to good talk and being the first to read his writings."

After spending time with the legendary writer as 1962 dawned, Kilgallen decided to answer many of those who believed her marriage was falling apart. She noted in her column that she and husband Richard had been frequenting her favorite New York City nightspots. Kilgallen said they were also "attending Broadway openings."

Regardless, Kilgallen's star continued to shine bright with appearances on the popular game show, *To Tell the Truth*, and articles she wrote for *Cosmopolitan Magazine*. To date, she had now written more than 6,000 "Voice of Broadway" columns—three and a half million words. She was without a doubt the most powerful female voice in the entertainment industry. Her fame extended into social and political life as well. If there had been a list of the 100 most influential women in the country, Kilgallen would certainly have been in the top 10.

Dorothy Kilgallen and
Ernest Hemingway at
the Stork Club, circa
early 1961.

Perhaps more importantly, Kilgallen was deeply in love with Johnnie
Ray. Alan Eichler, who managed Ray during the latter years of his life, told
this author it was a "genuine love affair, sexual in nature. Johnnie said he
actually gave Dorothy her first orgasm." Tad Mann, Ray's personal manager for nearly 40 years, said, "Dorothy and Johnnie likened themselves to
American royalty…. He was her Prince Charming."

Kilgallen not only was Johnnie Ray's lover but mentored the famed
singer as well. She suggested career choices and personal habits. Many saw
Kilgallen as a mother figure to Ray. He listened to her as she attempted
to improve his image. The 14-year age difference (he was 35; she was 49)
meant little to her. She was in love and cared less what others thought of
the affair.

Meanwhile, now that JFK was president, he deserved a regular mention in Kilgallen's *Journal-American* column. In July 1961, she rolled out

another exclusive, writing, "Warner Bros. has given up the idea of using a big-name star to play President Kennedy in [the film] *PT 109* based on JFK's book of the same name."

In the same column, Dorothy Kilgallen boosted the career of Marilyn Monroe. Kilgallen also exposed inside information about Marilyn's various love affairs. Kilgallen was fascinated with Monroe's sex appeal, her box office successes, and her numerous romances.

During this time, Kilgallen also arranged, through friendship with Presidential Press Secretary Pierre Salinger, a visit to the White House with son Kerry. When the eight-year-old redhead and his mother arrived, Salinger conducted the tour himself. While in the cabinet room, President Kennedy suddenly appeared. He invited Dorothy and Kerry into the Oval Office. While they sat and chatted, JFK looked at a bundle of letters Kerry had brought written to the president by Kerry's third grade classmates.

JFK gifted Kerry a number of presidential souvenirs including a ballpoint pen with the presidential seal inscribed and a gold pin in the shape of PT-109 that the president placed on the youngster's striped school tie. After reading Kerry's letter, JFK said, "That's very well written. Very well done."

Then, while winking at Kilgallen, the president added, "…I don't know whether Kerry is a Democrat or a Republican." Kilgallen responded, "I bet he is a Democrat now."

CHAPTER 9

On August 3, 1962, two months before the Cuban missile crisis, Dorothy Kilgallen became the first journalist to reveal Marilyn Monroe's relationship with "a Kennedy." She cleverly wrote in her column:

> Marilyn Monroe's health must be improving. She's been attending select Hollywood parties and has become the talk of the town again. In California, they're circulating a photograph of her that certainly isn't as bare as the famous calendar, but is very interesting. And she's cooking in the sex-appeal department, too; she's proved vastly alluring to a handsome gentleman who is a bigger name than Joe DiMaggio in his heyday. So don't write off Marilyn as finished.

When Marilyn died in Hollywood two days later, a startled Kilgallen, three years separated from her own death, questioned the investigation. She wrote:

> If the woman described as Marilyn's "housekeeper" [Eunice Murray] is really a housekeeper, why was [Marilyn's] bedroom such a mess? It was a small house and should have been easy to keep tidy.

Kilgallen also wondered:

> Why was Marilyn's door locked that night, when she didn't usually lock it? If she was just trying to get to sleep and took the overdose of pills accidentally, why was the light on? Usually people sleep better in the dark.

Adding to her suspicions, Kilgallen asked:

Why did the first doctor [arriving on the scene] have to call the second doctor before calling the police? Any doctor, even a psychiatrist, knows a dead person when he sees one, especially when rigor mortis has set in and there are marks of lividity on the surface of the face and body. Why the consultation? Why the big time gap in such a small town? Mrs. Murray gets worried at about 3 a.m. and it's almost 6 a.m. before the police get to the scene.

Continuing to question facts surrounding the Hollywood legend's death, Kilgallen closed the column with the statement: "The real story hasn't been told, not by a long shot." In a tribute column to Marilyn, Kilgallen wrote, "Sleep well, sweet girl. You have left more of a legacy than most, if all you ever left was a handful of photographs of one of the loveliest women who ever walked the face of the earth."

With her skepticism about the true cause of Monroe's death squarely in view, Kilgallen wrote a "Voice of Broadway" column mentioning an author who would play an eerie part in her death. She wrote, "Novelist Robert Ruark [author of *Honey Badger*] and his wife were conferring with their lawyers preliminary to an amicable divorce. The decree will be sought in Mexico." He was the same Robert Ruark who had written a scathing article entitled "Sinatra is Playing with the Strangest People These Days," chastising the singer for hanging out in Havana with gangsters like Lucky Luciano, whom Ruark called "scum."

Meanwhile, Kilgallen, expanding her coverage of high-profile cases around the world, flew to England in July 1963 to cover the explosive trial of Dr. Stephen Ward. He was an English osteopath (one patient was Winston Churchill), and a central figure in the "Profumo affair," a British political scandal triggering the resignation of John Profumo, Minister of War. The scandal contributed to the defeat of the Conservative government one year later.

Displaying her prowess for prophetic prose, part of Kilgallen's *Journal-American* column read:

There was a dinner party where a naked man wearing a mask waited on tables like a slave. The authorities searching the apartment of one of the principles in the case came upon a photograph showing a key figure disporting with a bevy of ladies. All were nude except for the gentleman in the picture who was wearing an apron. And this was a man who had been on extremely friendly terms with the very proper Queen and members of her immediate family!

Following the Ward case, in September, Kilgallen's *Journal-American* announced President Kennedy would visit Dallas for a campaign stop in November. She barely noticed since Kilgallen faced a libel case in court filed by Elaine Shepard, a Broadway and motion picture actress.

Shepard's presence in the press party during a President Dwight Eisenhower 1959 European tour triggered the action. Kilgallen wrote that "an actress" had an affair with a member of the White House staff" in one of the cities visited.

Shepard believed all signs pointed to her being the unnamed "actress" since she was the only actress present on the trip. Shepard was offended by Kilgallen's use of the words, "lewd and unchaste" to describe the actress' conduct. Shepard sued the famous columnist for three quarters of a million dollars, a huge sum in those days. Shepard's supporters said Kilgallen's nasty comments were another example of the muckraking journalistic style permeating her columns.

At trial, Elaine Shepard called Kilgallen's harsh words "humiliating and shocking." Kilgallen countered by asserting her comments did not target Shepard. A jury agreed in a trial overseen by Judge Thomas Aurelio. Years earlier, the judge had faced disbarment charges due to his "friendship" with New York gangster Frank Costello. A wiretap exposed the true extent of the friendship, one pointing to the mobster's ability to put judicial robes on obliging candidates. After Aurelio told Costello, "Thanks for everything," Costello said, "When I tell you something is in the bag [fixed] you could rest assured." Aurelio replied, "I want to assure you of my loyalty for all you have done for me. It is undying."

Kilgallen never wrote about that case. However, she clearly knew that underworld figures, through bribes and influence, controlled many of the New York City politicians, judges, and police with speculation that corruption had seeped into several administrative agencies including the NYC Medical Examiner's Office.

CHAPTER 10

Money never drove Dorothy Kilgallen's ambitions. Nevertheless, her success as a nationally known newspaper columnist, television star and renowned investigative reporter made her rich by 1963. Through various media ventures, her income was estimated at two hundred thousand dollars a year—1.5 million today—a mindboggling figure for a woman during that time, reinforcing Kilgallen's position as a true magnate without challenge. No doubt exists that if *Time* magazine had published a list of the highest paid females in the U.S., Kilgallen would have been near the top if not the very top.

Since husband Richard had fallen into depression due to his nightclub failures and alcoholism, Kilgallen was the family's sole breadwinner. Her hairdresser Marc Sinclaire called Richard, "Mr. Kilgallen." This label may have been a bit unfair. Competing with his celebrity wife and her ever-widening shadow had always been difficult for Richard.

As Kilgallen attempted to deal with a disappointing husband, she kept up with JFK's planned trip to Dallas. She was unaware that as September 1963 welcomed fall temperatures, President Kennedy and his brother Bobby, the Attorney General, discussed the visit. RFK attempted to convince JFK of the importance of appearing with Vice-President Lyndon Johnson. He was concerned that the president might dump him from the 1964 ticket. To assure LBJ that JFK had no such intentions, the Texas trip became important.

While Dallas made plans to welcome the president, during the late summer months, Kilgallen and her husband Richard had quarreled over her public display of affection for Johnnie Ray. Richard forbade her to see him. Kilgallen was heartbroken. Madly in love with Ray and desperate for affection, she continued the affair despite her husband's orders.

Always interested in JFK's private life, Kilgallen returned to the entertainment side of his presidency. In an October 1, 1963 "Voice of Broadway" column written two years and thirty-eight days removed from her death, she mentioned "President Kennedy was reported to have told Cary Grant that he liked [Grant's film] *Charade* so well he saw it twice."

In her "Voice of Broadway" column fifty-two days later, on November 22, Kilgallen did not write about the president's Dallas trip. Instead, she noted that underworld figures were circling a gambler playing a dangerous game.

> The Broadway post-mortem reports about a big show business figure are startling. He's said to have run up enormous gambling debts—ranging from $10,000 to $20,000—at every casino in Las Vegas, for a total estimated at $150,000. The shylocks are closing in on him, the gang boys are starting to display impatience, and some have blown the whistle to the Internal Revenue chaps, alleging that he'd accepted under-the-table cash in business deals. It all figured because he certainly is a swinger, but friends didn't realize the amazing amount of trouble he was in until they began comparing coast-to-coast notes.

Kilgallen did not divulge the name of the "business figure." Pressed by the authorities to do so, she refused.

That same morning, Kilgallen's *Journal-American's* front page had noted JFK's Dallas appearance. One time zone to the west, *The Dallas Morning News* posted the headline "Storm of Political Controversy Swirls Around Kennedy on Visit."

Kilgallen, watching television in the townhouse, saw JFK land in Dallas. The presidential motorcade headed toward Dealey Plaza. At 12:30 p.m. CST in front of the Dallas Book Depository, shots rang out toward the president's limousine. When Texas Governor John Connally heard the gunfire, he shouted, "My God, they're going to kill us all."

Kilgallen was stunned when news reports confirmed JFK's wounds. With tears in her eyes, she sat alone watching further television coverage. Like millions of Americans, she prayed that her beloved president JFK would survive.

Less than a four-hour drive away from Kilgallen's townhouse at Robert Kennedy's Hickory Hill home in McClean, Virginia, RFK, the second most powerful man in America, the one dubbed by White House associates, "Assistant President," received a telephone call from FBI Director J. Edgar Hoover. He told Bobby about the assassination attempt. A few minutes later, Hoover called again. With an unsympathetic tone, he informed Bobby that JFK was dead.

In her townhouse, a distraught Kilgallen watched as *CBS's* Walter Cronkite delivered sad news to the nation: "The President died at 1:00 p.m. Dallas time, 2:00 p.m. Eastern Time." Continuing to monitor the television coverage, Kilgallen learned of the arrest of Lee Harvey Oswald in connection with the assassination. At police headquarters after his arrest, police told the handcuffed Oswald he could cover his face with his hands if he wished to do so. To that suggestion, he told reporters, "Why should I hide my face? I haven't done anything to be ashamed of."

While Oswald was being interrogated, Kilgallen watched as LBJ took the oath of office on Air Force One. He became the 36th President of the United States. Besides him stood Jackie Kennedy, blood still visible on her pink Chanel suit.

Kilgallen paced the floor and began chatting with friends on the telephone. Meanwhile, at 4:45 p.m. EST at his Virginia home, a distraught RFK told his press secretary Ed Guthman, "There's so much bitterness; I thought they would get one of us, but Jack, after all he had been through, [I] never worried about it....I never thought it would happen. I thought it would be me...there's been so much bitterness and hatred...."

Unaware of Bobby's statement while seeking details about Oswald, Kilgallen called contacts in Dallas. Her investigative reporter instincts on high alert, she began to question why JFK was killed.

Despite the late hour on the east coast, Kilgallen watched the midnight press conference with Oswald in Dallas. The media gathered to learn more facts about JFK's alleged assassin. He had stated, "I didn't kill the President, I didn't kill nobody."

As the news conference commenced, Kilgallen heard D.A. Henry Wade say Oswald was a member of the anti-Castro Free Cuba Committee. Seconds later, Kilgallen listened as someone in the back of the room shouted, "Henry, that's Fair Play for Cuba Committee." He turned out to be Jack Ruby, owner of the Carousel strip club in Dallas.

Early the next morning, Kilgallen held young Kerry in her arms. Mother and son wept over JFK's death. In her column, Kilgallen recalled the visit with her son to the White House. In her column, she wrote, "The picture that stays in my mind is the one of this tall young man bending over a small boy, carefully scrutinizing envelopes until he came to the name 'Kerry Ardan Kollmar—Grade 3B.' This is the man who was assassinated in Dallas."

CHAPTER 11

At 11:15 a.m. on November 24, Dorothy Kilgallen watched television coverage of the transfer of Lee Harvey Oswald from one jail to another. Emerging from an elevator, two detectives flanked the grim-faced man. One journalist shouted, "Here he comes." Loving the president as she did, Kilgallen glowered at the alleged assassin.

Kilgallen noticed Oswald handcuffed to the left wrist of a detective, J.R. "James" Leavelle. He wore a white suit and a gleaming white Stetson hat. Detective L.C. Graves held Oswald's left arm. No officers were directly in front of him.

Behind Oswald's entourage, several police looked on. Eager to display to the world the alleged killer of JFK and of Dallas Policeman J. D. Tippit, police welcomed the swarm of reporters and photographers. All gathered for the photo-op.

As bright lights showered him, Oswald, arguably the most hated man in the world, smirked at three journalists shouting questions. He was snarly and silent. Beads of perspiration pockmarked his shiny forehead. The plan, according to police, was to transport Oswald in an armored car to the more secure county jail.

Pen and paper in hand, Kilgallen's eyes focused on Oswald's sullen expression. The prisoners' bruised, unshaven face reflected his struggle with police during his arrest. Kilgallen watched Oswald sneer as flashbulbs popped and floodlights glared in the background. She wondered what his motive was for killing JFK.

Television camera operators focused on the hectic scene. Millions of viewers, including Kilgallen, glared at Oswald. At exactly 11:21 a.m., they heard reporter Ike Pappas ask, "Lee, do you have anything to say in your defense?"

A second later as Kilgallen's eyes scanned the scene, a stout man wearing a nap-brimmed gray fedora, edged closer to Oswald. While he approached, JFK's alleged assassin's face seemed to register a glimmer of recognition. Conspiracy buffs later claimed Oswald, a white shirt peeking from under his dark crew neck sweater, recognized the man later identified as Jack Ruby. Others maintained that Oswald's expression was an acknowledgment of a pistol the assassin suddenly pointed at Oswald's midsection.

Like millions of others, Kilgallen watched in disbelief as the man, from a distance of about fifteen inches, pulled the trigger. The gunshot caused Detective Leavelle, his eyes reflecting disbelief, to recoil in horror. Robert Jackson snapped his Pulitzer-prize winning photograph at this moment.

Kilgallen screamed as Oswald moaned in anguish. His eyes gazed upward. He crumpled to the ground. The television image of the second assassination spread across the planet. Kilgallen watched as Detective Graves freed his hand from Oswald's arm. The detective grabbed the shooter and wrestled him to the ground like a defensive lineman tackling the fullback.

Graves grasped the revolver so the man could fire no more. Oswald was in cardiac arrest, with wounds to his kidneys, spleen, and aorta. The main suspect in the assassination of President John Fitzgerald Kennedy died a short time later at Parkland Memorial Hospital.

A shocked Kilgallen watched as police arrested the assailant. She walked around her townhouse in disbelief. *Two assassinations in three days,* she told herself. *Something doesn't make sense. Something's very wrong.*

* * * * *

While Dorothy Kilgallen attempted to make sense of the strange turn of events in Dallas, famed attorney Melvin Belli enjoyed lunch with friend J. Kelly Farris at Scoma's Restaurant at San Francisco's Fisherman's Wharf. A waiter told Belli that Ruby killed Oswald. Belli, dubbed by *Life Magazine* the "King of Torts" for his prowess as a personal injury attorney, boasted, Farris told this author, "Well, since Oswald's dead, I'll have to defend Ruby." Perplexed by the comment, Farris asked Belli to elaborate. He did not do so.

Certain the killing of Oswald confounded logic, Dorothy Kilgallen began to investigate the man she learned was Jack Ruby. She wondered why he was present in the Dallas Police Department basement for Oswald's transfer. Within minutes, she reached out to contacts in the department looking for answers.

Meanwhile, Jack Ruby, while being led to his jail cell, asked Detective Don Ray Archer if Oswald was dead. Recalling the conversation, Archer said:

> [Ruby's] behavior to begin with was very hyper. He was sweating profusely. I could see his heart beating....He asked me for one of my cigarettes. I gave him a cigarette. Finally, after about two hours had elapsed, the head of the Secret Service came up and I conferred with him and he told me that Oswald had died. This should have shocked [Ruby] because it would mean the death penalty. I returned and said, "Jack, it looks like it's going to be the electric chair for you."
>
> Instead of being shocked, he became calm, he quit sweating, his heart slowed down. I asked him if he wanted a cigarette and he advised me that he didn't smoke. I was just astonished at this complete difference of behavior from what I had expected. I would say his life had depended on him getting Oswald.

On the morning of November 25, Kilgallen, ever inquisitive about the assassinations, made plans to visit Dallas. At the same time, J. Edgar Hoover issued a memo to the Dallas Police Department. It stated that FBI headquarters in Washington D.C. should receive all DPD files. In essence, Hoover and the Bureau had taken over the investigation.

Unbeknownst to Kilgallen, Hoover also called White House aide Walter Jenkins. He told him, "The thing I am most concerned about and so is Mr. Katzenbach, is having something issued so we can convince the public that Oswald is the real assassin." Hoover instructed aide Clyde Tolson to "prepare a memorandum to the Attorney General setting out the evidence that Oswald was responsible for the shooting that killed the president."

On November 25, 1963, less than two years until Kilgallen's death, JFK's funeral took place in Washington D.C. Representatives from 90 countries attended. Kilgallen, watching on television, wept at the death of her friend.

All the while, Kilgallen's suspicions consumed her mind as to whether Oswald acted alone. She also kept wondering how Ruby was able to kill Oswald so quickly after his arrest.

At her home office desk in the "Cloop," Kilgallen typed columns focused on President Kennedy and wife Jackie. She praised the president for his dedication to civil rights and Jackie for being such a credit to the long line of first ladies. Using her powerful reputation, Kilgallen gathered information from Dallas sources. They promised secret police department files.

Meanwhile, at his home in Virginia, Robert Kennedy walked the grounds with his favorite dog, Brumus, a black Newfoundland. RFK's head bowed. He was stricken with grief. He had lost his brother, his best friend.

The next day, Kilgallen read a press release from J. Edgar Hoover at FBI headquarters: "Not a shred of evidence has been developed to link any other person in a conspiracy with Oswald to assassinate President Kennedy." Kilgallen shook her head in disbelief. Hoover, it appeared, was intent on closing any government investigation before it began.

CHAPTER 12

At the *Journal-American* offices, readers flooded Dorothy Kilgallen's desk with various theories about the JFK assassination. In her "Voice of Broadway" column, she wrote, "I wish I could acknowledge all of [the letters], but it is impossible so I hope those who wrote to me in the days following my columns on President and Mrs. Kennedy will accept my heartfelt thanks now."

While Kilgallen pored over the correspondence, Dallas County Assistant District Attorney Bill Alexander spoke with friends. He told this author he was surprised JFK was dead, telling the friends, "I had heard RFK was going to be killed because as many people as he had screwed, ones like local law enforcement that he stepped all over, or with people he hadn't kept his word with, underworld people like [Carlos] Marcello, politicians and the like. He just had too many enemies, many more than his brother."

As Alexander ruminated about JFK's demise, Kilgallen continued to receive information about Oswald and Ruby from her Dallas contacts. An assassination investigation file she had created thickened. Kilgallen was determined to probe the DPD and FBI investigations. She wanted to make certain the public learned all of the facts.

In the *Journal-American*, Kilgallen read the Page Five headline, "Famous Attorney Melvin Belli to Represent Jack Ruby." Kilgallen was suspicious and used her San Francisco contacts to investigate. She learned Belli's practice focused exclusively on civil cases instead of criminal matters. He had not tried a murder case in years. He had never tried a capital murder case like Ruby's. The information made her wonder why Belli had been retained to represent Oswald's killer. Kilgallen made plans to attend Ruby's trial.

At her townhouse, Kilgallen watched television coverage of Belli arriving at the Dallas airport. Reporters flocked to his side. He announced his representation of Ruby by telling the media Earl Ruby, Jack's brother, had hired him to represent Jack.[1] Belli never mentioned his mobster client and friend Mickey Cohen. Belli also failed to tell reporters he had represented Ruby's close friend and Cohen's girlfriend, stripper Candy Barr,[2] at the request of Cohen, before Judge Joe Brown a few years earlier. He was the same judge who would oversee the Ruby trial. Reporters thus neglected to connect Belli with Cohen or Barr. They missed the opportunity to question whether, due to Belli's friendship with, and representation of, a dangerous underworld figure, the Mafia could have been involved in the JFK and Oswald assassinations.

On the 29th, Kilgallen noted with interest President Lyndon Johnson's formation of the Warren Commission. It would investigate the JFK assassination. Kilgallen examined the list of Commission members. She began background checks on each.

Without exception, every journalist focusing on what had happened in Dallas appeared satisfied with J. Edgar Hoover's official statement that it was Oswald and Oswald alone who assassinated JFK. Kilgallen had strong beliefs to the contrary. Ever defiant when she believed any sort of cover-up happened, Kilgallen decided to question the official investigation with the

---

[1] Belli made several inconsistent statements regarding how he became Ruby's attorney in two different books he wrote, *Dallas Justice* and *My Life on Trial*. One version alleged that Earl Ruby watched him in an LA courtroom and was impressed enough to ask that Belli represent Jack Ruby. This proved to be false. When asked by this author about how Belli became Ruby's lawyer, Belli's associate Seymour Ellison attributed it to "a call from a Las Vegas businessman, someone in the entertainment industry."

[2] Candy Barr, stage name for Juanita Dale Slusher, was a top name stripper who appeared in Las Vegas and also at Jack Ruby's Carousel Bar. At one point, she was engaged to gangster Mickey Cohen, Melvin Belli's client. When Barr was arrested for narcotics violations and sentenced to a long prison term with Judge Brown presiding and Bill Alexander prosecuting, Belli was hired to appeal the case.

Within 10 hours after Ruby's shooting of Oswald, the FBI interrogated Candy Barr. The agents asked about her friendship with Ruby and any part in an alleged plot to kill the president. The interrogation lasted several hours. The next day, a *Dallas Morning News* article read: "Candy Barr, [a] well-known Dallas stripper who worked a few doors down from Ruby's strip club, told reporters she received a call from Ruby shortly before the JFK assassination. She said [Ruby] was trying to get in touch with Mickey Cohen or some other mobster. Ruby was certain that Juanita [Candy] would know how."

dogged determination she had employed during other high profile cases including the trial of Dr. Sam Sheppard.

With this in mind, her November 29 *Journal-American* column, entitled "The Oswald File Must Not Close," was a call to action loud and clear. Troubled by the circumstances surrounding the assassinations, the column launched what would become a full-scale investigation on her part. It would last until the day she died.

At the outset, Kilgallen's strong words aimed at the new president. She wrote:

> President Lyndon Johnson has been elevated so swiftly to his new high post that in one sense, he has been snatched up into an ivory tower. As Chief Executive, he is no longer in a position to hear the voices of ordinary people talking candidly. If he could walk invisible along the streets of the nation and listen to ordinary people talking, he would realize that he must be sure that the mystery of Lee Harvey Oswald is solved and laid before the nation down to the smallest shred of evidence.

The next six words Kilgallen used were most revealing. They were in complete opposition to those offered by Dallas Police Chief Jesse Curry and J. Edgar Hoover, cheerleaders for the "Oswald Alone" theory. Kilgallen wrote, "If Oswald is President Kennedy's assassin, he is the most important prisoner the police in this country had in 100 years and no blithe announcement in Dallas is going to satisfy the American public that the case is closed."

Continuing, Kilgallen wrote, "President Johnson has directed the FBI to look into every aspect of the case, but he must go a giant step further. He must satisfy the public's uneasy mind about this peculiar assassination of the assassin or he will start his term in office by making a dire political mistake that can cost him the 1964 election." In the next paragraph she added:

The case is closed, is it? Well, I'd like to know how, in a big, smart town like Dallas, a man like Jack Ruby—owner of a strip tease honky tonk—can stroll in and out of police headquarters as if it was at a health club at a time when a small army of law enforcers is keeping a "tight security guard" on Oswald. Security! What a word for it.

Further making her case for a full-scale investigation, Kilgallen added, "I will not try to speak for the people of Dallas, but around here, the people I talk to really believe that a man has the right to be tried in court. When that right is taken away from any man by the incredible combination of a Jack Ruby and insufficient security, we feel chilled." Continuing her strong diatribe, Kilgallen wrote, "Justice is a big rug. When you pull it out from under one man, a lot of others fall too."

Providing another indication of her suspicions, Kilgallen added:

That is why so many people are saying there is "something queer" about the killing of Oswald, something strange about the way his case was handled, a great deal missing in the official account of his crime. The American people have just lost a beloved President. It is a dark chapter in our history, but we have the right to read every word of it. It cannot be kept locked in a file in Dallas.

Kilgallen's laundry list of enemies expanded. It included the State Department, the CIA, the FBI, Fidel Castro supporters, the Russian government, and angered celebrities like Frank Sinatra. Added now were those who may have been involved in the John Kennedy and Lee Harvey Oswald assassinations. To the latter, a chill had to run up their spine—the most famous crime reporter of the time intended to search for the truth.

CHAPTER 13

Shortly after writing the column, Dorothy Kilgallen telephoned Melvin Belli in Dallas. She asked his intentions concerning Jack Ruby's defense. Belli was noncommittal while flirting with the famous journalist. He said he looked forward to meeting her at the Ruby trial.

Kilgallen continued to wonder how Belli became Ruby's lawyer when he was a civil attorney not a criminal lawyer. She knew there were many nationally known defense lawyers available more qualified to represent Oswald's killer. Among them were Charles Bellows, Charles Tessmer, and Jake Erlich.

At the Dallas jail, Ruby told Belli he killed Oswald so Jackie Kennedy and the family could avoid a trial. Belli dismissed the story. He ordered Ruby not to discuss his case with anyone.

Kilgallen's research confirmed Belli's prowess as a trial lawyer in high-profile civil cases. He had won large verdicts against such corporations as Coca-Cola and Cutter Laboratories. Clever as a trial strategist, Belli implemented creative methods to convince juries to award substantial plaintiffs' verdicts. He employed innovative "demonstrative evidence" courtroom exhibits. They included "Day in the Life" projections visualizing how severe the disabilities of his injured clients were on a daily basis.

While Kilgallen further investigated Belli and Ruby, at FBI headquarters on Dec. 6, 1963, J. Edgar Hoover spoke with a high-level agent. He told him no grand jury investigation of the assassinations was necessary.

Why? Because, Hoover asserted, it was not a Federal crime to kill the president unless a conspiracy existed. The Director insisted there was none.

Days later, Kilgallen's *Journal-American* reported that Robert Kennedy and LBJ met at the White House. Friction was apparent based on mistrust between the two powerful men. LBJ placated Bobby regarding his continuing to be attorney general. It was apparent RFK had little interest in promoting any of LBJ's agenda especially his pursuit of underworld figures. RFK left the Oval Office despondent. Bobby hated LBJ. The feeling was mutual.[1] RFK knew his days with the new administration were numbered.

On December 11, 1963, Kilgallen once again noted the assassinations in her *Journal-American* column. It was entitled "Still Live Topic." Dorothy Kilgallen wrote, "What happened in Texas on Nov. 22 and two days later is extraordinary, so it is inevitable that people should continue to discuss the events, debate them, and argue about them. But even I am amazed at the sustaining interest in the assassination and its aftermath."

Extolling her propensity for mixing with the rich and famous, Kilgallen then wrote of a party she attended. Stage and film director Joshua Logan (*Picnic, Bus Stop*) hosted. The guests included celebrated author Truman Capote, wealthy sportsman Alfred Vanderbilt, American impresario, theatrical showman and lyricist Billy Rose (*Me and My Shadow*), and the former president of Mexico. She wrote:

---

[1] Author Jeff Shesol wrote, "Lyndon Johnson and Robert Kennedy loathed each other. 'This man,' Kennedy said of Johnson, 'is mean bitter, vicious—an animal in many ways.' Johnson considered Kennedy a 'grandstanding little runt.' Their mutual contempt was so acute, their bitterness so intense and abiding, they could scarcely speak in each other's presence." In *LBJ*, a *PBS* documentary aired in 2006, John Connally said of the rivalry, "LBJ and Bobby hated each other," and Bobby Baker, Johnson's political adviser, added, "mutual dislike between LBJ and RFK was second to none in the world.

As I moved from group to group, it seemed to me that there was no one who did not want to talk, for a moment or for quite a long time about President Kennedy, Jacqueline's astonishing fortitude after his death, the killing of Lee Harvey Oswald, and the mysterious figure who shot him, Jack Ruby. One might think that this collection of sophisticates and celebrities might be "tired" of the topic by now, but they were not obviously.

On December 12, 1963, Kilgallen noted a *Journal-American* mention of a speech by American Bar Association president-elect Edward Kuhn. Regarding Belli's representation of Ruby, Kuhn told reporters, "Belli is not a criminal [defense] lawyer. He will make a circus out of this case."

While Kilgallen made plans to visit Dallas and meet Belli, in his San Francisco offices on the unseasonably balmy day of January 15, the famed civil lawyer examined legal treatises while preparing the Ruby defense. After several days of deliberation, he chose one realizing it would surprise the prosecution and the public at large. They expected him to throw Ruby on the mercy of the court and plead for a light sentence in light of millions of witnesses having seen Ruby shoot Oswald on television.

In New York City, Kilgallen continued to wrestle with Oswald's motive for assassinating JFK. She demanded more information from her Dallas sources. At the same time, RFK discussed who was responsible for JFK's death with CIA Director John McCone. During an interview for the John Lowery Simpson Oral History series, McCone stated, "[RFK] wanted to know what we knew about it and whether it had been a Cuban or perhaps Russian hit. He even asked me if the CIA could have done it. I mentioned the mob but RFK didn't want to know about it. I suspect he thought it was the mob. He said, ' They—whoever 'they' were—should have killed me. I'm the one they wanted.'"

Meanwhile, on January 22, 1964, Kilgallen discussed the assassinations with her *Journal-American* editor. She told him Jack Ruby was the key to solving the case. The editor said she should interview Ruby but that was probably impossible. Kilgallen explained that Belli was enamored of her. She believed through him, an interview with Ruby was likely.

Two days later, an anxious Belli, unaware that Kilgallen had launched a full-scale investigation into his law practice, visited Ruby in jail. Belli explained to his client that an insanity defense could be their best option. Ruby was dubious. He asked Belli whether he believed he was crazy. Belli begged the question. He then convinced Ruby their *only* defense was insanity. Ruby reluctantly agreed but wanted to tell his story. Belli warned Ruby that would be a huge mistake. When Belli left, Ruby was distraught but he decided he had to trust Belli. After all, the famous lawyer represented mobster Mickey Cohen, Ruby's idol.

At her home office, Dorothy Kilgallen's file on the assassinations swelled. She spent hours on the telephone tracking down leads on Jack Ruby. Then she bought an airplane ticket for Dallas. Kilgallen was about to cover her second "Trial of the Century."

CHAPTER 14

On February 12, 1964, 20 months before her death, Dorothy Kilgallen and more than 400 reporters from around the world flocked to the entrance of the Dallas County courthouse as rain pelted the sidewalk. At a few minutes before 9:00 a.m., Melvin Belli entered. A dour-faced Jack Ruby joined him at counsel table.

At the pre-trial hearing, Belli addressed Judge Joe Brown. Ruby's attorney informed the court of his intended defense: "Not guilty by reason of psychomotor epilepsy insanity." Hearing the news, Kilgallen's face froze in shock. Chief trial prosecutor Bill Alexander told this author, "I could not understand Belli's strategy. It made no sense."

Three days later, Kilgallen and Belli, both staying at the Statler Hilton Dallas hotel, dined together. Kilgallen asked if she could interview Ruby. Belli told her that was impossible since Ruby was crazy. Kilgallen disputed the claim. Belli was insistent.

On February 21, Kilgallen read with interest the latest issue of *Life* magazine. It featured the infamous photograph of Lee Harvey Oswald brandishing his rifle on the cover. The magazine touted headlines reading "Exclusive—Oswald Armed for Murder, In Full and Extra Ordinary Detail, The Life of The Assassin." Below the caption, the blurb read, "As Jack Ruby Goes to Trial, Cast of Characters: How the Law Applies."

In one accompanying photograph, Kilgallen noticed that Ruby stood with his hands clasped in handcuffs. He was dressed in a dark suit, white shirt and tie. His eyes stared blankly at the reader in an eerie fashion. The photograph caption read, "As Ruby goes to trial, the question before the court: Was This Man Sane?" District Attorney Henry Wade, when asked about the insanity defense, replied, "We think [this] is a case of cold-blooded, calculated murder."

In a biting *Journal-American* column of February 21, Kilgallen noted the government's refusal to provide the Ruby defense team documents requested. After quoting a governmental reply to Belli's co-counsel Joe Tonahill, she wrote:

> Say that again, slowly. Information concerning Oswald's assassination of the president will not be available. Perhaps it is dramatizing to say that there is an Orwellian note in that line. But it does make you think, doesn't it? It appears that Washington knows or suspects something about Lee Harvey Oswald that it does not want Dallas and the rest of the world to know or suspect....Lee Harvey Oswald has passed on not only to his shuddery reward, but to the mysterious realm of "classified" persons whose whole story is known only to a few government agents.
>
> Why is Oswald being kept in the shadows, as dim a figure as they can make him, while the defense tries to rescue his alleged killer with the help of information from the FBI? Who is Oswald anyway?"

To Tonahill, Belli boasted about gaining Kilgallen's cooperation. He also proudly pointed to the *Life Magazine* story's implication that Ruby was insane. Tonahill criticized Belli's insanity defense. Every one of his colleagues did as well. According to author interviews with Belli's associate Seymour Ellison, Tonahill and his daughter Rebecca, Belli refused to alter the strategy.

The same day, Kilgallen begged Belli to permit her an interview with Ruby. He once again told her this was impossible. Her persuasive charm began to chill his resistance. When Belli mentioned his interest in a career as an actor, Kilgallen sensed a trade of sorts. She could provide Hollywood contacts in exchange for his allowing the Ruby interview.

At his Virginia home far away from the Kilgallen/Belli rendezvous, RFK, despite the frigid temperature, sat with wife Ethel by the pool at his home. He read works by Albert Camus, Greek philosophers, and classicist Edith Hamilton [American educator and author] suggested by Jackie

Dorothy Kilgallen and Jack Ruby attorneys Melvin Belli and Joe Tonahill during the Ruby trial, March 1964.

Kennedy. From Hamilton's *The Greek Way*, RFK selected a passage to remember: "The gods who hated beyond all else the arrogance of power, had passed judgment upon them." Later, Bobby read one Bible verse from Genesis 4:10 that haunted him: "The voice of my brother's blood crieth unto me from the ground."

As Bobby mourned, Kilgallen's February 24[1] *Journal-American* column provided readers with inside information about the Ruby trial. Under the headline, "DA to Link Ruby to Oswald," she wrote:

> Among those who know the seamier side of Dallas show business, the betting is 10 to 1 that Dist. Atty. Hank Wade will produce witnesses who will testify that Jack Ruby and Lee Harvey Oswald were acquainted. Ruby has said repeatedly that he didn't know the alleged assassin of President Kennedy—but then Ruby's plea is temporary insanity and there are a great many things he doesn't remember, and isn't about to.

---

[1] On February 23, Kilgallen had written in her column, "Melvin Bell, Jack Ruby's lawyer, is threatening a giganctic lawsuit if a weekly magazine publishes a highly critical article about him in its present form." The weekly magazine was never identified and Bell never filed the lawsuit.

Kilgallen, having referred to Oswald as an "alleged assassin," then added:

> To quote one observer, "the operation of Jack's Carousel Club had its unsavory aspects but if Oswald checked in there a couple of nights a week, he could have made some extra money. That would account for his ability to take trips—like the one to Mexico—on a $50-a-week salary, and it also would account for his lying in a room in the heart of Dallas five nights a week and joining his wife and children in the suburbs only on Fridays and Saturdays."

On March 2, 1964, jury selection began for the Jack Ruby trial. Kilgallen had prepared herself for a high-profile case like this since the early days at the *Evening Journal*. To date, she had covered four of most headline-making trials of the twentieth century, Bruno Hauptmann, Dr. Sam Sheppard, Dr. Bernard Finch, and John Profumo. Kilgallen had written hundreds of articles and columns while learning the ins and outs of the criminal justice system.

Without question, the reporter whom Hemingway had called "one of the greatest women writers in the world," was the preeminent investigative reporter of her era, a skilled wordsmith who paid close attention to detail, to accuracy, to an undying search for the truth. Now Kilgallen, armed with unequaled credentials, was ready to cover the case of a lifetime on the grandest stage of all.

Predictably, Kilgallen, who believed women should challenge men regardless of the occupation, made her appearance amidst much attention. She was a national celebrity whose very presence added to the gala appearance of the trial. Autograph seekers lined the halls before deputies shooed them away. Noted columnist Bob Considine wrote, "Dorothy Kilgallen arrived in court yesterday and stopped the show. Judge Joe B. Brown, one of her fans, gallantly granted (yea, insisted) on an interview in his chambers. Melvin Belli, of San Francisco, and Joe Tonahill, of Jasper, Texas, took her to lunch at a nearby seafood house named Vincent's—whose oysters Belli declared are the best this side of his native city's Fisherman's Wharf."

Jim Lehrer of the *Dallas Times Herald* escorted Kilgallen around the courthouse. He later became a co-anchor on PBS' *News Hour*. Lehrer interviewed Kilgallen regarding Dallas' responsibility for JFK's death. She said, "I don't see why Dallas should feel guilty for what one man, or even three or five in a conspiracy have done."

To anyone involved in the planning and assassination of JFK and Oswald, this was a sure warning sign. Use of the word "conspiracy" by the famous journalist meant she intended to continue investigating the Dallas killings until she revealed the truth.

CHAPTER 15

On a cold and windy morning before court convened, Dorothy Kilgallen visited Dealey Plaza where President John Kennedy had been assassinated.

The famous journalist carefully noted the angle of the street in front of the Book Depository. She examined the exact spot where the shots rang out toward JFK. Looking upward, Kilgallen gazed at the sixth floor window where Oswald had allegedly fired his Carcano rifle. She walked toward the infamous grassy knoll area, and the overpass nearby. Whatever she concluded was included in the ever-expanding assassination file.

On the same day, Earl Ruby, still avoiding Kilgallen, met with Melvin Belli. Earl, at Jack's insistence, explained that his brother was disappointed with the insanity plea. He wanted another lawyer, Charles Tessmer, to be co-counsel. Belli yelled at Earl refusing any consideration of the matter.

While Kilgallen met privately with a Dallas Police Department source, J. Edgar Hoover and Clyde Tolson discussed the Warren Commission investigation at FBI headquarters. Hoover also mentioned his displeasure with Kilgallen's irreverent columns questioning the official account. The Director explained that any FBI information about the Kennedy family was off limits to reporters and the Commission. The Director emphasized again that Oswald acted alone. Hoover said they must head the Commission in that direction and only that direction.

The same evening, Melvin Belli sat alone sipping a drink at a bar in his Dallas hotel. He knew Kilgallen and others might learn his secret: that he was orchestrating, under threat to do so, a trial strategy that, if unsuccessful, could send Ruby to the electric chair. Realizing his integrity had been stripped away, he considered withdrawing from the case but knew such action was impossible. Those who had ordered him to represent Ruby were dangerous men. His only hope was that the convoluted insanity defense might prevail. He needed to convince the jury Ruby was crazy when Belli knew he was not.

At the defense counsel table in an otherwise empty Dallas courtroom, Kilgallen approached Belli's co-counsel Joe Tonahill with a request in mind. Despite the presence of 400 reporters from, among others, the *Chicago Tribune, San Francisco Chronicle, New York Herald Tribune, The National Observer, Life, Time,* and the *Saturday Evening Post,* she was determined to circumvent Belli's delay in permitting her an interview with Ruby.

How this happened was a credit to Kilgallen's ingenuity, her clever ability to slice through any formidable obstacle (Belli had forbidden Ruby to speak to any reporters and the judge had concurred) and get what she wanted. As smart and savvy a journalist who ever plied the trade, Kilgallen had landed on an introduction to Ruby due to her having learned of his friendship with a San Francisco opera singer. Somehow (the circumstances were never revealed), Kilgallen had communicated with the singer and she had asked the famous reporter to give Ruby a message. Armed with information no other reporter had uncovered, Kilgallen developed a plan.

In a videotaped interview (available at TheReporterWhoKnew-TooMuch.com), Tonahill, who had apparently gained Belli's permission for the interview, described how Kilgallen became Ruby's only interviewer at trial. "She told me she had had a contact with friend of Jack's from San Francisco," Tonahill said. "I believe it was an opera singer that he was very fond of. She wanted to pass a message along to him. I told Jack that and he said, 'I'd like to talk to [Kilgallen].'" Tonahill explained, "Jack had a bodyguard shield around him of four deputy sheriffs sitting behind him and everywhere he went and I told them Kilgallen wanted to ask him some questions and speak with him at recess and that he'd agreed to it. And they said 'okay.'" Tonahill added, "So when the judge declared the noon recess, Jack went over and spoke with her...in the courtroom right behind his

Dorothy Kilgallen whispers in the ear of Jack Ruby co-counsel Joe Tonahill during Ruby trial.

chair where he was sitting…there was a rail there and he got up and she was on the other side of the rail and Jack was on this side and they had a little conversation. I think the press had already left the courtroom." Asked how long Kilgallen and Ruby spoke, Tonahill replied, "About five minutes." [1]

Tonahill added, "[Kilgallen] started out saying this opera singer in San Francisco had spoken to her about Jack and she wanted to tell him something. I didn't pay much attention to what they were saying." Asked if Tonahill knew the name of the opera singer, he said, "No," but then added, "Jack was pretty enthusiastic about [the opera singer] so they must have been pretty close friends."

---

[1] Told that Earl Ruby denied Kilgallen ever interviewed his brother ("I asked Sheriff Bill Decker and he said she never had an interview with Jack"), Tonahill said, "I don't know why Earl would make that statement because it's absolutely untrue. Bill Decker, the sheriff, knew about the interview. The officers told him about it after I told them and they went to their boss and the boss said, 'Okay.'"

Once the interview began, Kilgallen looked into Ruby's weary face. She noticed his hands were shaking. She said they chatted for eight minutes. Kilgallen left the courtroom with pages of notes.

A DOROTHY KILGALLEN EXCLUSIVE

Nervous Ruby Feels "Breaking Point" Near

In her Dallas hotel room, a perplexed Kilgallen typed her *Journal-American* story for February 23, 1964. Under the banner "A Dorothy Kilgallen Exclusive," she chose the headline: "Nervous Ruby Feels Breaking Point Near." The first paragraph read, "Jack Ruby's eyes were as shiny brown-and-white bright as the glass eyes of a doll. He tried to smile but his smile was a failure. When we shook hands, his hand trembled in mine ever so slightly, like the heartbeat of a bird."

Continuing, the article, Kilgallen added, "'I'm nervous and worried,' he told me. 'I feel I'm on the verge of something I don't understand—the breaking point maybe.'" When Kilgallen told Ruby "I think you're holding up pretty well," he replied, "I'm fooling you Dorothy. I'm really scared."

To explain the circumstances surrounding how she garnered the exclusive interview, Kilgallen wrote:

> I had stayed behind because I had been told that Ruby would like to talk to me. In a short while co-counsel Joe Tonahill beckoned to me, and I went up to the defense table. "Jack would like to talk to you," he said. Jack rose politely to shake hands, his eyes glistening and his mouth smiling but the total effect inexpressively sad. "It's wonderful to see you Dorothy," were his first words…

Kilgallen ended the article by writing:

> I went out into the almost empty lunchroom corridor wondering what I really believed about this man.

Why Kigallen did not mention the opera singer involved was probably due to her protecting the woman's identity. Why she made it seem like Ruby asked to speak to her may have been to blunt any disparaging remarks from fellow reporters upset over the special treatment she received since interviewing Ruby was a scoop of immense proportions. Once again, the fearless Kilgallen had prevailed with determination unmatched among journalists of the day.

Meanwhile, on March 4, 1964, as Kilgallen looked on from a front row seat, Ruby trial testimony commenced. The prosecution, led by Henry Wade and Bill Alexander, paraded several police officers to the witness stand. They established Ruby's premeditation before killing Oswald. Witnesses included Detective Don Ray Archer. He quoted Ruby as saying "I intended to shoot Oswald three times." When this happened, Kilgallen stared at Ruby. She considered what the true motive might be for his killing JFK's alleged assassin.

At Belli's hotel that evening, Kilgallen and Belli discussed the trial. She requested a second interview with Ruby. Belli refused. Before she left the room, he changed his mind.

In the bar downstairs, Kilgallen wondered, as many of Belli's colleagues did: Why was he forging ahead with the absurd psychomotor epilepsy insanity defense? It made no sense. Based on her observations during the interview, Ruby, though scared appeared mentally stable. Why not simply plead Ruby guilty and let Judge Brown sentence him? Why risk the death penalty when a few years in prison might result if Belli could garner sympathy for his beleaguered client? After all, she knew, Ruby had killed Oswald, the most hated man on the face of the earth.

Proof of Kilgallen's suspicion about Belli's defense had first surfaced in a February 21, 1964 column. Recall she wrote, "...Ruby's plea is temporary insanity and there are a great many things [Ruby] doesn't remember and isn't about to." The "isn't about to" quote was revealing. It apparently meant she believed Ruby, regardless of his mental state, had to keep certain information secret. That directive, she knew, could only have come from Belli.

While Kilgallen attempted to unravel the mystery of Belli's defense strategy, at the Justice Department one day later, Warren Commission investigators met with Deputy Attorney General Nicholas Katzenbach. They discussed access to Justice Department files. Under orders from Robert Kennedy, Katzenbach agreed to cooperate with the defense lawyers but only to a limited extent.

Prior to court convening in Dallas, Kilgallen arranged to interview Ruby once again. Before she did so, Oswald's killer asked Belli to let him testify. Belli refused the request. He explained that the doctors were their best witnesses. He told Ruby he would get "tricked" if he testified. Ruby was upset. An argument ensued. Ruby told Belli that he was not crazy. Belli asked Ruby to trust him. Ruby reluctantly did so.

At court the next day, Kilgallen spoke with Judge Joe Brown. Like others, he was impressed with her celebrity status. He had asked for an autograph. She obliged. He agreed to allow her to conduct the private interview with Ruby away from the courtroom. Fellow reporters screamed at the news. They complained to Judge Brown about the special treatment. He had his public relations man placate them.

A small office nearby was chosen. Ruby's guards and Joe Tonahill waited outside after Belli had given the go-ahead. Kilgallen spoke to Oswald's cold-blooded killer for less than ten minutes. To friends, she acknowledged the meeting but, for reasons unknown, never the substance of the conversation. Whatever Ruby told Kilgallen remained a secret with the information noted in her ever-expanding assassination file.

On March 10, 1964, Kilgallen listened carefully to three psychiatrists Belli presented for the defense. They included Yale's Dr. Roy Schafer. He testified regarding Ruby's unstable mental state before he shot Oswald. Kilgallen was skeptical of his findings in lieu of the second interview with Ruby.

In her *Journal-American* story, Kilgallen described Ruby as "a gangster," referring to her having connected him to the Chicago "laundry shakedown rackets" in a previous December 1963 column. When Ruby learned of her depiction, he told Belli he was "upset" with what she wrote.[2]

With Kilgallen absent from the courtroom, *Dallas Morning News* reporter Wes Wise talked to Ruby. Wise asked Ruby if he wanted to testify. Ruby nodded "yes." He then told Wise, "But Belli knows best."

At the Justice Department, Robert Kennedy met with Kilgallen's friend, White House Press Secretary Pierre Salinger. Afterwards, he told

---

[2] Ruby stated in a medical interview, "I did like Dorothy Kilgallen until she wrote a column saying I was a gangster so I don't like her now."

a colleague that Bobby was the most "shattered man he had ever seen in his life. He [is] virtually non-functioning." Pulitzer Prize winning author Arthur Schlesinger agreed. He told Salinger RFK refused to involve himself in the question of who murdered his brother. Salinger said Bobby did not want any investigation. He had left Katzenbach to deal with the Warren Commission.

The next day, as Kilgallen looked on, Belli further questioned Dr. Roy Schafer about Ruby's mental state. While doing so, Belli mistakenly called his client Oswald. Judge Joe Brown shook his head in disgust. This was the fifth time Belli had mixed up his client with JFK's alleged assassin.

Kilgallen was also curious about Belli's miscues. In her hotel room, she worked on her book, *Murder One*. She was still uncertain whether the Ruby case would be included or part of a separate book.

At his hotel bar, a worn-down Belli sat with chauffeur and friend Milton Hunt. In a low tone, Belli startled Hunt confessing, as Hunt told this author, "The Ruby case is fixed; I'm just going through the motions. It's simply being staged for the sake of publicity." Belli, according to Hunt, added, "there's an inside thing, and no way to win, it's a whitewash." Troubled by Belli's admissions, Hunt wondered whether he should pass them along to the court, to Jack Ruby or the Ruby family. He did not do so.

During the late afternoon hours of the 12th, Belli stunned Kilgallen and the other reporters. He formally rested Ruby's defense without permitting him to testify. After the trial, Ruby affirmed to the media, "I wanted to tell my story."

Belli's decision caught not only Kilgallen and the media off-guard but the jury as well. Jury Foreman Max Causey later wrote, "The biggest shock of the trial came…when Mr. Belli rose to his feet and told the court, 'The defense rests'…I don't think we were any more surprised than the prosecution. I looked over [at them] to see what they were going to do now, and I noticed that they appeared to be taken completely by surprise."

In her hotel room the next morning, Kilgallen read the *Dallas Morning News* headline: "Final Arguments Set in Ruby Trial. Big Question: Was Ruby Crazy?"

CHAPTER 16

On the afternoon of March 13, 1964, Dorothy Kilgallen listened intently as Bill Alexander rose to address the jury. In a confident tone, he said, "I'm not defending Oswald. But American justice demands that he was entitled to protection from the law as a living, breathing American citizen."

Scowling, Alexander turned toward Ruby. As Kilgallen winced, Alexander shouted at him calling Ruby "the judge, jury, and executioner, one who committed a thrill kill, seeking notoriety." The harsh words caused Kilgallen to sympathize with Ruby's plight. Was he also a "patsy," the same word Oswald had used when questioned about his involvement in the JFK assassination? Was Ruby a sacrificial lamb, the fall guy for those masterminding the president's death?

After a long recess following Henry Wade's final argument, Melvin Belli addressed the jurors. Kilgallen took extensive notes. Belli proclaimed the important evidence from the doctors clearly proved Ruby insane. Belli told the jurors Ruby did not belong in prison. Belli asked for justice despite knowing that Ruby was getting anything *but* justice.

As the lawyers conferred over jury instructions, Kilgallen noticed Jack Ruby sitting by himself in the stuffy courtroom. His shoulders were slumped, his head bowed. Finally, Earl Ruby joined him. The brothers sat arm in arm. Kilgallen reviewed her notes about the final arguments. She realized Belli had never asked the jury to spare Ruby's life if he was found guilty.

The Ruby jury deliberated on March 14, 1964. Kilgallen sat in her hotel room confronting suspicions that something was terribly wrong with the trial. She sensed that Belli seemed to have thrown the case like a punch-drunk fighter. The telephone rang. The jury had reached a verdict. Racing toward the courthouse, she ran into Belli. Excited, he told her "No jury in the world will convict Ruby with less than three hours of deliberation."

Outside the courtroom, Bill Alexander told this author reporters surrounded him. One, he said, asked if Belli surprised the prosecution by not pleading for Ruby's life. Alexander explained to this author that he informed the reporters, "Yes, I am shocked," while adding that Ruby was "gonna get the chair," and that he felt "kind of sorry" for Ruby. He said Belli "took a good five-year murder-without-malice-case, and made it into a death penalty one for his client."

At 11:14 a.m., television cameras were set to record the Ruby verdict. Kilgallen sat nervously with the other journalists awaiting Ruby's fate. She could not take her eyes off him.

Two hours and 19 minutes after Wayne Causey was selected foreman (not all spent deliberating), the jurors were somber as they filed into the courtroom. They took their seats never glancing in Ruby's direction. Belli knew what this meant. He turned toward his client and whispered, "It's bad. Take it easy. We expected it all along and we tried this case for an appeal court. We'll make it there. I'll stick with you." Only half-hearing Belli's words, Ruby's face was ashen, any hope of freedom dashed.

A minute later, Foreman Causey handed the verdict form to Bailiff Bo Mabra. He in turn passed it to Judge Brown. After shuffling through the pages and reviewing it, the Judge read the words aloud without expression: "We the jury find the defendant guilty of murder with malice, as charged in the indictment, and affix his punishment at death." Judge Brown then quickly asked, "Is this unanimous. So say you all? Please hold up your right hands." All twelve jurors did so.

In the courtroom, the crowd appeared dazed and confused as to how to react. There was no eruption of cheering and no sobbing. Reporters scurried to write their stories. Each hid emotion behind blank faces. Ruby's sister Eileen, tears welling in her eyes, and his brother Earl bowed their heads. Ruby appeared dazed, a look of puzzlement and confusion apparent on his face. Had he really heard the words "affix his punishment at death?"

In her seat, Kilgallen gasped at the death penalty verdict. She continued to watch Ruby. Like Bill Alexander, she felt sorry for this condemned man. Ruby had killed Oswald, the most despised man in the world but execution was his fate.

Kilgallen's eyes met Ruby's. She shook her head. Handcuffed, Ruby left the courtroom. As he disappeared from view, Kilgallen told herself she would search for the truth. She was certain there had been a conspiracy. Typing quickly in the pressroom, she forwarded her report to the *Journal-American*. Then she headed for the hotel bar and a stiff drink.

On March 19, the Ruby family fired Melvin Belli.[1] One day later, Kilgallen's *Journal-American* "Voice of Broadway" column read, "The point to be remembered in this historic case is that the whole truth has not been told. Neither the state of Texas nor the defense put on all of its evidence before the jury. Perhaps it was not necessary, but it would have been desirable from the viewpoint of all of the American people."

Nearly a month later, on April 14, 1965, Kilgallen was at it again headlining her *Journal-American* column with the daunting words, "Why Did Oswald Risk All By Shooting Cop?" Although the logic requires careful examination, the column proves she was continuing to question the "Oswald Alone" theory even *after* the Ruby trial had ended. Kilgallen wrote:

> A mysterious and significant aspect of the events following the assassination of President Kennedy in Dallas has never been explored publically, although it must have occurred to crack reporters covering the case as well as authorities investigating the tragedies. The important question—why did Lee Harvey Oswald, presumably fleeing from the police after the assassination, approach Patrolman J. D. Tippit's car—in broad daylight

---

[1] In his book, *Dallas and the Jack Ruby Trial,* Judge Joe Brown said he had "talked to the jury" and they had told him "Belli offered them no alternative but either an acquittal or an extreme penalty." Brown also scolded Belli for never fitting the facts to the possibility of "murder without malice, a homicide committed under extreme passion created by passion or horror, or resentment or horror that renders a mind incapable of cool reflection" so the jury had a choice for a conviction carrying a maximum sentence of five years.

with witnesses standing by—and shoot the policeman three times, although he had not said a word to Oswald.

Oswald had managed to slip away from the scene and was—up to that point—not a reckless one. A man who knows he is wanted by the authorities after a spectacular crime does not seek out a policeman usually, unless he has decided to givehimself up, and certainly Oswald was not doing that. By shooting Tippit instead of trying to make himself inconspicuous, Oswald put himself in double jeopardy. His act almost guaranteed his arrest. Why? A whodunit fan would infer that the policeman knew something about Oswald that was so dangerous [the policeman] had to be silenced at any cost, even Oswald's chance at escape and freedom.

Kilgallen's relentless pursuit of the truth, her asking questions no other reporter was asking, caused author Mark Lane, whom she had first met when he was a New York state legislator, to write of Kilgallen: "She was a very, very serious journalist. You might say that she was the only serious journalist in America who was concerned with who killed John Kennedy and getting all of the facts about the assassination."

CHAPTER 17

In early April 1964 with the Jack Ruby trial in the rear view mirror, Dorothy Kilgallen met with attorney F. Lee Bailey in New York City. He was the appellate counsel for Dr. Sam Sheppard, the Cleveland physician imprisoned for killing his wife.

During a private conversation as spring temperatures abounded, Kilgallen provided Bailey with crucial information regarding Sheppard's trial never divulged before. More about the case would be included in Kilgallen's book, *Murder One*.

While Kilgallen added text to the manuscript, RFK spoke to JFK presidential confidant Ken O'Donnell about the Dallas assassinations. He recalled, "I mentioned the Syndicate—the Mob—as a possibility. I'm certain RFK thought the Mob had been involved. He suspected Carlos Marcello, the New Orleans capo to whom Jack Ruby had ties...All he kept saying was 'They should've killed me,' without indicating who *they* were."

In a far different case than Ruby's, that same month Kilgallen was shocked when NYC detectives arrested comedian Lenny Bruce. He had given a profanity-laced performance in Greenwich Village. The charges were based on a law prohibiting "obscene, indecent, immoral, and impure exhibition and entertainment that would tend to the corruption of the morals of youth and others." For each of the three charges against him, Bruce faced a maximum punishment of three years in prison.

Free speech was on trial. Many noted celebrities supported Bruce: Elizabeth Taylor, Richard Burton, Norman Mailer, Paul Newman, Bob Dylan,

Woody Allen, Susan Sontag and John Updike. Kilgallen added her name to the cause.

When Bruce's trial ensued, Kilgallen, a staunch defender of free expression, was a defense witness. Asked about the artistic merit of Bruce's act, she answered, "I think Lenny Bruce is a brilliant satirist—perhaps the most brilliant I have ever seen—and I think his social commentary, whether I agree with it or not, is extremely valid and important." Despite Kilgallen's plaudits, the jury convicted Bruce.

An appeals court reversed the decision. The reversal caused Bruce's trial counsel to exclaim, "I have to think that [Kilgallen] had a lot to do with the ultimate result of the case. The briefs that were filed placed an enormous reliance on Kilgallen, again because of what she is and what she stands for." Later, Kilgallen, her impact as a media icon once again revealed, caused a stir when she told reporters, "Lenny Bruce is a very moral man trying to improve the world and trying to make audiences think."

Meanwhile, day by day, Kilgallen continued to investigate the Dallas assassinations. She used her stature as an investigative reporter and media star to full advantage. One evening, a person close to the Warren Commission probe contacted her out of the hundreds of reporters who had covered the Ruby trial. He said he had a copy of Ruby's testimony before the commission and trusted her to reveal it to its best advantage. Respect for Kilgallen's character had won the day. She made plans for a clandestine meeting to receive the 102-page transcript.

Kilgallen told no one of her secret. Days later, the documents were in her hands. She knew she would have a chance to read Ruby's testimony before any other reporter did so. She could also publish it for the world to read.

When Kilgallen informed her *Journal-American* editors of the unexpected good fortune, they were ecstatic. The publisher decided to rush the documents to print as soon as possible. The paper would have an exclusive.[1]

---

[1] One may only imagine, in that day and age without hundreds of television outlets and no internet and thus any social media, what an incredible "exclusive" Kilgallen's access to, and exposure of, Ruby's Warren Commission testimony was in light of its historical importance. Perhaps later disclosure of the Nixon White House tapes by the *Washington Post* may provide a comparison but regardless, printing Ruby's testimony for the world to read must be considered a crowning moment in a journalistic career matched by few, if any, reporters before Kilgallen's era or since.

On August 9, 1964, the *Journal-American* published and *The Associated Press* circulated the story across the country and around the world in three parts. Included were comments by Kilgallen. Her opening words were:

> What you are about to read is the transcript of the testimony given by Jack Ruby to Chief Justice Earl Warren and other members of the Warren Commission investigating the assassination of President Kennedy....The transcript is 102 pages long and is a word-by-word account of the three-hour, five-minute interrogation of Jack Ruby—the third member of a triangle that has become an irrevocable part of history.

The initial copy employed the headline, "Stories Quote Ruby Saying Slaying Was His Own Idea." Excerpts included:

> Jack Ruby, in a purported secret testimony given to the Warren Commission, said it was strictly his own idea to kill Lee Harvey Oswald, accused assassin of President Kennedy. In a copyrighted story Tuesday by *Journal-American* columnist Dorothy Kilgallen, Ruby was quoted as having told Justice Warren June 7, 'I was never malicious toward this person. No one else requested me to do anything. I never spoke to anyone about attempting to do anything. No subversive organization gave me any idea. No underworld persons made any effort to contact me. It all happened that Sunday morning.'

On August 20, under the banner headline "In Tough Spot, Ruby Told Justice," and the sub-headline, "Club Owner Rips Lawyer on Motive," Kilgallen directly quoted Ruby as having told Chief Justice Earl Warren, "Boys, I am in a tough spot, I tell you that." Ruby, according to Kilgallen's reading of the transcript, then turned his wrath toward trial counsel Melvin Belli. Ruby accused his lawyer of distorting the facts as to whether Ruby's killing of Oswald was premeditated, swearing it was not.

Since Kilgallen had interviewed Ruby twice, and had labeled him a "gangster" in one of her columns, she was dubious of his Warren Commission testimony. She recalled his telling her he was "scared," and like a shrewd defense attorney always seeking the tiniest of clues to abnormal testimony, in an August 19 story, she focused on one aspect of Ruby's story that did not make sense to her. It was his insistence that he "went to a newspaper office and demonstrated a twist board for one of the employers" after learning of JFK's death. She wrote, "I find it hard to reconcile the picture of Jack Ruby performing on a twist board less than 24 hours after the President's assassination with the bereaved figure of a man [who says] he walked around in a state of emotional shock."

Commenting on Kilgallen's "scoop," an *Associated Press* article announced: "According to the *New York Times*, '[Warren Commission] officials have expressed distress concerning the *Journal-American* article which, on superficial examination appeared to contain verbatim secret testimony…Miss Kilgallen said she obtained the actual transcript of Warren's interview with Ruby from sources close to the Warren Commission in Washington."

A Warren Commission attorney was livid at the disclosures. He asked FBI Director Hoover to investigate the leak. In the *Herald Tribune,* the headline read: "Outcry Over Ruby Leak Brings a Federal Probe." Agents with orders to discover Kilgallen's source scattered about. Interviews were conducted with anyone who was in the room when the interviews occurred. Those close to the investigation—including attorneys, district attorneys, a jailer, and various secretaries—became suspects. True to her nature of protecting sources or anyone suspected of being a source, Kilgallen made a statement. The young girl turned woman whose father had always told her to tell the truth said the court reporter transcribing the Ruby interviews was *not* the source.

Addressing the FBI probe, Kilgallen, irritating Director Hoover and the Bureau, posted a *Journal-America* column entitled, "Maybe You Didn't Know."

She wrote:

From what I have read, I would be inclined to believe that the FBI might be more profitably employed in probing the facts of the case rather than how I got them—which does seem a waste of time to me.

At any rate, the whole thing smells a bit fishy. It's a mite too simple that a chap kills the President of the United States, escapes from that bother, kills a policeman, eventually is apprehended in a movie theater under circumstances that defy every law of police procedure, and subsequently is murdered under extraordinary circumstances.

The Warren report made a great effort to note that the FBI and the Secret Service were delinquent in their duty, and that the press media—TV, radio and newspaper— also were responsible for the confusion that made Oswald's murder possible. Baloney. Oswald was not killed by a newspaperman. He was killed by a nightclub owner well-known to the police—Jack Ruby. How could the Warren Commission pretend to forget that?

Dorothy Kilgallen

Maybe You Didn't Know...

NUMEROUS READERS HAVE WRITTEN to ask about this column's reaction to the Warren Commission report. My only possible answer: I have not read the entire Warren Commission volume—I have seen only what appeared in the newspapers, and that seemed fragmentary—so I do not consider myself qualified to evaluate the tragic picture. However, from what I have read, I would be inclined to believe that the Federal Bureau of Investigation might have been more profitably employed in probing the facts of the case, rather than how I got them—which does seem a waste of time to me.

In a subsequent *Journal-American* column titled "Search for the Truth," Kilgallen observed, "[The Warren Commission Ruby testimony] is a fascinating document—fascinating for what it leaves unsaid, as well as what it says." Commenting on Ruby's state of mind, she added, "He opened the floodgates of his mind and unloosed a stream of consciousness that would have dazzled a James Joyce buff and enraptured a psychiatrist. There was a great deal of fear inside Jack Ruby that Sunday in June [when he testified]. He feared for his own life, he feared for the lives of his brothers and sisters."

Kilgallen did not disclose whom Ruby feared. Nevertheless, her words put those to whom she referred on notice that she was not about to drop her investigation.

Regarding the Warren Commission agenda, Kilgallen wrote, "It seemed to me after reading the testimony three times that the Chief Justice and the general counsel were acutely aware of the talk both here and in Europe that President Kennedy was the victim of a conspiracy. They took pains to prove to themselves and the world that no conspiracy existed."[2]

On August 21, two FBI agents, each feeling the pressure to learn Kilgallen's source, visited her. They were upset when she told them (according to an FBI file secured through the Freedom of Information Act), "I would

---

[2] Larry J. Sabato, founder and director of the University of Virginia Center for Politics and author of *The Kennedy Half Century*, agreed with Kilgallen's statement. He wrote, "The Warren Commission was doomed from the start, because Washington power brokers, led by the new president [Johnson] himself, were far more interested in preserving domestic tranquility that in finding the full truth. They wanted a report that would calm citizen's jangled nerves by reassuring them that a lone nut named Lee Harvey Oswald had acted completely on his own."

rather die than reveal the source" during an hours-long interview at Kilgallen's townhouse. She did not have a lawyer present to protect her rights. Such statements were in line with the fearless journalist's credo, "Things said to a reporter in confidence should be kept in confidence."

On August 22, Kilgallen read newspaper accounts, including one posted in the *Boston Sunday Herald* under the headline "Jack Ruby's Stories Seen Ruin of Warren Commission." In the article, Melvin Belli blasted Kilgallen's premature exposure of Ruby's testimony before the Warren Commission. Belli stated that it had "destroyed the integrity" of the Commission's investigation.

Of more interest to Kilgallen was a Belli comment. He said, "Ruby pleaded with me not to put him on the [witness] stand. He told me 'If I go on they'll cut me to ribbons.'" Kilgallen knew that Belli had twisted the words around. She knew it was Ruby who wanted to testify and Belli who had forbid him from doing so.

The crack investigative reporter also realized that Belli's quote conflicted with Ruby's Warren Commission statement to Chief Justice Warren. She had exposed it in her *Journal-American* articles:

> I wanted to get on the stand and tell the truth [about] what happened that morning, [but Belli] said, "Jack, when they get you on the stand, you are actually speaking of a premeditated crime that you involved yourself in." But I didn't care, because I wanted to tell the truth. [Belli] said, 'When the prosecution gets you on the stand, they will cut you to ribbons.'

Kilgallen realized that Belli was lying. In addition to her February 1964 column alluding to suspicions about Belli's defense, and her questions about Ruby's contradictory behavior the day after JFK was shot, Belli's false statements in the Boston article triggered additional suspicion on her part as to the potential for a cover-up. This convinced her that the investigation into JFK and Oswald's deaths must continue unabated.[3]

On a daily basis, Kilgallen gleaned information from her Dallas sources. She learned that Jack Ruby had multiple friends among the Dallas police

---

[3] Earl Ruby later confirmed Jack's demands to testify, and Belli's refusal to let him do so. It was one reason Belli was fired shortly after the trial.

department. Many of them frequented his strip club, The Carousel.[4] Kilgallen's reputation and clout permitted her to receive the original police log as reflected in radio communications. It chronicled police activities by the minute directly after the shooting of the president.

Left out of the Warren Commission report, Kilgallen realized, was a startling disclosure. It detailed how Dallas Police Chief Jesse Curry, seated in the first car in the president's motorcade, reacted to shots fired. He told officers to "get a man on top of the overpass and see what happened up there." This story was printed in the *Journal-American* on August 23, 1964 under the headline, "The Police Mix-Up in Dallas."

After beginning the article with the words, "A previously unpublished and private report by the Dallas Police Department of events surrounding the assassination of President Kennedy conflicts sharply with some public statements of Dallas police officials, "Kilgallen then seized on the conflicting statements. She wrote that Curry's reaction and subsequent orders were at odds with what he told reporters 24 hours after the assassination. He had said the shots originated from the Book Depository building. In addition, Kilgallen wrote, Curry had informed reporters that his first order to officers was to have officers surround the Book Depository building. In conclusion, Kilgallen wrote, "…as we see from the Police Department's official version of events, Chief Curry's immediate concern was not the Depository, but the triple-tiered overpass overhead, which the President's car was moving at about eight miles an hour when the fatal shots were fired."

In effect, Kilgallen now called the Dallas Chief of Police a liar. The list of enemies grew—Curry, Hoover and the FBI, the CIA, The Justice Department, Warren Commission members and attorneys, and anyone implicated in the JFK and Oswald assassinations.

---

[4] Addressing Oswald's killer's popularity with police, Author Seth Kantor said Earl Ruby witnessed it firsthand. When Jack invited him along to police headquarters to "see some of my friends," Earl told Kantor, "it was 'Hi Jack, Hi Jack, Hi Jack' all the way down the hall" as they encountered officers.

CHAPTER 18

At FBI headquarters in Washington, J. Edgar Hoover displayed his personal anger at Dorothy Kilgallen. In the famed reporter's dossier obtained by this author through the Freedom of Information Act, the Director, in his own handwriting, posted piercing remarks in the margins.

The comments related to the facts she included and conclusions reached in the *Journal-American* stories. Hoover wrote "WRONG" in longhand next to her comment about the "man on the overpass." Hoover also wrote "WRONG" beside the famous columnist's specification of the time when Chief Curry ordered police to check the overpass.

Regardless of Hoover's efforts or anyone else's, Kilgallen was not deterred. Determined to learn the truth, she actually became an amateur detective. This included attempting to re-create part of what happened on November 22 in Dealey Plaza. To do so, she relied on the Warren Commission testimony of a steamfitter named Howard Brennan. He had provided a description of an alleged shooter permitting police to release a physical description.

Brennan told police he was sitting on a concrete wall as the presidential motorcade passed through the plaza. The wall was located a hundred feet from the book depository window. Brennen said he could see up into the 6th floor window where someone was holding a rifle. Believing this to be impossible, Kilgallen had her husband Richard stand at their townhouse window on an upper floor. He held a broomstick mirroring Oswald holding a rifle. She stood outside on East 68th Street at the same distance as

Brennan described. When she returned to the townhouse, she informed Richard that her conclusion was correct: Brennan could not have seen into the window, could not have seen anyone holding a rifle.

The scientific aspects of the experiment were questionable, but Kilgallen's obsession with continuing to probe every aspect of the JFK assassination was clear. She was the only journalist in the world actively disagreeing at the time with Hoover's self-proclaimed "Oswald Alone" theory. Nothing could stop her from pursuing every lead through sources only a reporter of her stature could garner.

Concerned about surveillance, Kilgallen and Mark Lane carried on a clandestine relationship. She told him, "Intelligence agencies will be watching us. We'll have to be very careful." When they spoke on the telephone, it was from different telephone booths. They even used code names—hers was "Robinson," his "Parker." During meetings at Kilgallen's home, Richard listened to their conversations.

Intent on keeping the debate alive, Kilgallen published a stream of allegations about the ineptness of the investigations, including that of the Warren Commission. This caused her to believe that any one, or all, of the 18 townhouse telephone lines could be tapped.

On September 3, 1964, Robert Kennedy resigned as attorney general. In a *Journal-American* column published ten days later, Kilgallen, fourteen months removed from her death, wrote:

> This column owes a great debt of gratitude to the thousands of messages of congratulations that came after the stories on the Jack Ruby testimony before the Warren Commission. They came from William Randolph Hearst, Jr., Walter Winchell, editors and publishers all over the nation, rival columnists…and citizens in many states in the Union who hailed my paper and me for 'courage' in printing the articles.
>
> Of course, there was courage involved, but mostly it was the simple urge to print the story…. Thank you very much, from an incorrigible reporter to whom the front page is quite a bit like the Star-Spangled Banner.

Eleven days later, Kilgallen's *Journal-American* reported the Warren Commission report's release. It concluded, among other matters:

"The Commission has found no evidence that either Lee Harvey Oswald or Jack Ruby was part of any conspiracy, domestic or foreign, to assassinate President Kennedy."

There was "no direct relationship between Lee Harvey Oswald and Jack Ruby."

"No evidence [existed] that Jack Ruby acted with any other person in the killing of Lee Harvey Oswald."

Concluding, the Commission wrote, "On the basis of the evidence before the Commission it concludes that Oswald acted alone."

Despite minimal information, one section of the report read, "Based on its evaluation of the record…the Commission believes that the evidence does not establish a significant link between Ruby and organized crime. Both State and Federal officials have indicated that Ruby was not affiliated with organized crime activities. And numerous persons have reported that Ruby was not connected with such activity."

In her "Voice of Broadway" column, and to anyone who would listen, Kilgallen called the report, "laughable" and continued her assassination probe with Jack Ruby as the focal point. She learned of his three prison attempts at suicide in late 1964. First, Ruby stood 20 feet from a concrete wall. His face soaked with perspiration, he ran as fast as possible head first into the wall. He hoped to crack open his skull. He did not.

Ruby's second attempt involved use of an electric light socket. A few burns on his hands were the result. The condemned man's third try involved using his pants legs to hang himself. The knot he devised was not sturdy. A guard, always on watch, squelched Ruby's intended plan.

Hearing of Ruby's suicide attempt anguished Kilgallen. She continued to ponder the shocking statement Ruby made after appearing before the Warren Commission: "The world will never know the true facts of what occurred. My motives. The people who had, that had so much to gain and had such a material motive to put me in this position I'm in would never let the true facts come above board to the world." Ruby's admission only reinforced Kilgallen's belief that Oswald's killer was part of a conspiracy and cover-up.

More certain every day of her suspicions, Kilgallen was not shy about sharing them. She told friend Marlin Swing several times, "This had to be a conspiracy." The same message was relayed to Johnnie Ray, *What's My Line?* associate producer Bob Bach, and her makeup man, Carmen Gebbia. When asked about her conclusions by her lawyer Mort Farber, Kilgallen said boldly, "I'm going to break the real story and have the biggest scoop of the century."

In a December 10, 1964 "Voice of Broadway" column, Kilgallen plugged the upcoming book by her friend Mark Lane. She wrote, "Mark Lane, the attorney who leads the opposition to the Warren Commission's report on the assassination of President Kennedy, is studying thousands of pages of testimony in preparation for his book on the tragedy. Titled *Rush to Judgment*, it will be published by Grove Press in the spring, and promises to contain many hitherto unrevealed 'surprises.'"[1]

Kilgallen never mentioned what the "surprises" were. With the assassination file[2] in hand as the winter months of 1964/65 turn to spring and summer, Kilgallen traveled to Europe. In Zurich, she told friends she was writing *Murder One* while resting to improve her health. When she returned to the U.S., husband Richard and Johnnie Ray were impressed with Kilgallen's appearance. Ray stated, "She was plumper. Her color was higher."

Back on the trail with only a few more months to live, Kilgallen searched for more clues about Jack Ruby's ties to a conspiracy. When she saw Mark Lane, Kilgallen told him she was going to visit Dallas again adding, "I expect I am going to learn a lot this time."

In mid-June, Bob Bach booked Kilgallen on ABC's *Nightlife* program. She expected to talk about the JFK assassination. In anticipation, she carried with her the hefty investigation file. To her displeasure, moments before Kilgallen went on the air, a producer warned her not to discuss the JFK assassination: it was "too controversial." She argued that it was the only reason she had agreed to be a guest.

The next day, Kilgallen learned of a Texas hearing considering Jack Ruby's sanity scheduled as part of the appeal process. Ruby told a Federal court judge, "I never had any defense…I never had any defense."

---

[1] Mark Lane's book, *Rush to Judgment*, was released in 1966 by Holt, Rinehart and Winston.
[2] Kilgallen friend Jean Bach said of the file, "We wondered about the folder she had. She brought it to the *What's My Line?* dressing room and said, "here's all the stuff I've learned. I'm working on it and nobody can have a look at it."

On September 3, 1965, Kilgallen, three months before her death, published her final column about the JFK and Oswald assassinations. She wrote, "Those close to the scene realize that if the widow of Lee Harvey Oswald (now married to another chap) ever gave out the 'whole story' of her life with President Kennedy's alleged assassin, it would split open the front pages of newspapers all over the world."

Most importantly, Kilgallen sent a clear signal to anyone fearing her continuing investigation. She wrote, "This story is not going to die as long as there's a real reporter alive—and there are a lot of them." She did not identify who they might be. Perhaps this was a call for help. Perhaps some reporter would aid her cause. It did not happen.

As September appeared, Kilgallen spent time at Barbara Walter's father Lou's Latin Quarter nightclub located at Broadway and West 47th Street. Always wary of those who might spread rumors about her blurring the boundary between her job as an entertainment columnist and personal friendships, she apparently watched Johnnie Ray perform from backstage.

In October 1965, New York City was hit with a newspaper strike. Kilgallen appeared on the popular WPIX radio program *Hot Line!* hosted by noted author Gore Vidal. It featured Kilgallen and revered television producer and talk show host David Susskind. Social issues were the subject with mention of the JFK assassination prohibited.

Shortly thereafter, Kilgallen traveled to New Orleans. Her hairdresser Marc Sinclaire,[3] prominent in New York Society circles to the extent of having his own press agent, described in a videotaped interview the bizarre set of circumstances regarding the visit: "She didn't tell me why we were going. She just asked me if I could go with her, and I said 'yes.' She told me how I was to travel, where I was to go, what I was to do. And I'd never

---

[3] Sinclaire's name often appeared in the NYC newspapers. Besides Kilgallen, he did the hair of Phyllis Cerf and when they visited the U.S., Princess Margaret and her husband, Anthony Armstrong Jones, the Earl of Snowden. Kilgallen mentioned Sinclaire in her "Voice of Broadway" column, writing, "The newest coiffure rage in Paris is 'the Maure'—a more elaborate and sophisticated version of the ponytail. New York hairdresser Marc Sinclaire has been doing it for months only he calls it 'the Tom Jones' in tribute to the hairdos worn by lovelies in the English film of that name." In the videotaped interview, Sinclaire notes that European hairstylists were copying his creation during "the year of the hairdresser." During that year, he said, "We were almost celebrities in our own right."

Marc Sinclaire, Dorothy Kilgallen's hairdresser and close confidant.

been to New Orleans before, so I didn't know anything about it." (Selected excerpts from Sinclaire video and audiotaped interviews may be viewed at TheReporterWhoKnewTooMuch.com)

Concerning the overall plans, Sinclaire added, "We didn't even travel on the same plane together. I went directly to my hotel, we talked [on the phone], and then I went over to her hotel and had dinner and then I went back to mine." Sinclaire then said, "And the next morning, I was supposed to do her hair and make-up and she called me at my hotel and she said, 'I want you to go to the airport, I've left a ticket for you, and I want you to go back to New York, and never tell anyone you came to New Orleans with me.' And I said 'okay' and I left." Summing up, Sinclaire added, "I knew enough not to ask any more. There were certain things where she drew a blank wall and she didn't want me to know any more about it."

In another videotaped interview, Sinclaire told a similar story, "[Six weeks before she died], she [Kilgallen] went down [to New Orleans] on a plane and I went down on another at the same time. And I stayed at a different hotel than she did. We were going to have dinner that evening and I'd done her hair ...She called me and she said, 'I want you to leave immediately. I don't want you to tell anyone you were ever here with me. I don't want anyone to know you were ever here with me. And don't ask me any more questions' and I got on the plane and flew back to New York." He added, "I was upset. I didn't know why she was sending me away. And she didn't tell me until she got back." Asked what he learned, Sinclair said, "I did know from Dorothy finally that there was a conspiracy [to kill JFK]. That it was a group of people, not one. She told me."

Sinclaire added another strange element to the trip. Asked if he later viewed a New York City newspaper photograph of Kilgallen standing beside two men in New Orleans, he said, "Yes" and agreed that the newspaper was probably the *Daily Mirror*, a tabloid in circulation since the major New York City newspaper workers were on strike. Sinclaire then said he didn't know who the two men were and never saw the photograph again. "It was a small photograph," he said, "and she had on a suit and she was very well-done and I looked at it because she was in it and [the caption] said, 'Dorothy Kilgallen in New Orleans.'" Asked his reaction, Sinclaire said, "I find it strange that she would be photographed in New Orleans especially after what she told me to leave and I find it strange that she was photographed at all—I don't think she wanted to be photographed...I'm not sure now that I think about it, I'm not sure that photograph was posed for. I think it was caught."

Recalling once again the New Orleans trip in an audiotaped interview, Sinclaire said, "I don't know who she was meeting [in New Orleans]. She didn't tell me much about that meeting, period, never did. And I knew enough not to ask anymore. There were certain things where she drew a blank wall; she just didn't want me to know anymore about it. Maybe she was frightened at that point."

A month later, as the day of her death neared, Kilgallen planned another trip to New Orleans. *What's My Line?* make-up man Carmen Gebbia noted Kilgallen's excitement and asked "Is it Kennedy?" She replied, "Yes, and it's very cloak and daggerish. I'm gonna meet a source whom I do not know

Dorothy Kilgallen at the time of her death.

(NY19-Nov. 8)-DOROTHY KILGALLEN DIES-Dorothy Kilgallen, 52, above, widely known newspaper columnist and radio and television personality, died unexpectedly in New York today. Cause of death was not known immediately. She was the wife of producer Dick Kollmar and the daughter of newspaperman James Kilgallen.(APWirephoto) (s21520f1s)1965(See AP wire story)(EDS: A 1964 file photo)

but will recognize who is going to give me information about the case." In a videotaped interview with her second hairdresser Charles Simpson, he said Kilgallen told him...I used to share things with you...but after I have found out now what I know, if the wrong people knew what I know, it would cost me my life."

Curiously, on November 4, 1965, four days before Kilgallen died, an *Associated Press* article appeared regarding an important development in Jack Ruby's case. A portion read, "[Dallas] District Attorney Henry Wade said today his office is willing to recommend that Jack Ruby's death sentence be reduced to life imprisonment." Among Wade's comments were, "There is an advantage to keeping Ruby alive for interviews and historical purposes. There are still a lot of unanswered questions." Wade did not elaborate and no follow-up article appeared. Ruby's sentence was never commuted to life imprisonment.

On Saturday, November 6, two days before she died, Marc Sinclaire spoke with the famed columnist. He recalled, "We talked for about an hour. Her life had been threatened."

During the early evening hours of the 7th, Kilgallen readied herself for her final *What's My Line?* program (www.youtube.comwatch?v=6gn6jS1UK78). When the program ended at 11:00 p.m., Kilgallen and Bob Bach sped by limousine to P. J. Clarke's for a nightcap. She ordered her drink of choice, vodka and tonic. The table where the two sat was located near the rear exit. As midnight neared toward the day of her death, Kilgallen told Bach she had a "late date." They parted when he walked her to her limousine.

An hour later, Kilgallen entered the nearby Regency Hotel bar. She sat in a booth near the back. Kurt Maier, the piano player, recalled her still being in the bar at 2:00 a.m. Kilgallen was, he said, joined by a man.

Hours later, Dorothy Kilgallen, "the most powerful female voice in America," was found dead, at age 52, lying in a bed at her East 68th Street townhouse. Her JFK assassination file was missing. It disappeared, and has never been recovered.

CHAPTER 19

The *Journal-American* published news of Dorothy Kilgallen's death in its late afternoon edition of Monday, November 8, 1965. The short article stated, "Jim Kilgallen said his daughter apparently suffered a heart attack, her first."

Kilgallen's final "Voice of Broadway" column appeared on its usual page. A side note indicated she wrote it, "early in the morning." The Hearst syndicate repeated the news in small towns and large city publications across the country. Readers reacted with anguish over news of Kilgallen's death. The accomplished woman whose words had been woven into America's fabric, who had touched people's way of life on a daily basis for years on end would do so no more, struck down as she was in the prime of life.

Tributes to Kilgallen pored across the newswires. Louis Sobel, after opening his column with "Shocking, Shocking, Shocking—the Sudden death of Dorothy Kilgallen," wrote in the *Journal-American:*

> Dorothy Mae Kilgallen was a newspaper woman considered so eminent in her field that her untimely death at 52 tugged Page One coverage from most of the country's newspapers and two-column obituary in the conservative *New York Times....*Indeed, few newswomen have received as much attention in their lifetime from national news magazines—such as *Time* and *Newsweek*—as did this slender but aggressive girl reporter.

Writing for the Hearst Headline Service, noted columnist Bob Considine said:

> It seems to me that when a reporter dies, all of us are reduced....I saw more of Dorothy Kilgallen in her role of reporter than in her role as a historian of New York night life. To me, she was one of the finest reporters I ever knew. On a straight, going-away, give-and-take news story, Dorothy could give the ablest man reporter one hell of a contest. She had a keen ear for the fumbled testimony dropping from the lips of a witness, a murderer or a supplicant. No one should ever underestimate the value of a keen ear. Keen ears have passed down every truth by which we live. She had the keenest.
>
> Because of her television fame, her good clothes, the fact that she sometimes arrived at an assignment in a limousine, some of her contemporaries thought of her as a dilettante. She was not. She was a reporter.
>
> A reporter who became a part of every story that she ever covered. She was as interested in the accused in a trial as she was in the prosecution and the judge and gave them equal time and attention. She did enormous favors for reporters of lesser renown and means that she worked with. She came from the ablest newspaper stock possible, Jimmy Kilgallen, and she did him proud.

In a follow-up column, Considine added:

> There were two Dorothy Kilgallen's, three really, if you count the Dorothy Kilgallen of *What's My Line?* In the latter role, she was one of the best known women in America, chic, witty, trenchant and an absolute master of ferreting out the occupations of the mystery guests. Then there was Dorothy Kilgallen, the "Voice of Broadway," saucy, provocative and superbly informed about what was happening in the worlds of the theatre, cafe society, Hollywood, TV, Washington, London, Paris and Timbuktu.
>
> The image of Dorothy as a journalist who drove up to assignments in a Rolls, which she did now and then, cannot evaporate in any reporter's mind the memory of her hard-digging, scrappy, dogged determination as a reporter.... She had become more famous than most of the people she was covering.

As the hours passed into the evening of November 8, more tributes appeared, each extolling the virtues of Kilgallen, the gifted wordsmith who had no equal. While this happened, Junior NYC medical examiner Dr. James Luke, for reasons never explained, decided to perform an autopsy despite no apparent evidence of foul play.

To date, the autopsy report and those pages included in the official report as addendums under the title "Report of Death," have not been published. Obtained by this author from the National Archives, the pages, a combination of typed and handwritten, are most revealing as to the facts gathered and conclusions reached by Dr. Luke concerning the purported cause of the famous reporter's death.

The starting point to examining the documents is the "Report of Death" pages presumably written following Dr. Luke's presence at Kilgallen's death scene.

Of interest on this page are the times listed to the left of Dr. Luke's signature and to the right of the handwritten "11/8/65" above the typed "Date and Time." Translated, this apparently meant the time of death was 1:40 p.m., the "examiner" [medical examiner] had been notified at 2:45 p.m., and the examiner had arrived on the scene at 3:10 p.m., staying until departing at 4:15 p.m., an hour and five minutes later. Beside "Pronounced Dead by" was the name, "Dr. Heller, 11 E. 68th Street."[1]

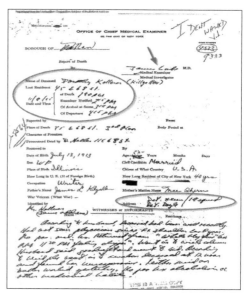

"Place of Death" is noted as 45 E. 68th Street, 3rd Floor," which coincides with the notation of her "Last Residence" at the same address. "Name of Deceased" is listed as Dorothy Kollmar (Killgallen)—misspelled. Her

---

[1] No explanation apparently exists as to why Dr. Saul Heller, a physician who apparently only practiced neurology and psychiatry on Park Avenue during his 50+ year career, pronounced Kilgallen dead.

occupation is noted as, "Writer," with identification by "Mr. Kollmar (same address)."

The designation of 1:40 p.m. as the time of death is confusing but may have been intended to disclose when Dr. Heller pronounced Kilgallen dead. How Dr. Luke knew this since he apparently did not arrive until 3:10 p.m. is unknown.

To the right and below the date and times on the report are names of two NYPD detectives who apparently visited Kilgallen's townhouse: "Det. Green and Det. Doyle/19 Squad." The latter is an apparent reference to Manhattan's 19th Precinct.

Under "Witnesses or Informants," the following information exists:

According to husband, deceased had been well recently. Had not seen physicians since Fr [fractured] shoulder last year. [Undistinguishable] Returned from "What's My Line?" [Undistinguishable] P.M. 11:30 pm "feeling chipper." Went to write column. Husband said goodnight and went to bed. According to maid, she went in to awaken deceased at 12 noon and found her unresponsive. Neither maid or butler worked yesterday. [Undistinguishable] alcoholism or other medicinal habits.

Who gathered the information from the witnesses, Dr. Luke or the two detectives, is unknown. Richard contributed the fact that his wife had been "well recently," that she had returned home from *What's My Line?* at 11:30 p.m. in good spirits ("feeling chipper"), that she left him to write her column, and that he went to bed.

According to the report, the maid discovered Kilgallen's body. She and the butler had not worked the day before. Who told the detectives about the "alcoholism or other medicinal habits" is unclear due to the undistinguishable words but may logically be attributed to Richard.

Most important regarding this report page, one whose entries are all handwritten, is the maid discovering the body. This fact, as will become evident, adds to the intrigue surrounding events on the day Kilgallen died.

The following page once again pertains to the circled 9333 case number.

Under the heading "State the circumstances and particulars of death..." the following pertinent text appears in Dr. Luke's handwriting:

Scene – orderly elegant apartment. Papers in order. Deceased a middle aged WF lying on back in bed, head on pillow. Robert Ruark's new book by side, clad in blue bathrobe and nothing else. Covers up to chin.

Hair dyed brown
Long eyelashes
Chest – ō
[Undistinguishable]
[Undistinguishable] obese

Rigidity complete
No trauma
No signs violence

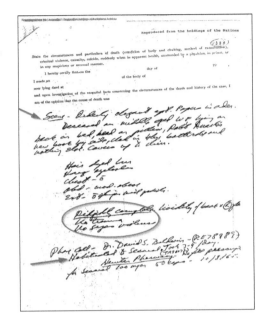

Phone call – Dr. David S. Baldwin (9RE78989)
Habituated to Seconal. Took 3-4/day
(TR86072)
<u>Hunter Pharmacy</u> – He fill prescription for Seconal 100 mg –
50 caps – 10/8/65.

Significant is the location of Kilgallen's body ("lying on back in bed, head on pillow," presence of Robert Ruark's book and what she was wearing—"blue bathrobe," apparently nothing underneath. Also of interest, "covers up to chin," and the presence of "long eyelashes."

The mention of Kilgallen's being "obese" appears in conflict with her general appearance. Most importantly, Dr. Luke's conclusion that there was "No trauma" and "No signs violence" excludes physical abuse as the cause of death. The indication that she may have been "habituated to Seconal," apparently meant Kilgallen was known to be a habitual user of sleeping pills.

Mention of Dr. Baldwin, Kilgallen's personal physician, and the Hunter Pharmacy, with the notation "He fill prescription for Seconal 100 mg – 50 caps – 10/8/65," indicates either Dr. Luke or one of the detectives called or visited the pharmacy to check on her use of Seconal. If "Took 3-4/day" were correct, the supply of the barbiturate would have run out well before the day of Kilgallen's death since even three a day would have only lasted until approximately October 24.

At this point, one may conclude that Dr. Luke, based on the evidence gathered and certain physical evidence present at the death scene, believed Kilgallen had died accidently due to a drug overdose. All of his handwritten notations point in this direction prior to the official autopsy being performed. The culprit, he assumed, had been Seconal and since Kilgallen had a prescription for that drug and was a habitual user, Dr. Luke apparently felt accidental death was a safe bet.

The next page of the official documents is the autopsy report reads.

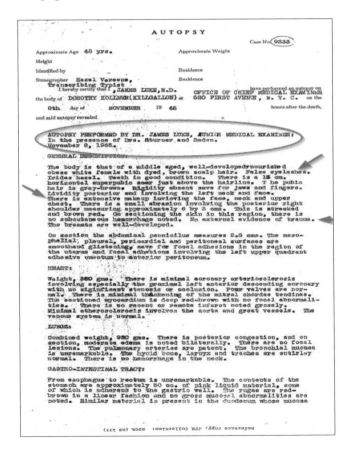

Since "Hazel Vereene" is listed as "Transcribing Typist," it appears Dr. Luke dictated this information into a recorder presumably as the autopsy proceeded. The text then reads

AUTOPSY PERFORMED BY DR. JAMES LUKE JUNIOR
MEDICAL EXAMINER
In the presence of Dr. Sturner and Baden.
November 8, 1965

Also of note is the indication that Kilgallen, erroneously aged at 48, is once again described as "obese" while no figure is listed under "Approximate Weight." Her eyelashes are described as being "false." She is described as having, "extensive makeup involving the face, neck and upper chest." A second indication appears that there was "no external evidence of trauma."

Page two attached to the one marked "autopsy" contains details regarding Kilgallen's bodily functions but nothing of major significance regarding cause of death. Page three reads:

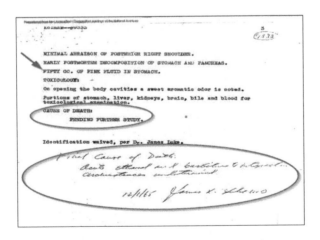

Above the word, "Toxicology" appears "FIFTY CC. OF PINK FLUID IN STOMACH." Then the typed words following "CAUSE OF DEATH: PENDING FURTHER STUDY." There is no date beside the notation but the first page of the autopsy report confirms Dr. Luke's dictation happened on the same day the autopsy was performed, November 8, the day Kilgallen died.

Below the typed words, "Identification Waived, per Dr. James Luke," appears, in Dr. Luke's handwriting:

Final Cause of Death:
Acute Ethanol and barbiturate intoxication…
Circumstances undetermined.

12/1/65 James R Luke M.D.

Since it appeared from Dr. Luke's "Report of Death" notations that he had adopted an accidental death theory based on information collected at Kilgallen's death scene, why had he concluded the autopsy report with the words, "Cause of Death: Pending Further Study"? Did "Further Study" mean awaiting the toxicology results from the ME lab? Or had something else changed his mind so that he could not definitively conclude that Kilgallen had died accidently from the alcohol and drug overdose, presumably from ingesting too many Seconal pills?

Notice that the "Final Cause of Death" on this page beneath the typed information includes the handwritten date "12/1/65." Simple mathematics suggests nearly three weeks passed between when Dr. Luke dictated the words, "Pending Further Study" on November 8th and when he wrote in longhand, "Final Cause of Death: Acute Ethanol and barbiturate intoxication…Circumstances Undetermined" on the first of December.

Presumably, "Further Study" indicated Dr. Luke awaited toxicology results based on testing of Kilgallen's bodily fluids. If so, what specifically did he learn on or before December 1 causing him to undermine the "Final Cause of Death" by including the words, "Circumstances Undetermined"?

An important clue to answering this question is a subsequent handwritten page attached to the page marked "autopsy." Notice that once again, Kilgallen's case number, 9333, is included proving this page was part of the official documents.

Under the words "Dorothy Kollmar," Dr. Luke organized the toxicology text results according to *Microscopic* and *Chemical.* Under *"Microscopic,"* "No pathology" is written next to "Heart, Stomach, Adrenals, cerebellum, cerebrum, brain status, Kidneys," etc. Below these notations under *"Chemical,"* is listed:

Alcohol – Blood – 0.15
[Undistinguishable]
Eye Fluid – 0.15
[Undistinguishable]
Brain – 0.1
[Undistinguishable]
Stomach – Tr

Besides these words are:

Barbiturates –
[Undistinguishable]
(liver, brain)
UV – 2.4 [Undistinguishable] eO
(liver)
1.6 [Undistinguishable] eO
(brain)
[Undistinguishable]
[Undistinguishable] same level as
seconal, tuinal

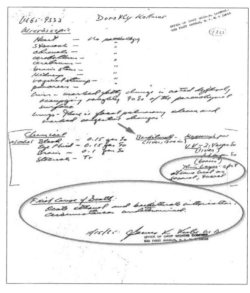

Below were the following words in Dr. Luke's handwriting:

Final Cause of Death:
Acute Ethanol and barbiturate intoxication
Circumstances Undetermined
11/15/65 Dr. James R. Luke, MD

Stamp: Office of Chief medical examiner
520 First Avenue, NY, NY 10016

Regarding blood alcohol content—the measuring stick for whether someone is legally intoxicated, i.e. drunk—Kilgallen's is listed as 0.15. If this notation was made at 3:10 p.m. or a bit later when Dr. Luke presumably arrived at her townhouse, this means her actual blood alcohol content would have been much higher dependent on the actual time of death especially if it was several hours earlier. Because of the time lapse, there is no accurate way to know how much alcohol Kilgallen consumed prior to, or after, she returned to her townhouse. However, it should be noted that on the second page of the autopsy report not reprinted here, there was the notation that Kilgallen's liver was "fatty," but not "cirrhotic." This apparently meant the famous columnist did not suffer from liver disease caused by heavy drinking.

How the blood alcohol level affected Kilgallen's cause of death is important but dependent on the type and quantity of drugs in her body at the time she died. Information as to these factors is located to the far right of the word "*Chemical.*"

Beside "Barbiturates" is an undistinguishable word and below that "(liver, brain)." Below and to the right of these words are "UV" and then two numbers—2.4 for liver, and 1.6 for brain.

Below this information are two undistinguishable words, one that may be "Layers" and the other "Spot." Below appear the words "at same levels as" and then, significantly, the words, "seconal" and "tuinal," handwritten by Dr. Luke.

The appearance of the word "tuinal" may in fact be the smoking gun with regard to confusion surrounding the true cause of Kilgallen's death. Recall that while Dr. Luke's writing on one other page indicated she had a prescription for "seconal" from her personal physician, Dr. Baldwin, no such prescription is noted for Tuinal, a toxic combination of two active ingredients, amobarbital sodium, a sedative-hypnotic, and secobarbital sodium (Seconal/sleeping pills). Tuinal can be very dangerous when abused as the window between the dose causing drowsiness and the one causing death can be very small. Its effect is accelerated when alcohol is added to the equation. Physicians prescribing Tuinal strictly forbid its use with any alcoholic beverage.

Why is the mention of Tuinal of critical importance to clarifying Kilgallen's exact cause of death? Because, just as Dr. Luke knew, Tuinal being present was a clue that something was wrong, something unexplainable presumably causing doubt in Dr. Luke's mind as to the actual cause of death and the circumstances surrounding it.

When the autopsy revealed Tuinal's presence, it is safe to imagine that Dr. Luke was spooked, that he must have been perplexed by the startling discovery. "What to do?" he must have wondered since while the presence of Seconal (the sleeping pills Kilgallen used habitually) in her system pointed directly at accidental death, the presence of Tuinal, a much more dangerous drug and one she had no prescription for, dented that theory.

The presence of Tuinal most likely accounts for Dr. Luke hedging his "Final Cause of Death" to include the words "Circumstances Undetermined" since he could not figure out how that drug had been discovered in her system unless—and this is huge—there was more to her death than it being accidental. If no presence of Tuinal had been detected, Dr. Luke would not have written, "Circumstances Undetermined" because there would have been no reason to do so since the presence of Seconal was predictable based on knowledge of her usage and the prescription. However, now he must have realized the Tuinal discovery caused concern and he thus added the words, "Circumstances Undetermined" to the mix.

Notice that on this page, Dr. Luke wrote the date, "11/15/65," an indication that he decided on that date to fix the "Final Cause of Death" as "Acute Ethanol and barbiturate Intoxication" while including the words, "Circumstances Undetermined." Since the same words appear on the official "autopsy" page with the date, 12/1/65," he must have written them in his own hand two weeks later or simply made a mistake regarding the date. Either way, it appears Dr. Luke was either lazy, confused, or hiding something.

Since discovery of the Tuinal in Kilgallen's system had clouded the issue of official cause of death, what documents did Dr. Luke release to those who had the authority to view them? In New York City in the 1960s, the requirements for receiving the autopsy report, aside from police officials or the District Attorney's office, if requested, involved request from any next of kin including spouse, siblings, parents, grandparents, and uncles and aunts.[2] There is no means of confirming whether any of these family members attempted to secure a copy.

Regarding release of the document to the media, or leaking of the autopsy report, it is also impossible to know if this happened although, as will be revealed, some news outlets appeared to quote from it. If anyone,

---

[2] In 2015, this author attempted to secure Kilgallen's autopsy report from the NYC medical examiner's Office. Even 50 years later, this request was denied since the author was not a "next of kin."

family members or the media, was able to read the report, one must wonder if they even noticed the presence of Tuinal in Kilgallen's system, and if so, whether they realized its importance toward understanding the true cause of her death. To date, this author, despite extensive research of several NYC newspapers published during the time of Kilgallen's demise, has seen no disclosure of Tuinal being discovered in her system or any reprint of the autopsy report or its accompanying pages in part or in its entirety.

One additional possibility is that Dr. Luke may have not included the toxicology results indicating the presence of Tuinal when releasing the final autopsy report. His motive for doing so will become clear based on startling facts about the ME's office uncovered by this author.

Regardless, the presence of Tuinal in Kilgallen's bloodstream during her autopsy calls into question every theory proposed for five decades and counting concerning the circumstances surrounding the death of the famous reporter and media star. Closer inspection of the drug will provide further clarification but first it is important to understand the utter confusion regarding the cause of Kilgallen's death from the very first media reports published on the day of, and those following, November 8, 1965.

CHAPTER 20

Tuesday, November 9th's *New York Journal-American* edition updated the shocking story under the headline, "Dorothy Kilgallen Dead: Cause Not Determined Yet." The accompanying text read, "An autopsy Monday night failed to determine the cause of death. Dr. James Luke, examiner, said further tests would be made."

This quote coincides with Dr. Luke's notation in the ME documents of "Pending Further Study." Since the reporter directly quoted him, it appears he, or she, had not actually read the documents but simply secured the quote from the Junior medical examiner. Also, what "tests" were anticipated is left to speculation since Dr. Luke did not disclose the specific tests in the documentation. In addition, there is no mention of either Seconal, or more importantly Tuinal, being in Kilgallen's system.

Meanwhile, confusion as to the circumstances surrounding Kilgallen's death began immediately. Why? Because according to various media reports, the discovery of her dead body happened *twice*, by *different* people at *two* different times. These conflicting accounts continued as newspaper reporters gathered facts as filtered in from various sources, many with little credibility. Certainly the sensationalism surrounding the famous reporter's death added to the confusion. However, as will be revealed, misinformation about Kilgallen's death continues to this day since those reporting on such matters simply rely on false facts, much of it on the internet or through inexperienced individuals with no regard for the truth.

Concerning discovery of her body, accounts published by the *Journal-American* on November 9 included the statement: "She was found by a maid who went to wake her about noon." A day later, the newspaper revised that account. It reported, "[Kilgallen] was found dead when her hairdresser arrived at 12:45."

In the *New York Herald-Tribune*, reporter Albin Krebs stated that "the hairdresser," named for the first time as Marc Sinclaire, was the one who had discovered Kilgallen's body. Krebs later said, "I'm certain I got the information from a family source, probably the husband."

The police report, apparently obtained by the *Journal-American* and signed by 19th Precinct Detective John Doyle (mentioned in the ME documents along with Detective Green), stated, "DOA was found by maid Marie Eicher between 12 and 1 p.m. lying on back in bed clad in night clothes." A subsequent note stated, "Pronounced DOA by Dr. Saul Heller, 11 E. 68th Street: ME [medical examiner] Dr. [James] Luke present at scene."

Simultaneously, the *Journal-American* published this notation, one it reported was included in the official autopsy report: "According to the maid, she went in to awaken deceased at 12 noon and found her unresponsive." This is verbatim from the ME documents causing speculation Kilgallen's newspaper either secured a copy of the official report, one was leaked to it, or they again quoted Dr. Luke. Regardless of how the reporter secured the information, it was incomplete to the extent of not divulging any details concerning specific barbiturates Kilgallen ingested including Seconal and Tuinal. One may imagine that if a newspaper reporter learned of these details, he or she would have printed them causing the belief that Dr. Luke was the source of the information and that the *Journal-American* did not have a copy of the ME report. Or, if they did, the page denoting the presence of the two drugs was not included, either by mistake, or more likely, intentionally.

Also of interest were the various times quoted as to when Kilgallen's body was discovered, "noon," (maid) "between 12 and 1 p.m. (maid), and 12:45 p.m. (hairdresser Marc Sinclaire). In one newspaper account on the 9th, the day after Kilgallen died, Dr. Luke is quoted as saying she died "between 2 and 4 a.m."

* * * * *

On November 10, the *New York Times* printed, "A medical examiner's report stated that Miss Kilgallen died of 'the effects of a combination of alcohol and barbiturates,' neither of which had been taken in excessive quantities." Whether the *Times* reporter had ever actually read the entire ME's report, was summarizing, or was simply quoting someone in the ME's office is unclear. Since this exact language including "excessive quantities" is not noted in the ME documents, the latter seems likely.

Five days later, on the 15th, the *Journal-American* and *New York Post* quoted Dr. Luke. Regarding the cause of Kilgallen's demise, he said, "The death of Dorothy Kilgallen, *Journal-American columnist and famed TV personality, was contributed to by a combination of moderate quanti*ties of alcohol and barbiturates." Notice that this date is the same one included on the page where Seconal and Tuinal are listed as well as the "Final Cause of Death" conclusion including "Circumstances Undetermined."

The *New York Post* published Dr. James Luke's findings regarding Dorothy Kilgallen's death.

In a November 16 article in the *New York Herald-Tribune*, this quote appeared:

> Dr. Luke would not speculate about the form in which Miss Kilgallen had taken the barbiturates. "We'd rather leave that up in the air," he said. "We don't want to give that out—well, just because..." He said that combining alcohol and sleeping pills was a common form of accidental death. Miss Kilgallen had taken on "moderate amounts" of alcohol and the drug before her death, Dr. Luke said. He wouldn't give any figures.

Notice this evasive statement includes the words "the drug." However, Dr. Luke, based on his own handwriting in the ME documents, knew this was not true, as the second drug, Tuinal, had also been discovered in her system. Whether the other two attending physicians at the autopsy, Dr. Sturner and Dr. Baden, knew about the Tuinal, is unknown. If they did, they would have been as perplexed as Dr. Luke at Kilgallen having ingested the Tuinal.

Some ten-plus years after the famous reporter died, author Lee Israel[1] interviewed Dr. Luke for her 1979 book, *Kilgallen*. Israel asked Dr. Luke what "moderate" meant regarding her ingestion of alcohol and barbiturates. He replied, "The pills were not what we might expect to find in cases that were suicide." Dr. Luke also admitted he knew back in 1965 that there were 50 cubic centimeters of 'pink fluid' found in Kilgallen's stomach. Dr. Luke explained he sent the liquid to the ME toxicologists for examination. If this happened, Dr. Luke told author Israel he did not receive a report.

Criticizing his own toxicology department, Dr. Luke informed Israel that he was certain of the presence of Seconal in Kilgallen's stomach but appeared to question procedures as being adequate at the time. He admitted there were problems with laboratory personnel suggesting, "Capabilities were not what they should have been."

While Israel's questions to Dr. Luke were relevant, nowhere in her book is the indication she asked him about the presence of Tuinal in Kilgallen's system. Israel does mention ME documents and indicates that she viewed the autopsy report. Surely, if the author read those documents or showed them to Dr. Luke, both would have been curious about the presence of Tuinal but she never mentioned it while quoting Dr. Luke. This lends credence to the possibility Dr. Luke may have excluded the page including mention of "Tuinal" from any documents released at the time. Why he may have done so will be clarified later.

To her credit, author Israel further considered the barbiturate question. She revealed that while researching her biography of Kilgallen she had interviewed a chemist in the New York medical examiner's office during a clandestine meeting at a local pub. Apparently protecting her source, Israel did not divulge the chemist's name instead stating that he

---

[1] Author Disclosure: Lee Israel, who died on December 24, 2014, wrote, and Delacorte Press, a Random House imprint, published *Kilgallen: A Biography of Dorothy Kilgallen* in 1979. Unfortunately, in the mid-2000s, Israel's reputation was soiled when she was charged with forging letters from famous people and selling them to unsuspecting buyers. Israel, who was experiencing difficult times in her private life, pled guilty and was sentenced to house arrest and five years probation. In 2008, her book *Can You Ever Forgive Me?* detailing the sordid chain of events was published. Despite Israel's deceptive practices nearly three decades after writing *Kilgallen*, there is no indication she fabricated any of the *Kilgallen* text. Some material is incomplete but reference notes at the end of the book appear credible. Unfortunately, this author was unable to speak with Ms. Israel before she died in 2014.

was the "confidant and right-hand man" to Dr. Charles J. Umberger from 1967 to 1972.

Dr. Umberger was the NYC medical examiner's office Director of Toxicology in the Department of Pathology at the time of Kilgallen's death. Israel noted his reputation for preserving hundreds of toxicology specimens in his laboratory (forensic cryonics). He did so in case future scientific breakthroughs might aid in a fresh examination of various causes of death. Why Dr. Umberger singled out Kilgallen's case is curious. Speculation may be that he wasn't satisfied with Dr. Luke's conclusions and decided to preserve evidence for later analysis.

Known to colleagues as "Joe," Dr. Umberger retired in 1972. He died five years later. Regarding the chemist, Israel said he told her Umberger hinted to him that Kilgallen had been murdered, a startling revelation if true. The chemist also said Umberger admitted he had evidence proving the murder that he kept secret from the ME Department of Pathology.

Relying on the excuse that he was wary of the toxic politics weaving through the medical examiner's office at the time, Dr. Umberger was careful not to divulge his findings. However, subsequently, in 1968, *three years* after Kilgallen's death, he shared his raw data with the chemist. Dr. Umberger asked him to examine "a basic beaker with an extract from Dorothy's brain, and another beaker labeled 'drink.'" Also provided to the chemist were "two glasses which had contained alcoholic beverages." They were discovered at Kilgallen's bedside table. Dr. Umberger told the chemist his examination had indicated one was a "drink" glass from which "the alcohol had evaporated, [which] was hers [Kilgallen's]" without indicating how he knew this to be true.

* * * * *

In 2007, a significant article entitled *Who Killed Dorothy Kilgallen?* appeared in the magazine, *Midwest Today,* written by Sara Jordan and published by her father Larry. The article was part of a series devoted to celebrities born in the Midwest (recall Kilgallen was born in Chicago).

Based on their extensive research and information supplied by investigative reporter Kathryn Fauble and her associate, the article identified the chemist as John Broich.[2] After admitting he had examined the Kilgallen tissue samples, he revealed to Dr. Umberger that the basic beaker contained three dangerous barbiturates: secobarbital sodium (Seconal), pentobarbital sodium (Nembutal) and a combination of secobarbital sodium and amobarbital sodium (Tuinal). This was confirmation of what Dr. Luke had discovered three years earlier, Seconal and Tuinal, but also added a third drug to the mix, Nembutal which Dr. Luke did not mention in the ME report. In addition, Broich reported that a specimen taken from the glass attributed to Kilgallen contained traces of Nembutal. There was no explanation given as to the examination procedure for determining how it was known alcohol had evaporated from that glass.

According to John Broich's version of what happened in 1968, he presented his discoveries to Dr. Umberger.[3] Broich said the doctor "grinned" and told him, 'Keep it under your hat. It was big.'"

* * * * *

In his audiotaped interview supplied by Kathryn Fauble, John Broich revealed a troubling state of affairs existing in the ME's office in the mid 1960s.

> There was some talk…whether [Kilgallen's] body had been moved and a whole bunch of stuff. But I don't know if it was ever resolved. I do remember that things were kinda screwed up. I think things were probably

---

[2] Besides giving Sara and Larry Jordan information about Kilgallen's death, during 2014, 2015 and 2016, Kathryn Fauble provided this author with copies of several audiotape and videotape interviews conducted over a period of years with eyewitnesses, including Kilgallen's hairdressers Marc Sinclaire and Charles Simpson, and John Broich, regarding the circumstances surrounding Dorothy Kilgallen's death. Ms. Fauble also forwarded additional information about Kilgallen's life and her death through articles, photos, letters and other material. The quality of the interviews is exceptional. The interviewer is straightforward and the subjects are permitted sufficient time to tell their stories. Excerpts from some of the interviews are posted at www.TheReporterWhoKnewTooMuch.com so the credibility of those interviewed may be considered.

[3] In April 1967, Dr. Umberger was a witness in the celebrated second trial of Dr. Carl Coppolino. Defended by F. Lee Bailey, Coppolino was found guilty of murdering his wife Carmela. Forensic evidence played a large part in the conviction and Dr. Umberger and a colleague were given credit for developing a technique to detect deadly levels of succinylcholine byproducts in Carmela Coppolino's tissues.

pretty unreliable. I wouldn't trust anything, you know what I mean? When I was [employed by the ME's office], very few of the people knew what the hell they were doing. I was paranoid as hell when I was there. You never knew what was going to happen from one day to the next.

Broich further elaborated his sentiments about the medical examiner's office by stating, "It was not unusual for the M.E.'s office to screw up a case. Weren't too many people there who could get a job anywhere else. And there were people working there who didn't belong there. Downright dishonesty was there." Regarding Kilgallen's death, Broich added, "Dr. Luke loved headlines. Loved to see his name in print. And Joe (Dr. Umberger) hated Luke." [4] Finally, Broich said, "I remember there were some cloudy issues concerning who found the body and stuff like that. When Luke wrote, 'circumstances undetermined' on the report, it meant he didn't really know what had happened." Broich also stated, "Regarding the Certificate of Death, it was most unusual for Dominick DiMaio to sign it for Dr. Luke since he was deputy chief for Brooklyn and Kilgallen died in Manhattan."

A predictable question to ask is why Dr. Umberger and John Broich never divulged their findings in 1968. These results, if accurate, could have potentially paved the way for a fresh investigation of Kilgallen's death. Broich, like Dr. Umberger, blamed it on office politics, but this excuse was less than truthful as further evidence will indicate. Regardless, first, there had been no investigation. Now there was an apparent cover-up of evidence deliberately concealed by Dr. Luke but discovered by Broich and Dr. Umberger. These actions were misleading to the authorities and to the public, and worse to Kilgallen, who deserved a fresh investigation of her death.

To gain another perspective of what transpired in 1965 with regard to Kilgallen's manner of death, author Israel had contacted Dr. Michael Baden in 1978. He was then chief medical examiner for the City of New York. Dr.

---

[4] The root of discontent between Dr. Umberger, Ph.D and Dr. James Luke, M.D., is noteworthy. According to an anonymous source, this author learned that the two men were party to a "hateful feud" that continued after Dr. Luke left the ME's office. According to the source, when Dr. Luke's competence became an issue in Oklahoma during a court hearing, Dr. Umberger testified, "the man isn't qualified to wash test tubes at any laboratory."

Baden, who worked at the NYC ME office at the time of Kilgallen's death, later became quite famous when he was involved in several high-profile celebrity cases including John Belushi, O.J. Simpson, and Michael Jackson. In 2014, Baden provided autopsy analysis in the controversial Michael Brown police shooting death in Ferguson, Missouri.[5]

Israel apparently gave Dr. Baden raw data based on Dr. Luke's autopsy report without specifying the exact makeup of the raw data. Nevertheless, Dr. Baden said the "percentage of barbiturate found in Dorothy's brain and liver indicated that the body reposited the equivalent of 'fifteen to twenty' Seconal capsules."

Dr. Donald Hoffman, a senior chemist in toxicology at the ME office beginning in 1969, also provided an opinion. Apparently examining the same raw data Dr. Baden scoured, Dr. Hoffman said Dr. Baden's estimate was reasonable. Elaborating, Dr. Hoffman added, "The formal data indicate that it was acute poisoning due to alcohol and barbiturates and that the barbiturates alone could possibly have killed her."

In late 2015, this author interviewed Dr. Hoffman, still teaching at John Jay College in New York City at age 75. First, he confirmed earlier statements he made including his agreeing with Dr. Baden about the amount of drugs in Kilgallen's system. Dr. Hoffman, a member of the toxicological team at the NYC medical examiner's office from 1969-1996, also called the techniques used in the medical examiner's office "crude" during the early 1960s. "This limited," Dr. Hoffman asserted to this author, "the scope of the overall procedure as to identifying specific barbiturates found in a person's system during the post-mortem analysis. And this could impact upon the issue of whether the barbiturate or barbiturates detected were those prescribed to, or otherwise, available to the decedent. If not, it raises obvious questions about the circumstances surrounding the drug intake."

Dr. Hoffman added that these techniques "lacked the analytic sensitivity, specificity and confirmatory nature available during later years.

---

[5] Attempts by this author to interview Dr. Baden were not successful despite several tries to do so including emails sent to him that were not answered.

This damaged the reliability of testing causing any conclusions to be questionable."

Regarding the estimation that Kilgallen ingested "the equivalent of 15–20 Seconal capsules," Dr. Hoffman agreed this "pointed toward suicide or foul play." Most importantly, he said high barbiturate levels "ruled out that the person had just taken one or two pills" but instead meant he or she had taken "a lot more."

Asked whether the UV (ultraviolet) numbers, 2.4 for liver and 1.6 for brain, included in Kilgallen's autopsy report were important, Dr. Hoffman concluded they were, adding that the numbers were "high, and indicative that the screening tests used picked up significant amounts of the barbiturates." Dr. Hoffman also concluded the presence of both the Seconal and Tuinal caused there to be "a lethal dose of barbiturates" and when combined with the amount of alcohol in her blood triggered "a serious threat to Kilgallen's health."

Turning to the traces of Nembutal (pentobarbital) on the drinking glass on the nightstand next to Kilgallen's bed, Dr. Hoffman told this author, "This opens the door as to how she came to ingest it. The presence of the pentobarbital itself on the glass clearly implies that she reasonably could have ingested a liquid containing this drug. If so, then how did she come to have it in the first place since she was prescribed Seconal? Could someone have put it in her glass unknown to her? If someone wanted to 'spike' her drink, would he or she have just dropped in the capsules? Possible but that assumes [Kilgallen] would have been too distracted to know. Risk for the perpetrator?"

Asked the difference between someone ingesting a barbiturate capsule and the powder extracted when it was removed from the gelatin covering, Dr. Hoffman stated, "The only reason I can think of as to why a person would do that is if they thought the powder being disbursed in a liquid took effect quicker, absorbed into the person's system quicker." He added, "This would have to be done deliberately, not by accident since you have to open the capsules. It could not be done accidently unless the person was highly under the influence of alcohol but regardless combining the

John and Eileen Broich

barbiturate with alcohol increases the danger moving in the direction of central nervous system failure."

Asked to comment on the professionalism of Dr. Umberger, Dr. Hoffman told this author he was one of the "founding fathers of forensic toxicology." Of John Broich, Dr. Hoffman said Broich was "an excellent toxicologist, sharp, had good intuitive knowledge."

The conclusions reached by Dr. Charles Umberger, John Broich, Dr. Michael Baden, and Dr. Donald Hoffman are quite noteworthy, but only Dr. Umberger and Broich broach the subject of Tuinal being present in Kilgallen's system. They do, however, verify that Kilgallen ingested far more than the "moderate amount" of drugs Dr. James Luke specified in 1965.

Neither John Broich nor Dr. Umberger believed Kilgallen died accidently. While Broich did not discuss this belief in the 1990s interview, a January 2015 audiotaped interview this author conducted with Broich's widow Eileen confirmed his allegations. She first called her husband "a man full of ideas, bright, outspoken, a true scientist." She then praised Kilgallen as "a woman ahead of her time."

Mrs. Broich described the atmosphere in the medical examiner's office during the days preceding Kilgallen's death as "mean-spirited." She added, "Some people felt threatened by others and wanted reports to be fudged regarding cause of death."

"From time to time," Mrs. Broich said, "people with influence and money caused fear to exist in the office." However, she swore her husband and Dr. Umberger, a close friend of the family "were men of integrity, honest men who went by the book." Regarding Kilgallen's death, Mrs. Broich said her husband told her Dorothy was "bumped off," the Mafia term for killing a target.

As to why she felt her husband did not divulge his belief that Kilgallen was murdered, Mrs. Broich blamed "paranoia" in the medical examiner's office. Was this true or were there other reasons for John Broich and Dr. Umberger, like Dr. Luke before them, failing to disclose evidence that could have clarified how Kilgallen died? Answering this question requires considering the degree of danger to Kilgallen by ingesting a combination of Seconal, Nembutal and Tuinal with alcohol while keeping in mind the three possible causes for her death: suicide, accidental death, or murder.

In essence, Kilgallen's death must be investigated in the same way she would have done so based on her career as the premiere crime reporter of her era. The starting point must be to understand the deceased's state of mind as of November 1965. This provides a roadmap to learning how the iconic journalist and television star died, and more importantly, why.

CHAPTER 21

Conflicting reports cause inconsistencies regarding Dorothy Kilgallen's mental state at age 52.

Certainly, her marriage to Richard was a marriage in name only. They led separate lives while acting like a happy couple when they appeared in public. There was some indication Kilgallen's reliance on alcohol had increased. Reports surfaced that someone had seen Johnnie Ray and her falling-down drunk in public. One friend swore he saw them passed out on a New York Street corner. Some acquaintances insisted Kilgallen had a drug problem. They suggested her dependence on sleeping pills had increased over time.

Eyewitness Joe Tonahill, co-counsel with Melvin Belli during the Jack Ruby trial, disagreed. In a videotape interview, Tonahill was asked whether he believed Kilgallen was "a troubled woman on the downhill of her life" with drug or alcohol issues. He answered, "She wasn't struggling with any substance abuse problems or anything. I went to dinner with her at the 21 Club [in New York City] in July 1965. She didn't drink much, maybe one vodka tonic. That was about it." He added, "She didn't show any indication of being an alcoholic to me. Or any drug use. She had a good mind and her mind was working. Very realistically and very effectively." (Tonahill interview excerpts available at TheReporterWhoKnewTooMuch.com)

Tonahill, who said Kilgallen asked him to contribute content for her book on the assassinations, also disclosed that just a week before her death, she spoke to him about appearing on a radio talk show together to discuss the assassinations and Ruby. He intimated that she was as sharp as ever.

Confirmation of Tonahill's opinion, it may be recalled, is possible through observations by both husband Richard and Johnnie Ray after Kilgallen returned from a trip to Europe during the spring/summer 1965. Ray, in fact, stated, "She was plumper. Her color was higher."

On the financial front, speculation in New York City circles suggested Kilgallen's position as the noted columnist for the *Journal-American* may have been in jeopardy. The reason: the newspaper had fallen on hard times and might fold.[1] Kilgallen's hairdresser Marc Sinclaire addressed this point in an audiotaped interview: "That wouldn't have changed her life much. She was still being syndicated across the country and was working on television and had book offers."

Speculation aside, on the positive side, Kilgallen still enjoyed her lofty status as one of the most eminent personalities in America. Her *Journal-American* columns were as popular as ever. Weekly appearances on *What's My Line?* thrilled millions of fans. They counted on her to ask the tough questions other panelists avoided.

Most importantly, Kilgallen continued to write drafts of the *Murder One* manuscript. There is some confusion as to whether she would have included the Ruby trial in a second book or in *Murder One*. Joe Tonahill said later he believed Kilgallen intended the Ruby trial to be part of *Murder One*. In a videotaped interview Marc Sinclaire stated, "I saw her open notes on the assassination and look at them. *Murder One* wasn't the book she had in mind [for them]."

As noted, Kilgallen's file on the Dallas killings was missing at the time of her death and never recovered. This means there is no certain way to pinpoint what actual evidence Kilgallen uncovered although revisiting the columns and articles she wrote following the assassinations provides clarity. Of special interest are the columns previously noted, "The Oswald File Must Not Close," "Still Live Topic," "DA to Link Ruby to Oswald," "Nervous Ruby Feels Breaking Point Near," "Why Did Oswald Risk All By Shooting Cop?" and "Maybe You Didn't Know." Close reading of these

---

[1] The *Journal-American* ceased publishing in April 1966, six months after Kilgallen died. Afternoon newspapers experienced difficulty competing for advertising revenue due to early evening newscasts including Walter Cronkite's.

columns and Kilgallen articles provides a window into her mindset, hints of what exclusive information she had learned about the JFK and Oswald assassinations that could be exposed at the proper time.

Kilgallen apparently did not keep a diary or personal journal. It might have been a gateway into her mindset within days of her death. Fortunately, one clear indication of Kilgallen's outlook toward life is possible. It comes through the status of *Murder One* although that book, like Kilgallen's death, is shrouded in mystery. Why? Because when the book was finally published by Random House (she had been given a $10,000 advance) two years after Kilgallen died, questions arose as to whether most of the text may actually have been written by her for the book. In April 1978, Mrs. Phyllis Wagner, formerly Mrs. Bennett Cerf, informed author Lee Israel (in a letter this author has read) that Kilgallen had not completed much, if any, of the manuscript.

Mrs. Wagner wrote, "The book was very important to Dorothy—the thought of being between hard covers delighted her..." Mrs. Wagner added, "[But] she missed deadline after deadline—each time promising to bring something in shortly. Finally, she produced a chapter or so...I believe it was the day she died, that Bennett told her that he read it and that he liked it."[2]

Regarding the book being published, Mrs. Wagner wrote, "After her death, at the suggestion of Richard Kollmar ...her research [was] turned over to editor Allan Ullman to finish—I have no idea how much material he received or how little of it he used...or how much. [The book] was written. It was okayed by Richard Kollmar and it was published."

Recall hairdresser Marc Sinclaire confirmed that Kilgallen was working on the book. Also, producer Joseph E. Levine [award-winning film producer of *The Lion in Winter* and *The Graduate*] said Kilgallen had shown him *Murder One* text since they had a meeting on November 3, 1965 to discuss film/television adaptation.

Most importantly, following the "Dorothy Kilgallen to the Reader" section at the beginning of the published book, it was mentioned that this

---

[2] Mrs. Wagner's comment apparently means Bennett Cerf read whatever Kilgallen had written while she waited for her final *What's My Line?* program. This was actually the day before Kilgallen died.

section "…accompanied the draft manuscript from which the present book was edited." This was an indication Kilgallen had written a substantial portion of the book text.

The superb writing style and word selection not only indicates Kilgallen was the author, but how competent she was as an investigative reporter who knew legal strategies as well as a seasoned trial lawyer. It further confirms that she certainly had developed skills permitting her to be at the top of her game in November 1965. No less authority than the celebrated attorney F. Lee Bailey, attorney for Dr. Sam Sheppard and later for Patty Hearst and O. J. Simpson, said of Kilgallen, "She was a very bright and very good reporter of criminal cases. The best there was."

Questioned about his daughter's prowess as a reporter, Jim Kilgallen told a journalist, "She had an unerring instinct for news…a brilliant style of writing. She was accurate and had a flair for the apt phrase. She had an uncanny ability to produce scoops and an inordinate speed in turning out copy." Appropriate in terms of her dogged style as an investigative reporter, Bennett Cerf, as mentioned, praised Kilgallen when he issued a statement about her death: "A lot of people knew Dorothy as a very tough game player; others knew her as a tough newspaper woman. When she went after a story, nothing could get in her way."[3]

Murder One, published under Kilgallen's name, received excellent reviews with at least four printings available for the bestseller. King Features Syndicate called it, "The best true crime book of the year…but only for adult readers." Kirkus Reviews reported, "…to equal parts of murder and mayhem [in *Murder One*] add a double portion of sex, flavor with leaden innuendo, and cover the intellectual gap with big pieces of the trial record."

Random House certainly believed *Murder One* was top notch based on the front cover copy. In bold red letters, the title appeared and below it, "By Dorothy Kilgallen" in black print.

---

[3] Kilgallen told *Variety*: "Ever since I was a little bittie girl around the newspaper I have been allowed to use my typewriter and my own head, and any opinions expressed have been entirely mine. When I have to get permission to write about something that interests me, then I will exit quietly from the field of journalism."

Beneath this lettering was posted in a black circle with white lettering the words, "Six On-The-Spot Murder Stories by American's Most Famous Crime Reporter." To the immediate right of the circle were the titillating titles Kilgallen had chosen for chapter headings. Each was printed in bold black letters:

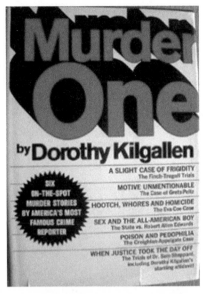

A Slight Case of Frigidity:
The Finch-Tregoff Trials

Motive Unmentionable:
The Case of Greta Peltz

Hootch, Whores and Homicide:
The Eva Coo Case

At the time of her Death, Dorothy Kilgallen was writing *Murder One* chronicling famous trials she had covered during her career.

Sex and the All-American Boy:
The State vs. Robert Allen Edwards

Poison and Pedophilia:
The Creighton-Applegate Case

When Justice Took the Day Off:
The Trials of Dr. Sam Sheppard including Dorothy Kilgallen's
Startling Affidavit

The back cover indicated the celebrity status Random House believed Kilgallen still enjoyed two years after she died. It featured only a black and white photograph of Kilgallen sitting on a desk, telephone pressed to her ear. On the inside cover flap copy, the following appeared:

The image of Dorothy Kilgallen as a brilliant, remarkably well-informed member of TV's *What's My Line?* panel and caustic columnist whose "Voice of Broadway" was devoured daily by millions tends to obscure her record of more than thirty years as one of the nation's top crime reporters. Her byline in the Hearst newspapers was a guarantee of sharp, accurate and highly readable journalism. From 1934 to 1965 she covered many of the sensational murder trials that once shocked and fascinated the American public.

No bleeding-heart sob sister, she went after a story with a vigor and tenacity that frequently bettered the best of her colleagues. And she never hesitated to voice an opinion—or a doubt. Indeed, at the close of the Dr. Sam Sheppard's first trial, Hearst papers ran banner headlines, DOROTHY KILGALLEN SHOCKED, above her account of that peculiar verdict.

Commenting on her career, Bill Slocum, another journalistic great, had written, "No reporter in the history of journalism ever approached her ability to sell papers when the readers knew she was covering a news story. When she was reporting on a trial, newspapers throughout the country fought to buy her coverage."

These plaudits, ones that clearly spell out how Kilgallen was a giant of her profession, intrigued readers as to her coverage of six intriguing murder cases. Reading excerpts from what Kilgallen wrote about each case provides great insight into her razor-sharp mind. This is especially true when it comes to dissecting the important morsels of evidence significant to the outcome of the cases.

Indicative of this skill was Kilgallen's shrewd sense of insight into criminal cases and the criminal mind as evidenced in the high-profile Dr. Sam Sheppard murder trial, a shining moment in the famous journalist's career. The title of the *Murder One* chapter, quite similar to the *Journal-American* column she wrote, was, "When Justice Took the Day Off."

When the trial had ended, the headline read, "Dorothy Kilgallen on Sheppard Trial: ASTOUNDED BY VERDICT SEES REVERSAL POSSIBLE." Kilgallen then wrote, "There were a number of reasons for my startled reaction to the jury's verdict. Basically, the state had failed to present...anything resembling a conclusive case that established 'beyond a reasonable doubt' the doctor's guilt. The evidence submitted was flimsy beyond belief, much of it was remote from the commission of the crime, much of it sheer speculation. The motive attributed to Dr. Sam was clearly poppycock."

Exhibiting her ability to take readers into the case with her, Kilgallen vividly detailed the trial. It almost seemed like Dr. Sheppard was a longtime acquaintance: "As he walked with the deputy sheriff across the leaf-covered lawn, their wrists were so close the handcuffs barely showed, he was hatless and ramrod straight in a light brown and tan small-checked topcoat. Burberry style, which he wore unbuttoned. Except for the stern set of his jaw and his pallor, he looked almost collegiate; he might have been, standing in the icy wind, not seeming to notice it, the local high school's football coach." Regarding how Sheppard's dead wife Marilyn appeared in court photos, Kilgallen wrote, "She was beautiful. So lovely and so bruised. So gentle looking, with her eyes closed, sleeping under the vermillion gashes…No picture ever printed of Marilyn Sheppard…has shown her to be as lovely as she was in death—discolored and slashed and broken."

Sheppard's defense, Kilgallen noted, revolved around his telling police "that someone had been in the house; that he had heard Marilyn scream and ran upstairs. When he got there he was struck and knocked out." Kilgallen felt it important that the prosecution admitted, "[Sheppard] had an injury to the face around the eye and he complained that his neck hurt" after the incident.

Throughout the trial, Kilgallen, through her gall and persistence, spoke to witnesses who would speak to no one else. Due to her reputation, she had the capacity to get others to trust her. These included Dr. Sheppard's brother Richard and even Dr. Sheppard himself. When Richard told her, "I know what Sam's like; I know he's incapable of violence," Kilgallen believed him.

Kilgallen berated Dr. Sheppard's defense counsels for basic ineptness. They were not asking the questions she would ask; not making the points she would make. To indicate how shaky the case against Dr. Sheppard was, Kilgallen honed in on several aspects of supportive testimony for the accused. There were nine in all. However, it was defense counsel William Corrigan, Jr. who was the recipient of Kilgallen's sharp tongue. She catalogued one critical mistake he made, writing, "Corrigan's motive for this sensational line of questioning (he delved into whether the Sheppards' first child was illegitimate) which in effect handed the state its motive for a crime of fury on a silver platter and tied with a ribbon bow—was not clear."

When Dr. Sheppard testified, Dorothy Kilgallen listened intently. She was impressed when he declared, "…I'm certainly going to do all I could to get to the bottom of this. I won't rest until I find out who killed my wife."

Without doubt, Kilgallen had gained the respect of attorneys she wrote about in her articles. They admired her professional credibility and astute courtroom savvy. One specific example arose during the Sheppard trial. It involved defense attorney Arthur E. Petersilge's final argument. Rising to address the jury, he, for all practical purposes, copied Kilgallen's words in her *Journal-American* story a few days earlier. She had written, "Five months after the murder of Marilyn Sheppard, the state does not know how she was killed, with what weapon she was killed, or why she was killed. Yet on the basis of this flimsy evidence, the state is asking you to send Sam Sheppard to the electric chair."

Kilgallen continued to believe in Dr. Sheppard's innocence. This was despite the prosecution's insistence that he was "an adulterer, perjurer, and cold-blooded murderer who deserved no mercy for the murder of his pregnant wife." When the jury returned a guilty verdict, Kilgallen wrote in the book, "Astounding was the word for the verdict in the case of Dr. Sam Sheppard. It may have been a correct verdict—but in my opinion, it was a verdict wrongly arrived at and therefore frightening. I heard the same evidence the jury heard. I saw Dr. Sheppard on the [witness] stand. I listened to the summation on both sides. I could not have convicted him of anything except possibly negligence in locking his back door. So I was aghast at the verdict."

Kilgallen's strong words were not enough to save Dr. Sheppard from prison. While he languished, the famed journalist lived with the knowledge that she had evidence that could free him. This was because before the trial, in an exclusive interview with Judge Edward Blythin, she saw firsthand his bias toward Dr. Sheppard.

The chance to inform F. Lee Bailey, Dr. Sheppard's appellate counsel, what Judge Blythin had told her in confidence, happened when they met in New York City. True to her assuring the judge she would not divulge their conversation, Kilgallen had never mentioned the substance of the conversation until he died.

In the affidavit she provided Bailey, Kilgallen said the judge summoned her to his chambers. He then told her, "I am very glad to see you, Miss Kilgallen. I watch you on television very frequently and enjoy the program. But what brings you to Cleveland?" She replied, "Well, [the case] has all the ingredients of what in the newspaper business we call a good murder. It has a very attractive victim, who was pregnant, and the accused was an important member of the community, a respectable, very attractive man. Then, added to that, you have the fact that it was a mystery as to who did it."

Judge Blythin, Kilgallen told Bailey, replied, "Mystery? It's an open and shut case." "Well, what do you mean, Judge Blythin?" Kilgallen asked. "Well, he's guilty as hell. There's no question about it," the judge proclaimed.

Based on Kilgallen's disclosure of judicial prejudice and that of a court clerk who heard a similar remark, the United States Supreme Court reversed Dr. Sheppard's conviction. The opinion read, "We have concluded that [Dr. Sam] Sheppard did not receive a fair trial consistent with the Due Process Clause of the Fourteenth Amendment and, therefore, reverse the judgment." Most legal observers at the time, as noted, believed that Kilgallen's reputation as a credible reporter turned the tide in Sheppard's favor on appeal.

In a subsequent trial, a jury acquitted Dr. Sheppard. Years later, DNA tests confirmed that he had not killed his wife. The case became the basis for *The Fugitive* television series starring David Jansen as Dr. Richard Kimble. A film of the same name starred Harrison Ford. The death of Marilyn Sheppard remains unsolved.

Most importantly, Kilgallen protected the prejudicial words spoken to her in confidence in the Sheppard case by Judge Blythin. This speaks highly of her integrity. Throughout her career, Kilgallen was a reporter who knew how to keep a secret. This laudable trait had permitted her to stare down FBI agents when they investigated her for disclosing Jack Ruby's testimony to the Warren Commission *before* its date of release. Kilgallen may have been a complicated woman with enemies abounding, but she could be trusted, a characteristic she took to the grave.

CHAPTER 22

As mentioned, three possibilities exist regarding the cause of Dorothy Kilgallen's death: the famous reporter, columnist and television star committed suicide, she died accidently by consuming the drugs and alcohol, or she was murdered.

To date, the possibility Kilgallen committed suicide bears little merit. The famed journalist and television star did not appear to be a desperate woman without hope who took her own life.

In fact, Kilgallen had much to live for outside her celebrity media status. In addition to the publication of *Murder One*,[1] her continuing probe of the JFK and Oswald assassinations provided excitement in her life. The longstanding affair with singer Johnnie Ray had blended into more of a friendship than a love interest. Both parties benefited from the change in status. There was no pressure on either of them. In October 1965, a month before she died, Kilgallen flew to Las Vegas on a private plane to see Ray perform. While there, they enjoyed mutual friend Tony Bennett's songfest at the Riviera Hotel.

Kilgallen was also fast-forwarding a new love affair with Ron Pataky, an Ohio newspaper columnist who visited New York City on a regular basis. Most importantly, on the night before she died, those who saw and spoke with Kilgallen provided a rosy picture of the media star. Among them was

---

[1] Besides Kilgallen being excited about the book, apparently she was expecting photographers from Twentieth-Century Fox to visit with her regarding a *Murder One* movie deal on the day she died.

What's My Line? moderator John Charles Daly. After learning of her death, he told reporters: "Dorothy was just full of beans last night. She was in great spirits."

Daly's perspective is confirmed in Kilgallen's final appearance on the *What's My Line?* program. (www.youtube.com/watch?v=6gn6jS1UK78) Actress Joey Heatherton was the mystery guest. Kilgallen's questioning of her and the additional contestants, including a woman who was a football newspaper columnist and one who sold dynamite, was sharp and sassy. Wearing a low-cut dress and appearing as glamorous as ever, Kilgallen laughed at her fellow panelist's remarks. She sat next to future *Odd Couple* star Tony Randall.

Throughout the program, Kilgallen smiled and appeared as lively as ever with no slurring of words. At the end of the program as the football writer left the stage, Kilgallen kidded Bennett Cerf. Exhibiting her sarcastic sense of humor, she asked whether he might have used the expression "forward pass" when addressing the attractive writer. Instead, Cerf had asked about the woes of his favorite team, the New York Giants.

During his videotaped interview, hairdresser Marc Sinclaire was asked about Kilgallen's character, that some people said she was an alcoholic and a drug addict. He answered, "They'd like you to believe that. They'd like you to believe she drank. She did drink. She was tough lady. She was able to go out with gangsters and people like that so she had to be like that. But how could she do the body of work that was done, that everybody professes to, that you can find on tapes and be an alcoholic and a pill pusher? How do you do that and she's on television three or four times a week? How do you do this without [someone] knowing?" Asked what the *What's My Line?* producer's reaction would have been if they believed she was an alcoholic and drug user, Sinclaire replied, "They would have taken her off the air immediately. They couldn't have let her on drunk."

Later in the interview, Sinclaire added, "Go look at the tapes a week before she died, she looks beautiful, she's walking around, looks beautiful. I had dinner with her twice that week. I went out for cocktails with her twice that week…she had a limo driver who knew her. The people in the restaurants knew her. People at the theater knew her. How do you hide this pill and drug habit that they say she had?" Asked if Kilgallen's face was puffy, her figure "shot," Sinclaire said, "You can look at the tapes. Was she bloated, was her figure gone? No, she wore a form-fitting dress. She looked beautiful."

Additional proof Kilgallen was in good form following her final *What's My Line?* program exists through the recollection of Dave Spiegal, a NYC-based Western Union office manager. Bob Considine of the Hearst Newspaper Syndicate first quoted him a few days after Kilgallen's death:

> Miss Kilgallen called me at 2:20 in the morning. She sounded great as usual. She said, 'Good morning, Mr. Spiegel, this is Dorothy Kilgallen. Would you send a messenger over to the house to pick up my column and take it to the *Journal-American*. I'll leave it in the regular place, in the door.' I said, 'it's a pleasure' and sent the messenger. It [the column] was there, as usual.

Based on Spiegel's interview, there was nothing mentioned about slurred words, drunken behavior, or depressive attitude as evidenced by her ability to tell Spiegel the column was available in the "regular place." This was apparently a metal box of some sort located just outside the front door of Kilgallen's townhouse hidden in the shadows since there was a small entranceway from the sidewalk to the front door. Today her leaving the column there would be risky. In 1965, doing so was apparently a safe bet.

Further indication of the unlikelihood Kilgallen committed suicide is a lunch date she made with her friend, music producer Dee Anthony, who knew her well enough to have been invited to Kilgallen's townhouse for Christmas parties—one attended, he recalled, by actress Jayne Mansfield. During an interview in the 1990s with an associate of investigative reporter Kathryn Fauble, he had complimented Kilgallen stating, "She was the kind of friend where I didn't need to see her every day; I wanted nothing from her and she wanted nothing from me."

On the Friday before she died, Anthony, who managed famous artists such as the Spencer Davis Group, Traffic, Jethro Tull, Joe Cocker, and Peter Frampton, said Kilgallen had a handwritten note delivered to his

Manhattan address. It read, according to Anthony, "You stinker. I haven't seen you in ages. Let's have lunch on Monday."

Certainly, Kilgallen could have changed her mind over the weekend and taken her own life. However, by all accounts, her committing suicide did not fit with the demeanor of the tough, crusty columnist, investigate reporter, television and radio star. In fact, it appears from her own writings that she had no intention to do so. This seems clear based on the Preface she apparently wrote for the 304-page book, *Murder One*, the one she showed Bennett Cerf on the evening of her final *What's My Line?* program.

It was entitled, "Dorothy Kilgallen to the Reader." After describing how publisher Bennett Cerf[2] urged her to write the book, she wrote, "The result was this collection of the six famous murder trials that I covered as a working member of the press (one of my colleagues once called me a 'newspaperman in a $500 dress' but don't you believe it!')."

Kilgallen then focused on the Sam Sheppard murder case by noting, "at long last it [is] being reviewed by the Supreme Court of the United States....No one knows how many months will pass before the Court announces its decision. Meanwhile, the show—or in this case the book—must go on." Below this sentence were the words, "Dorothy Kilgallen, New York City, 1965."

While Kilgallen's words indicate the book was on track to be published, the editor added the following caveat: "On December 8, 1965 [obviously a mistake about the correct date of death], Dorothy Kilgallen passed away. Only a little while before, she had discussed with us the possibility of delaying publication of her book until the Supreme Court had disposed of the Sheppard case so that she could bring her account up to date."

The editor's comment clearly suggests the mindset of a woman with no inclination to commit suicide. Instead, she anticipated waiting to update the chapter until the Supreme Court announced its decision in the Sheppard case. That could have taken months. In fact, it took until June 1966 for the justices to render their decision.

---

[2] At the end of the letter, Kilgallen called Bennett Cerf "as pleasant a slave driver as I have ever known."

This evidence by Kilgallen's own hand, along with the observations of others who knew her best, make death by suicide to be all but impossible. As Kerry Kollmar's tutor and family companion, Ibne Hassan told this author, "She was very cheerful about life. She was working on her book, very enthusiastically. She was determined to finish it."

Hairdresser Marc Sinclaire had his own reasons for doubting Kilgallen killed herself. In his videotaped interview, he stated, "Suicide is out of the question. It's just out of the question. She was Catholic and you know what that means..."[3]

* * * * *

Dealing with the second of the possible causes of death—Kilgallen accidently causing her own demise due to excessive alcohol and barbiturates—is trickier especially in view of the death scene at Kilgallen's townhouse.

One eyewitness important to considering what happened is Detective John Doyle. As noted, he was the lead detective from the 19th Precinct. His memories of November 8 were vivid. Why? Because Doyle recalled there had been a $400,000 burglary heist at NYC's Sherry Netherland hotel and a burglary at the famous Delmonico's restaurant. These happened during the time Kilgallen died.

Assigned to both crimes with his partner, Detective Doyle told author Lee Israel he had testified in court about the cases. He said he was informed of Kilgallen's death at about 3:00 p.m. on November 8. Doyle was upset since word reached him that the body was discovered two hours earlier (1:00 p.m.).

When Detective Doyle entered the residence, he recalled seeing Dorothy's father Jim. Also present was motion picture star Joan Crawford and Kilgallen's husband Richard. Doyle described him as drunk ("In no shape

---

[3] As part of a multi-part feature story about Kilgallen in the *Journal-American* following her death, Louis Sobel reported that producer Joseph E. Levine and Kilgallen met with lawyers on Wednesday, Nov. 3, five days before she died, about legal issues concerning *Murder One* becoming a television series. This would provide another indication that Kilgallen had no intention of committing suicide since the television negotiations, with apparently a six figure option price on the table, were ongoing. Sobel also noted that Kilgallen had plans to travel to London on November 11, the Wednesday after she died.

or form. He was completely inebriated. I don't even think he knew his own name."). Richard's conclusion, according to Doyle, was that his wife had fallen asleep while she was reading in a half-sitting position. He also noted the reading light was on.

Regarding his visit to Kilgallen's townhouse, Detective Doyle said he and his partner were waiting for the medical examiner to appear. He also reported Kilgallen was in bed and that on a nightstand was an empty bottle of Seconal that had contained 50 100-milligram capsules. Doyle and his partner later visited the Hunter Pharmacy on nearby Madison Avenue. This confirms the account provided by Dr. Luke in the ME official documents.

Doyle said while he was at the pharmacy, he viewed Kilgallen's Seconal prescription history for the previous three or four years. He concluded the amount prescribed made him believe she took an average of two per night. This was true even when she was overseas.

Detective Doyle reported that the empty vial should have been marked as evidence. However, he said, it never made it to the police station or the medical examiner's office. Doyle did not know what happened to the vial.[4]

If one considers the death scene as described by eyewitnesses (among them, Dr. Luke and Detective Doyle) along with the physical evidence of discovering the Seconal vial together with the knowledge that Kilgallen had a prescription for that drug, then, as suggested, the accidental cause of death may be viable. However, the presence of Tuinal noted by Dr. Luke, the presence of Seconal, Nembutal and the Tuinal noted by John Broich, and the analysis by Dr. Baden as confirmed by Dr. Hoffman that Kilgallen's system contained the "equivalent of 15-20 Seconals" throws the proverbial monkey wrench into the equation.

Based on the deadly quantity of barbiturates ingested by Kilgallen, the question to answer is whether she could have accidently swallowed this many pills since deliberately taking them has been shown to be highly unlikely. It also appears quite unlikely Kilgallen accidently overdosed since

---

[4] Curiously, according to researcher Kathryn Fauble, within a month of Kilgallen's death, Detective Doyle, the father of six children, resigned without a pension from the police force. He left New York City and opened a restaurant near LaGrangeville, New York. Describing a brief interview with Doyle, Fauble told this author he "sounded to us like a tough guy from Brooklyn—Goodfellas style."

while she had the prescription for Seconal, and took, according to Detective Doyle, two per night on average, there was no prescription for either Nembutal or Tuinal and no evidence that she had ever ingested these barbiturates. Giving Kilgallen the benefit of the doubt based on her being one of the most intelligent women of her era, it is logical to presume that only one possibility exists regarding the true cause of her death: someone else was involved with her taking the pills, and by doing so, committed murder.

Curiously, while several people suspected foul play including potentially Dr. Luke, and, for certain, Dr. Umberger, a powerful governmental organization also showed interest in how Kilgallen died. How do we know? Because during the late 1970s, a request from G. Robert Blakey, Chief Counsel and Director of the House Select Committee on Assassinations, was received by the New York medical examiner's office. This investigatory body was formed to consider new evidence about the JFK and Martin Luther King assassinations collected since the 1960s.

Blakey's request was forwarded to Dominick J. DiMaio, M.D., chief medical examiner. Dr. DiMaio wrote back to Mr. Blakey on April 13, 1978, "Enclosed you will find the complete file on Ms. Kilgallen who died on November 8, 1965."

In response to an email request from this author regarding the HSCA interest in Kilgallen, Robert Blakey wrote, "Our look [into Kilgallen's death] was not substantial. In any event, we thought it was 'fishy.' But we were not able to solve it and do JKK [JFK and Martin Luther King] assassination investigation at the same time."

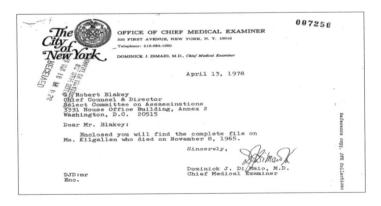

Whatever Blakey or the Committee had discovered, and if and how it used the information supplied by DiMaio, is unknown. Blakey confirmed to this author that there is no mention of Kilgallen, or what she discovered through her extensive investigation of the JFK and Oswald assassinations in the Committee's final report. Any opportunity to include eyewitness accounts from one of the premiere investigative reporters in history, a competent, credible journalist whose compilation of facts about what happened before, during and after the JFK and Oswald assassinations is unmatched, had been lost.

CHAPTER 23

If Dorothy Kilgallen was murdered, what was the killer or killers' motive for doing so? Did those responsible carry a strong grudge and decide revenge was in order due to something she wrote? Was it personal based on Kilgallen's actions during the months leading up to her death? Or, did the reporter know too much about important matters, ones threatening exposure of those in her crosshairs requiring her to be silenced?

Any fresh investigation of a cold case 50 years old requires focus on motive. It also requires considering the homicide detectives' remaining best friends: means, opportunity, and benefit from the crime. Certainly use of these tools would be of much more help in determining how Kilgallen died if the case were considered in a court of law. Then witnesses could appear with proper cross-examination.

With respect to who may have caused Kilgallen's death, the suspects must include husband Richard Kollmar as well as Frank Sinatra and other celebrities criticized through the years in Kilgallen's *Journal-American* columns and articles. Since she was obsessed with the assassinations investigation, those suspected of being involved in JFK's killing (the CIA, the State Department, the Russians, Cuban dissidents, and President Lyndon Johnson) are suspects. Also of interest are two individuals with much to gain from Kilgallen's death: FBI Director J. Edgar Hoover and New Orleans Mafia Don Carlos Marcello.

While many in the entertainment world mourned Dorothy Kilgallen's death, many did not. Along the way to her reaching the summit of being the most successful and best-known newspaper columnist of her era, the hard-charging Kilgallen made enemies. Her daily words could be career poison. Some were insulted with a scathing review or being slighted with no mention in the column. Others may have been upset with a curt remark about their private life. Still others objected to an inside story about them they believed crossed the bounds of professionalism. Any one of them could have killed her, or had her killed. Police, or the D.A., if they had investigated Kilgallen's death at all, could have followed up on any threats. They did not do so.

One celebrity objecting to Kilgallen's journalist credo was Christina Ford, the second wife of Henry Ford II, chief executive officer of the Ford Motor Company. During his videotaped interview, Marc Sinclaire said Mrs. Ford was incensed with Kilgallen writing about Jackie Kennedy instead of Lady Bird Johnson following Lyndon Johnson being sworn in as president. "Mrs. Henry Ford didn't like the Kennedy's, a lot of people did not like the Kennedy's and wanted them out of office, you have to understand what I am saying," Sinclaire stated. "She gave me a toy gun once and told me to give it to Dorothy to dry her eyelashes with. And it was a very vulgar gun and if it had been real, it could have blown Dorothy's head off. I threw it in the trash can. I wouldn't have taken it to Dorothy." Sinclaire added he did not think Mrs. Ford had anything to do with Kilgallen's death but the gun implied Ford believed someone should kill Kilgallen.

Many suspects exist with strong dislike for Kilgallen both on a personal as well as professional level, but chief among those who hated her is singer Frank Sinatra. It was a well-publicized public war. Kilgallen pounded his reputation on a daily basis for months at a time. He struck back.

That Kilgallen and Sinatra's battle became personal is a given. Kilgallen not only blasted his career and his private life but also his close friendship with members of the Mafia. At one point when Sinatra's career was languishing, Kilgallen printed his New York City address. When he moved, she printed it again. Sinatra, in turn, had a tombstone with Kilgallen's name embossed delivered to her office. Whether it was sent in jest or portended of evil intent, was unknown.

In February 1956, Kilgallen, as noted, had infuriated the *My Way* singer by penning "The Real Frank Sinatra Story" by making fun of his girl-friends and alluding to his Mafia connections.[1] In another seething column answering a reader complaint about JFK being friendly with Sinatra, she chastised the singer for being, "a successful tough guy who refers to women as 'broads' and gets off airplanes with a drink in his hand…in the true Sinatra fashion, no rules and plenty of booze and girls anywhere you look."

At a Copacabana appearance in New York City, Sinatra, called by Elvis Presley "a cretinous goon," hit Kilgallen with a nasty diatribe of his own. As a part of his act, Sinatra told the audience, "Dotty Kilgallen couldn't be here tonight. She's out shopping for a new chin." He then added to laughter and applause, "C'mon, let's all chip in and buy Dorothy a new chin" before lifting his glass toward the fans. "This is a toast to my enemies," Sinatra shouted before spitting the whisky to the floor. He then added, "That one was for Dorothy Kilgallen."[2]

When friends told Sinatra, the son of a Sicilian-born fireman, he was berating Kilgallen too often, he roared, "I'm not being rough enough." During a performance at the Sands Hotel, he held up a car key while asking the cheering audience "Doesn't this look like Dorothy Kilgallen's profile?" Later, Sinatra, while performing at the Villa Venice outside Chicago with Dean Martin and Sammy Davis Jr. said, "I've met many, many male finks but I never met a female fink until I met Dorothy Kilgallen. How's that for an opener? I wouldn't mind if she was a good-looking fink. The town where she came from had a beauty contest when she was 17 years old and nobody won."

After Sinatra learned of Kilgallen's death from his PR man, Jim Mahoney, Sinatra showed little concern. He calmly said, "Dorothy Kilgallen's dead. Well, guess I got to change my whole act."

---

[1] Sinatra was attacked in various columns for his underworld connections. This included his appearances at the mob-controlled Sands Hotel in Las Vegas. There, according to his FBI file, Sinatra "pimped" for John Kennedy. The notation read, "It was a known fact that the Sands Hotel was owned by hoodlums and that while the Senator [Kennedy], Sinatra, Peter Lawford were there, show girls from all over town were running in and out of the Senator's suite."

[2] Sinatra was severely criticized by columnists Walter Winchell and Louis Sobel for his nasty remarks. Sobel called them "in bad taste" and "inexcusable."

To say that Kilgallen's enemy had Mafia connections in New York City, and around the country, is an understatement. Sinatra's *close* friendships include gangsters Charles "Lucky" Luciano, Sam Giancana, Frank Costello, "Bugsy" Siegel, Mickey Cohen, and Tampa crime boss Santo Trafficante. In 1947, Sinatra had flown to Havana. There he frolicked with all of the heads of the U.S. crime families including Carlos Marcello, Mickey Cohen and others.

FBI reports obtained by this author through the Freedom of Information Act confirmed Sinatra gave Melvin Belli's client, Mickey Cohen, $20,000 ($150,000 in today's currency marketplace) following his release from prison. This happened after New Orleans Don Carlos Marcello had also given Cohen cash when the gangster visited him once he was paroled.

Sinatra's connections to Frank Costello and Mickey Cohen stretched from coast to coast. In California, Sinatra became close friends with Cohen after the gangster assumed control of the L.A. Mafia.

Kilgallen knew all about Belli's client and close friend Cohen since he was a newspaper favorite. Columnists called him "colorful" and always available for a spicy quote. Cohen had helped Sinatra when the crooner went through difficult times: "I love Frank," Cohen said, "I have a very great respect for him, and even when he was at his worst, I was his best friend."

Frank Sinatra's links to New York City crime boss Frank Costello were widespread. The singer joined the Mafia kingpin ringside for feature boxing matches at Madison Square Garden. Like Belli, whom close friend Milton Hunt told this author was "an unofficial member of the San Mateo [California] mob," Sinatra enjoyed the mysterious aura of gangster. His association with them made him feel as dangerous as the killers, robbers, and racketeers he admired.

Evidence of Sinatra's violent temper exists in the number of brawls he engaged in during his career. On many occasions, he was saved from conviction and imprisonment. Crime victims and witnesses suddenly disappeared or dropped charges when paid to do so. One person who witnessed the Sinatra method of dealing with those who crossed him was Kennedy family friend Peter Lawford, married to Patricia Kennedy, JFK's sister.

Lawford, a member of the infamous "Rat Pack" with Sinatra, boasted of his relationship with the singer. However, a violent argument between the two men happened after Lawford dined with Sinatra's love interest, Ava Gardner. Lawford said of the crooner, "I was panicked. I mean I was really scared. Frank's a violent guy and he's good friends with too many guys who'd rather kill you than say hello."

If Sinatra wanted to rid himself of his archenemy Kilgallen, his "good friends" in the underworld could have handled the task. Motive was a given since he detested her and he certainly had the means and opportunity to rid the world of the famous reporter. Without doubt, the bitter Sinatra benefited from her death. There was no more Dorothy Kilgallen to badmouth him, his private life, and his Mafia connections.

Whomever Sinatra, whose mother Dolly had said of him, "Yes, my son is like me. You cross him, he never forgets," directed to kill his enemy could hide the crooner's involvement so there was no link to the singer. However, proving Sinatra ordered Kilgallen's death is difficult if not impossible 50 years after she died but he must remain a strong suspect. Perhaps in the future, someone close to the singer will provide evidence that he was complicit in Kilgallen's demise. If this happens, he will finally be held responsible for silencing his longtime nemesis, the courageous reporter who sought to expose the truth about Sinatra's diabolical ways.

* * * * *

By all accounts there was no question Kilgallen and husband Richard were at odds in their marriage with the *New York Post Daily Magazine* reporting in 1960, "[They] go their separate ways for the most part." Certainly, the marriage was in name only in late 1965. Richard was a ghost of the man he had been when Kilgallen married him, an alcoholic with very little means of making an income. He was a "kept" husband who was depressed, having tumbled from being a successful businessman and Broadway producer, to a lonely man fallen from grace. The *Post Daily Magazine* called Richard "a muddling amateur" as a producer.

To many, Richard was a laughingstock, a failure, a man with little hope who kept up the pretenses of a happy marriage, one pockmarked with his affairs and being a drunk. Charlotte Manson, a successful radio actress who knew both Kilgallen and her husband, said Richard's "whoring" was well known. Apparently Richard boasted to Manson of his female conquests at parties she hosted.

After 14 years of marriage, the couple was headed in different directions; Richard was a has-been while Kilgallen was at the top of her profession, in good health, and highly successful. Kilgallen had lost respect for Richard and the marriage—appearing so vibrant during the Edward R. Murrow television interview—had disintegrated. For all practical purposes, it was a sham.

Author Lee Israel, after speaking with Richard's attorney Edgar Hatfield, discovered Kilgallen's philandering husband had actually impregnated several women. Hatfield confirmed he worked out financial settlements with many of them. No mention was made of whether any of Richard's conquests had a child or if Kilgallen knew of the pregnancies.

An additional account of Richard's dalliances came from pianist Lee Evans who performed at Richard's Left Bank restaurant. He reported Richard rented a third floor apartment where he met the women. Evans noted none of the affairs was long term but many were one-night stands.

According to Kilgallen, the two rarely met since "Dick works every night except Sunday and I'm out at least four nights a week to cover [Broadway] openings and usual rounds of a columnist." She also mentioned, "When I'm home and Dick isn't, I occasionally have friends in. He came home at four a.m. and was very amused to see me let seven men out the front door! We had been playing cards. Just a couple of years ago, I learned to play poker and blackjack."

Unhappy, Richard spent time at a neighborhood bar and prowled New York City seeking female companionship and understanding of his plight. Both of the nightclubs he had owned, the Left Bank in Manhattan and Paris in the Sky in East Orange, N.J., finally closed. He spent most of his time collecting classic Victrola records, toy banks, and sculpted hands. He mostly quit accompanying Kilgallen on the New York City social scene.

When he did go with his wife, he embarrassed her with his drinking. This behavior provided the rationalization for the famous journalist seeing other men, first Johnnie Ray, and then Ron Pataky. In essence, Kilgallen was the famous one; the television star, the respected columnist and the crack investigative reporter. Richard, whom Marc Sinclaire called, as noted, "Mr. Kilgallen," was a forgotten man.

Key to understanding Richard's state of mind is hairdresser Marc Sinclaire, the eyewitness come to life in startling videotaped fashion decades after Kilgallen's death. Sinclaire revealed facts about Richard, portraying him as a desperate man threatened by actions his wife intended to take shortly before she died. If Kilgallen had succeeded, Richard would have been in even more dire straits than before or at least he believed he would be.

The starting point is to note the shocking statement Kilgallen's mother Mae made at her daughter's funeral after she and Richard posed for a photograph appearing in the *Journal-American*. Glancing at the photo, Sinclaire, during his videotaped interview, said, "They [Mae and Richard] had a big fight. It says down at the bottom of [the newspaper page] that they are fighting and [Mae's] pointing a finger at Richard and said 'You killed my daughter and I will prove it' and Jim Kilgallen took her away."

By all accounts, no one, not the police or the District Attorney, ever investigated Mae's claim. To them, the bold accusation was simply that of a grieving mother looking to blame someone and poor Richard was caught in her crosshairs.

In no publication to date, has Mae's accusation been given credence. That is, until now triggering two significant questions: Was Mae right—did Richard kill his wife? And if so, why?

Based on credible accounts, at the center of the rough edges of the Kilgallen/Kollmar marriage was singer Johnnie Ray. With Richard leading his own private life amongst a boatload of beauties, Kilgallen had become "smitten" with the rock and roll singer. Exactly when the romance finally produced sexual fireworks appears to be in question, but the extent of the sexual explosion was not.

Lee Israel, based on interviews with Johnnie Ray, believed Kilgallen was deeply in love with Ray, and the sexual nature of the relationship was

Marc Sinclaire points at *Journal-American* page chronicling Mae Kilgallen/ Richard Kollmar confrontation.

torrid since Kilgallen and Richard had not had sex in several years. Kilgallen's friend Jean Bach backed up this comment using nearly the same words Israel noted stating, "Dorothy was terribly in love with Johnnie. Anything that he introduced was interesting to her. She was on cloud nine because it was all so perfect."

One indication of Kilgallen's true love for Ray, who sent Kilgallen lavender roses from time to time, was her gifts to him from expensive stores like Bergdorf's and Cartier. Recall Ray's manager Alan Eichler stating there was a "genuine love affair, sexual in nature." Ray's biographer Jonny Whiteside said that one guest at Ray's "63rd Street" parties told Whiteside, "[Kilgallen] drug [Ray] out of the living room into the den, in which there happened to be a long leather couch. We would sit in the living room and listen to all the activity that was going on in the den. It was lust out of control..."

Apparently, Kilgallen did little to keep secret her relationship with Ray from Richard or anyone else. The couple was seen necking in a corner booth at P.J. Clarke's. A television columnist reported seeing the two kissing at both El Morocco and the Stork Club.

As the continuing love affair was thrown in Richard's face, he must have been embarrassed beyond imagination. He was terribly unhappy while she pranced around New York City having replaced Richard not with a heterosexual but instead a known bisexual. One may only imagine the jealousy and rage boiling up inside Richard and finally that jealousy and rage boiled over during an early 1960 confrontation.

It happened after Kilgallen and Ray appeared together one evening at Richard's Left Bank nightclub, and "necked." When the bartender confronted Richard and asked him what he was going to do, Richard simply ordered another drink despite being humiliated.

At the couple's townhouse, Richard, drunk, apparently caught Ray and Kilgallen fondling each other in the Black Room and a screaming match ensued. Richard threatened to kill the singer if he ever saw the two together again. Ray defended Kilgallen and said it was her choice. Kilgallen reportedly told her husband she wanted to leave with Ray who told Israel, "I thought very fast. I knew that if she were to walk out—and she was ready—everything would collapse for her." Ray then explained that Kilgallen would lose the television show, the newspaper column, all that she had worked for if there was a scandal, but that Kilgallen didn't care. Apparently, Ray reasoned for both of them and said to Israel, "And I thought about Kerry. I told her, 'I'm gonna have to walk out and leave you here.'"

Kilgallen reluctantly accepted Ray's advice while promising Richard she would not see the singer again. The loss of Ray as her true love affected Kilgallen's health and she did not appear on the couple's radio program. When Richard, whose mental state was shaky at best, appeared drunk, the show was cancelled.

Despite Kilgallen's promise to Richard, she continued to see Johnnie Ray. His biographer Jonny Whiteside wrote, "Johnnie and Dorothy began to meet out of New York City as much as possible." Whiteside then quoted Jimmy Campbell, Ray's musical director, regarding the specifics of a rendezvous in Washington D. C., writing, "We all went out that night and then came back to our hotel. John said, 'I'll call you when I'm finished....'

So about four hours later, I get a call [and he said], 'I'm down in the bar, come on down and help me out of here, Jesus Christ, am I worn out.'" Campbell then added, "[Dorothy] loved him."

At the time, or since, no one considered the full significance of the Kilgallen/Ray love affair other than how it had inflamed Richard to the point of threatening physical violence against Ray, the threat to kill him. Yes, Richard was drunk at the time but the reaction to seeing Ray fondling his wife and her reciprocating sent him into a rage. His jealousy must have exacerbated beyond comprehension indicating he could act violently if pushed to the limit, if somehow threatened by Kilgallen's actions.

A clarification may be possible as to why Richard acted so violently toward Johnnie Ray. During his videotaped interview, Marc Sinclaire was asked why Kilgallen did not leave her husband. Sinclaire answered, "[She told me] she would never divorce Richard because he had been too kind to her."

What did Kilgallen mean by this statement? A clue appears through Sinclaire's further disclosures. Asked if Kilgallen was worried about young-est son Kerry within a month before she died, Sinclaire replied, "Yes, after a picture of Kerry appeared in the paper, a large picture of him alone in the middle of Central Park, she was very worried that Kerry would be kid-napped. Obviously, she didn't allow that kind of picture to be taken and be put in the paper of him all alone playing baseball but he wasn't even playing baseball, he was just running across a field means that someone was follow-ing him." Sinclaire added, "[Kerry's] name did not appear with it...[it was] frightening [to her] because he was alone."

Confirmation of Sinclaire's mention of Kilgallen's concern for Kerry after the Central Park incident comes from the October 31, Halloween night 1965 *What's My Line?* episode Guest panelist Steve Allen introduces Kilgallen by saying, "Her little boy is out trick or treating by limousine. How do you like that for class?" Sinclaire confirmed Kilgallen protected Kerry due the "threats and surveillance." (www.youtube.com/watch?v=_T6XLJU phyA&feature=youtu.be)

During the same conversation, Sinclaire said Kilgallen was concerned about people "spying on her." Asked to explain, he said, "Yes, she knew that [was happening]. She wasn't worried about the phones in the Cloop; she was worried about phones in the rest of the house. And she was carrying around a big packet of papers with her that she said pertained to the JFK assassination."

Alarmingly, Kilgallen had other fears at the time. Sinclaire acknowledged that while he readied her for the *What's My Line?* program, they often simulated the game. "I played it all the time [with her]," he said. "We would play the game, Donnell (Simpson) was there and we'd play the game around her." Asked if Kilgallen mentioned threats on her life, Sinclaire answered, "Yes, she told me, this is a couple of weeks before she died, or maybe three or four weeks, I'm not sure of the time anymore. But she told me she was going to get a gun because her life was being threatened and she was scared for her life and for her family."

Regarding a lengthy conversation two days before Kilgallen died, Sinclaire said, "I was at her house almost every night that week, the week before she died. She was worried about her life.... She said, 'I have to get a gun because someone's going to kill me.' And I jokingly said, 'Oh Dorothy, who would want to kill you?' So that started a conversation. And then time elapsed over us talking about this and she said, 'Well, I had to draw a new will.'"

Continuing, Sinclaire said, "It was embarrassing to talk about her death. But we were talking about it and she said, 'I don't know if Richard would take care of Kerry. He wouldn't take care of Kerry, keep Kerry close to him, and so he was going to need money.' She didn't mention Jill and she didn't mention Richard Jr. She didn't mention any of those people. She just mentioned Kerry. She said she drew up a new will and that Kerry would have a different inheritance. The will was drawn up by her lawyer but I don't know what happened to it or who knew about it."

Sinclaire, with some hesitation, revealed a secret focused on who was Kerry's real father. Asked again if Kilgallen would have divorced Richard, Sinclaire stated, "[the marriage] had been over for years. They would have stayed married. She would have never divorced him." Asked why Kilgallen would not divorce Richard, Sinclaire elaborated by repeating, "I asked her why she didn't divorce Richard and she said she could never do that to Richard, that Richard had been too kind to her. And I think that had something to do with Kerry." Asked if Kilgallen ever told him that the dark-haired Richard was not Kerry's father, Sinclaire said, "Yes, she did. She said that Johnnie Ray was the father of her youngest child."

Regarding any resemblance between Ray and Kerry, Sinclaire stated, "Yes, I saw a strong resemblance, coloring, freckles, things like that." This similarity in appearance coincides with Kilgallen describing Kerry in her *TV Radio Mirror* interview as a "husky, six-year-old with freckles across his nose who loves Dennis the Menace." Also, in a September 1954 *Good Housekeeping* magazine article Kilgallen wrote about Kerry's birth, her first sentence reads: "My baby has red-gold hair..."[3]

Sinclaire, arguably Kilgallen's best friend and confidant regarding her innermost secrets, the friend she trusted the most, did not believe people in New York City knew the truth. He said, "And I think that [Ray being Kerry's father] is what she was referring to when she said she couldn't divorce Richard because Richard had done too much for her." Asked if "Richard had to pretend to be Kerry's father," Sinclaire replied, "No, she never said that. And this was at the very end of her life that she told me this" while admitting later Kilgallen told him Richard had performed a "fatherly acting job." Asked if she would have wanted him to repeat the story about Kerry being Ray's son at the time, Sinclaire said, "Oh, no, I would never have repeated it and I'm very long in repeating it now. I'm not really sure why she told me that."

If what Kilgallen told Sinclaire about Kerry being Johnnie Ray's birth son, is true, this apparently meant Richard had raised Kerry—born when Kilgallen was 41 and when the couple was, as author Lee Israel explained, "going in separate directions on several levels" after 14 years of marriage— as his own son. He did so despite apparently knowing the truth or at least suspecting it to be the truth.

---

[3] If one compares childhood photos of Kerry with childhood photos of Johnnie Ray, there appears to be significant similarities between their respective noses. While Dorothy and Richard's noses have some sharp curvature, neither Kerry's nor Ray's has that feature but instead a more rounded shape.

Kilgallen, whom friend Marlon Swing said was "smitten, overwhelmed by the electricity of [Ray's] new [musical] style" as early as 1952[4], appeared to have no reason for birthing Richard's child based on the marital discord and her lack of respect for her alcoholic husband with several accounts suggesting they no longer had sexual relations. Marc Sinclaire, in an audio-taped interview, alluded to this by stating, "I would imagine that anyone coming [into the home] would think Richard and Dorothy led a married life which they had ceased to do long before [the 1960s]." Sinclaire, asked when he learned Kilgallen and Ray had begun an affair, stated it happened when Sinclaire first moved to New York City at the "end of 1952." Since Ray was gay and Sinclaire's gay friends on Fire Island were proud of Ray's accomplishment, they were quick to tell Sinclaire the couple was "meeting in hotels" while keeping the affair secret.

In *Cry*, author Johnny Whiteside, wrote, "Dick had shied away from performing his husbandly duties for years resulting in a pent-up yearning which Dorothy released with stupendous, and increasingly careless, ardor." Whiteside added that Ray told him, "God, she was starved for affection. Sometimes I didn't know how to handle it."

Another clue to recall is that "Dickie" and Jill had been born two years apart (1941 and 1943) and Kerry in 1954, eleven years later. It is thus logical to ask whether Kilgallen had intended to become pregnant, at least with Richard, at the advanced age of 41. If Sinclaire was right that her affair with Ray had begun as early as the latter part of 1952, it is possible that Kerry, born on March 19, 1954, was in fact Ray's son.

Despite Richard ignoring his not being Kerry's birth father, and instead helping raise Kerry, at some point, for whatever reason, Kilgallen became concerned Richard would not continue to "take care" of Kerry if she died. Whether Richard made this clear or not, is unknown. However, it appears some action on his part must have caused Kilgallen—at the time concerned

---

[4] According to researcher Kathryn Fauble, stand-up comedian George Hopkins, a friend of Johnny Ray's, reported Kilgallen met Ray at a 1952 press party for the singer at the New York Sheraton Astor Hotel near Times Square and "asked others what they thought of Johnnie." The date of the party is uncertain but apparently was in close proximately to Kilgallen's "Voice of Broadway" column where she praised Ray's hit song, "Please Mr. Sun."

enough that someone might kill her that she discussed buying a gun—to make sure Kerry was financially stable if she died, triggering her to tell Sinclaire she was drawing up a new will.

Those believing Ray was *not* Kerry's father include Alan Eichler, Ray's manager before he died. He told this author Ray never acknowledged Kerry as his son. There is also no specific mention of the matter in Jonny Whiteside's biography, *Cry* (apparently written with Ray's approval), or in Lee Israel's *Kilgallen* biography. Israel does refer at one point to Kerry being "redheaded." Johnnie Ray, fair-skinned, had light brown hair. A 1994 letter from Ray's sister Elma to researcher Kathryn Fauble's assistant denied Ray had fathered Kerry. [5]

However, if what Sinclaire said Kilgallen told him is true and Kerry's father was Johnnie Ray, and Richard knew it, this may explain the near-violent confrontation between Richard, Kilgallen and Ray resulting in Richard threatening to kill the singer. And it may be possible Ray never knew Kerry, six-years-old at the time the quarrel happened in 1960, was his son. Of interest is his saying, "And I thought about Kerry" during the confrontation. Why Ray only mentioned thinking about Kerry and not "Dickie" or Jill is unknown.

Most importantly, Kilgallen's worry Richard would not care for Kerry and her love for her son makes her committing suicide unlikely. If anything, she would have wanted to remain alive to protect Kerry.

Regarding Kilgallen's having a new will prepared, after the interviewer told Sinclaire that the *NY Times* reported Richard inherited everything, the hairdresser said, "Yes, I read that." Asked if this meant the new will never surfaced, Sinclaire said, "Yes, that's correct." In a separate audiotaped interview, Sinclaire added, "[There's] another will somewhere. Richard must have destroyed it."

---

[5] This author's attempts to further confirm Johnnie Ray as Kerry's father in accordance with Kilgallen's statement to Sinclaire have been unsuccessful. So as to alert Kerry to the publishing of this book, several messages for him were left both with business colleagues in Georgia, and through his Facebook page during 2015 with no response. This author also informed Kerry's sister Jill that the three siblings could read the book's manuscript for accuracy or comment, but unfortunately, no response was received.

Sinclaire also divulged that two or three months before Kilgallen died, she visited Switzerland, a trip confirmed by family tutor Ibne Hassan. Sinclaire said, "[Before leaving] she set out some books and diaries and tapes and papers. And some jewelry. I think she had a safe deposit box in Switzerland." He added, "The way I know about it is that the things were spread out on the bed. They were going into a suitcase." Speculating on why she may have taken the items abroad with her, Sinclaire said, "She didn't trust Richard financially. I don't think she would have told him that she was going to do something financially in Europe."

Research by this author regarding any new will, why Kilgallen took various personal items to Switzerland, and whether she had a safe deposit box there has not been fruitful. By a will signed in 1941, Richard inherited virtually everything. In 1966, Richard sold the townhouse for $290,000 [$2,100,000 in today's dollars]. Dorothy's various insurance policies provided Richard with another $90,000 and the three children shared $85,000 from a Goodson-Todman (production company for *What's My Line?*) profit-sharing dividend. No mention of any of Kigallen's cash savings is included although Marc Sinclaire stated in a videotaped interview, "The money was there. Dorothy made a lot of money. We're not talking about money in today's terms; if it was put into today's terms, it would be millions."

Additional benefits to Richard after Kilgallen's death ("benefits from the crime" if he was involved in her death) included royalties from *Murder One!* when it was published two years later. On the downside, when Kilgallen died, Richard was the one who lost the family wage earner since it was Kilgallen's salary from *What's My Line?* the *Journal-American* and other means that were paying the family bills. Still, even though Richard had no income, Sinclaire was surprised when Richard ended up marrying Anne Fogarty, Kilgallen's acclaimed clothes designer. Sinclaire said in his video-taped interview, "I found that very strange. Certainly Dorothy didn't know that Richard had any inklings toward Anne or Dorothy would have told me. And Anne wouldn't have remained her friend although I don't think Dorothy would have cared what Richard did."

When asked why Richard, who knew his marriage was a failure by this time, seemed overly distraught when Kilgallen died, Sinclaire said bluntly,

"He needed the income [she provided]." Regarding his reason for marrying Fogarty, Sinclaire said, "More income."

The question is, was Kilgallen worth more to Richard dead or alive? In lieu of Richard's shaky mental state, could his learning Kilgallen planned to change her will to protect Kerry have infuriated Richard enough that he might cause her harm? Did he realize he might be destitute if he was left out of the will causing him to consider evil actions towards his wife?

Perhaps Kilgallen had a premonition of some sort regarding Kerry's well-being since on Kerry's internet blog entitled "Testing the Waters" (kerryslifeblog.blogspot.com/2009/04/sweet-jane.html, viewed November 2015), he admitted being "thrown out of my house at age sixteen." This would have happened around 1970 when Kerry was sent away, as he admitted to author Lee Israel in 1975, to a foster home, a cruel act that would have broken Kilgallen's heart. Why Richard, who committed suicide a year later, kicked Kerry out of the house is unknown.

According to the same blog entries, relations between Richard and Kerry deteriorated on the day Kilgallen died. Kerry wrote that he returned home and, "as I entered the black room on the third floor, I sensed, even from behind him, my father's misery. He sat as he always did, perched on the right side of one of the pair of black, silk-covered loveseats, his shoulders stooped and rounded, elbows leaning on his knees...hovering over a beer. He sipped one after the other."

When Kerry reached out to his father, Kerry wrote, there was no contact. Kerry said he went upstairs and "sat on the edge of my bed thinking. I wondered what my father was thinking about. I wondered why he wouldn't talk to me, particularly in this time of death and sadness. Didn't one comfort their child when times were hard? Did he not even care about me? Or was it, perhaps, that he hurt so deeply, that he couldn't find the words or even a gratuitous gesture. Could he not come out of himself long enough to offer a hug to his eleven-year-old son who had, after all, just lost his mother?" Summing up, Kerry had written, "This day would mark the beginning of the end of my respect for my father." This may mean Kerry never knew what his mother told Marc Sinclaire, that Kerry's father was really Johnnie Ray.

If so, Kerry learning of his mother's intention to protect him if she died should warm his heart indicating a deep love for her youngest son. Her confiding in Sinclaire may have been the only divulging of the secret, one she shared with Richard but no one else.

Richard's unsteady state of affairs apparently had extended through the days when he was married to Fogarty. Sinclaire, when asked whether Richard should have been more stable but instead continued to haunt NYC bars including the Madison Avenue Café, the hairdresser said, "It sounds like someone who is very unhappy about something." When asked whether Richard's shaky state of mind was indicative of a man who possessed "the secrets to the JFK assassination" through Kilgallen's files (insinuating the information she had gathered could be valuable), Sinclaire said that made little sense.

If Richard never confiscated the assassination file, then that "something" Richard was "unhappy about" could have been complicity in Kilgallen's death. If it was, how involved was he?

Clues appear in author Lee Israel's book and when considered with other evidence from both primary and secondary sources, there appears to be a plausible means by which Richard could have ended his wife's life based on jealousy and greed, two common homicide motives. Certainly Richard had the opportunity to kill Kilgallen since not only was he in the townhouse at the time of her death but the servants had Sunday off and did not return until after 6:00 a.m. Monday morning. That meant, other than Kerry, and tutor and family companion Ibne Hassan—their rooms were on the 4th floor where noise from the third would have been difficult to hear—no one was present who could have witnessed Richard's evil actions.

One may only speculate as to how Richard could have been complicit in Kilgallen's death. However, the circumstances surrounding *his* drug use point to a plausible explanation since he was known to have ingested various barbiturates while continuing his alcoholic ways during the years prior to Kilgallen's death.

The question then to be asked is what specific drugs were part of Richard's daily ingestion? Clarity is provided by none other than Kerry Kollmar who told author Israel his father "had vats of pills around, containers of

Tuinal large enough to pickle mice." This suggests Richard certainly had the means by which to spike Kilgallen's drink or trick her into taking more pills than her heart could stand since Tuinal was one of the drugs discerned in her blood stream. To this point, during March 1965 when Kilgallen was hospitalized for a fractured left shoulder, Pearl Bauer, an assistant to Kilgallen's secretary Myrtle Verne, said "[Richard brought Kilgallen] pills and liquor that damn near killed her."

Since Kilgallen did not have a prescription for Tuinal, common sense dictates Kilgallen could have secured Tuinal pills from Richard. This scenario is certainly possible but because of the amount of barbiturates in Kilgallen's blood, she must have taken several pills. Alternatively, Richard may have succumbed to a fit of jealous rage over Kilgallen's enjoying the good life and her threat to change her will, leaving him with less if she died. In this state of mind, he could have decided to add the Tuinal noted in the ME report to her drink during the early morning hours of Kilgallen's death. This could have happened when she was distracted or in the bathroom.

Another possibility exists as to how Richard could have been complicit in Kilgallen's death. Recall Pearl Bauer's statement that Richard brought Kilgallen pills and liquor when Kilgallen was hospitalized for the fractured shoulder. Perhaps Richard provided too much Tuinal from his "stash." This could have happened if Kilgallen asked for a sleeping aid when she arrived home. Unfortunately, when Richard returned to the bedroom, he discovered the dosage had rendered her unconscious. Believing he had contributed to her death, and afraid of being charged with a crime, an intoxicated Richard had to think quickly regarding how to cover up his actions and to do so staged the death scene. Whether Richard enlisted the help of James Clement, the butler, or the maid Marie Eichler, is unknown.

If Richard accidently on purpose (deliberately) spiked Kilgallen's drink with the powerful Tuinal along with the other barbiturates, he was guilty of premeditated murder. If he simply mixed too much Tuinal and the other drugs into her drink causing her death, the charge could have been manslaughter.

Marc Sinclaire's discovery of Kilgallen's body a few minutes after 9:00 a.m. must have been a shock to Richard since as Sinclaire, referring to

Clement, stated in his videotaped interview, "James was very nervous because I wasn't supposed to be there. I was not supposed to find the body.... They didn't expect me to come; no one knew I was coming [to the townhouse."

Recall the police were not notified of Kilgallen's death until mid-afternoon, much later than Sinclaire appeared on the scene. And when they did, by all accounts including that of actress Joan Crawford, Richard was in a sad state. Phyllis Cerf, wife of Bennett, told Sinclaire, "Richard was dead drunk. They were trying to sober him up." Jean Stralem, a friend of the Kollmar's said, "Dick was in his chair crying. So drunk! So upset! So in tears!"[6] The question is: was Richard drunk and upset over the loss of his wife or because he somehow was responsible for her death?

Richard's conduct after Kilgallen died is riddled with inconsistencies including what he told Dr. Luke within a short time after the medical examiner appeared on the scene. Recall that listed under the section, "Witnesses or Informants," he said Kilgallen had returned home from *What's My Line?* at 11:30 p.m. "feeling chipper" before writing her column, saying "goodnight" and going to bed.

Based on other accounts, Richard's statements were false. Bob Bach had been with Kilgallen after midnight at P.J. Clarke's, several witnesses saw her at the Regency Hotel Bar past that time, and Dave Spiegel, the Western Union manager, spoke to Kilgallen at 2:20 a.m.

What Richard said about Kilgallen's JFK assassination file adds to suspicion that he was involved in her death. Three days after she died, Jean and Bob Bach invited Richard to dinner. Bob asked, "Dick, what was all that stuff in the folder Dorothy carried around with her about the assassination?" Richard replied, "Robert, I'm afraid that will have to go to the grave with me."

Later, Kilgallen's friend Mark Lane, with whom Kilgallen shared her JFK assassination investigation findings, asked Richard about the file. He said, "I'm going to destroy all that. It's done enough damage already." Lane

---

[6] There is no explanation as to why Joan Crawford, Jean Stralem, or any others were present at the Kilgallen townhouse BEFORE the police arrived. Who called them and when is a mystery.

apparently did not follow up with a question as to why the file had "done enough damage already." Since Richard never commented on the file publically, confusion reigns as what happened to file, if in fact Richard possessed it after Kilgallen died.

More crucial, Richard argued quite extensively against any autopsy being performed. In fact, Johnnie Ray biographer Jonny Whiteside wrote of "Dick's vociferous refusal to allow an autopsy." Had Richard done so out of love for his wife or because he was afraid of what the autopsy results might indicate regarding the barbiturates discovered in her blood? If it was the latter and he had spiked her drink with the killer drugs, he must have sweated until the final medical examiner's report was issued.

With all of these facts in mind, and since Richard's propensity for violence was a given based on his threatening to kill Johnnie Ray, was Richard capable of murdering his wife? At her funeral, as previously discussed, Kilgallen's mother accused him of doing so, but no investigation resulted based on her comments. Since Richard committed suicide, he cannot defend himself from any accusations and his children, for reasons known only to them, will not comment.

Based on interviews with the couple's friends, Lee Israel was dubious Richard could have murdered Kilgallen. Summarizing her thoughts, the author wrote, "He did not appear to have the 'balls' to do a crime of such magnitude."

Marc Sinclaire also expressed doubt during his videotaped interview that Richard killed Kilgallen. Sinclaire stated, "I don't think he could have done it." Asked if a more powerful person did, he said, "I think it was more than one person who did it, was involved in Dorothy's death."

Fifty years later, no clear-cut evidence exists proving Richard Kollmar murdered Kilgallen. This is true despite his having motive (jealousy of her continued success both personally and professionally; and greed with the potential loss of inheritance if she changed her will), means (being in the townhouse when Kilgallen died with easy access to her), opportunity (townhouse empty except for Kerry and Hassan who were asleep in their 4th floor rooms), and benefit from the crime (no more humiliation existing due to Kilgallen's love affairs and success; and no reduction of inheritance from a new will). Any prosecutor, if Richard had been charged, would have certainly targeted his unruly/desperate state of mind, his having threatened to kill Johnnie Ray and Kilgallen's mother's funeral accusation.

Added to the mix regarding Richard's potential responsibility for Kilgallen's death is information supplied by tutor Ibne Hassan in a 1978 interview. Asked about the circumstances at the townhouse just after Kilgallen's body was found, he said, "…Jill and her husband had also come. And they were discussing different family problems. And Mr. Kollmar was there [and to Jill] he said, 'Well, Jill, there was no argument; there was nothing.' She said, 'Well, Dad we are not blaming you or anything.'" Hassan did not comment further regarding what the "family problems" were or why Jill had reason to assure her father that she did not blame him for her mother's death.

Aside from considering Richard as the murderer, Lee Israel, based on her extensive research, believed one person was responsible for Kilgallen's death. The author wrote, "It must be considered probably that, if [Dorothy] was murdered, the crime was done to silence her, by a kiss-and-tell representative of whatever faction it is that did not want the facts about the JFK assassination to emerge."

If Israel is right, who was this person who killed or participated in the murder of the famous journalist, investigative reporter extraordinaire, and *What's My Line?* television star?

CHAPTER 24

Any discussion of foul play being the cause of Dorothy Kilgallen's death must pass through her obsession with one particular case among the hundreds she covered as an investigative reporter. Some may be more memorable than others, but one stands out with certain priority: the JFK and Lee Harvey Oswald assassination investigations.

Suspects have abounded since the events in Dallas unfolded in 1963. They include the CIA (speculation JFK was going to dissolve the agency), the Russians (hated JFK as a result of the Cuban missile crisis), Cuban dissidents (hated JFK because of the Bay of Pigs fiasco), the military establishment (hated JFK since he could end the Vietnam War by reducing military spending), and Lyndon Johnson (feared JFK would remove Johnson from the 1964 Democratic presidential ticket.) Regarding the latter, recall that Kilgallen, in her column, "The Oswald File Must Not Close," demanded that the new president "satisfy the public's uneasy mind about this peculiar assassination of the assassin." Her doing so must have caused LBJ and his handlers to keep a close eye on Kilgallen's future columns/articles. However, like the others mentioned above with the possible exception of the CIA as noted later, it is most difficult to connect any to Kilgallen's death without further evidence surfacing.

Directing attention to one specific person who feared Kilgallen's JFK investigation more than any other, requires due care. It begins with understanding how passionate Kilgallen was about discovering the truth regarding who killed the president. It was not business, but a personal matter for her, one highly personal due to the never-to-be forgotten experience with the president that touched her heart and soul.

Recall this happened when JFK treated Kilgallen's young son Kerry with affection when they visited the White House. She had never forgotten his kindness toward her son. After the assassination, Kilgallen wept with Kerry in her arms for a man they both loved. Recall she then wrote in her *Journal-American* column: "The picture that stays in my mind was the one of this tall young man bending over a tall small boy, carefully scrutinizing envelopes until he came to the name Kerry Ardan Kollmar - Grade 3B. This was the man who was assassinated in Dallas."

Kilgallen friend Marlon Swing confirmed she had a special friendship with John Kennedy dear to her heart. The CBS producer recalled the night he and Kilgallen returned from a [Broadway] opening and were sitting in her office. "The phone rang," Swing said, "And it was very late, 1:30, almost in the morning. It was [Ted] Sorenson, special counsel to the president— no small potatoes. They were talking and I heard Dorothy say, 'Oh, really, say hello to him too.' Jack Kennedy had walked into the room, asked who [Sorenson] was talking to and when he learned it was Dorothy said, 'Say hi for me.'"

Bob Bach, Kilgallen's friend and *What's My Line?* producer, noted another time when JFK and Kilgallen met and the details he added indicate more than a passing friendship. "[At the Stork Club]," Bach stated, "[I] watched with a mischievous thrill as Jack Kennedy, a young senator out late with someone other than his wife, 'touched base' with Dorothy: 'Hello, Dorothy [he said]. Do you remember the night we played charades at your house? What fun it was!'"

The sum of these encounters meant that from the moment Kilgallen learned JFK died, her quest to discover who killed her friend, and why, was a top priority. To be certain, the affection she felt for the president was the driving force behind her investigation. Kilgallen felt she had a duty, a responsibility out of friendship with the slain president, to learn the truth.

It is clear that the "Oswald Alone" proclamation from Dallas Police Chief Jesse Curry and then FBI Director J. Edger Hoover provided a pat explanation for JFK's assassination. However, when Jack Ruby shot

Oswald, Kilgallen's investigative instincts kicked in. Her years of experience as an investigative reporter proved valuable. Kilgallen knew something was wrong; something did not make sense. She had to learn more about what had happened in Dallas. To that end, Kilgallen immediately told her *Journal-American* editor she intended to cover the Jack Ruby trial.

Recall that when that trial began in early March 1964, questions she had been pondering began surfacing during a jury selection discussion with journalist Jim Lehrer when she mentioned "one man, or even three or five in a conspiracy..." This was a revealing statement proving that from the very first day of Ruby's trial, Kilgallen was wary of official accounts. Other reporters accepted Chief Curry and Hoover's "Oswald Alone" proclamation. Kilgallen did not.

Using her fame and reputation to the fullest, Kilgallen immediately ingratiated herself into the defense camp. This is where lawyer Melvin Belli controlled Jack Ruby's fate. That she did so with the defense and not the prosecution is quite relevant. It indicates the answers she sought mainly dealt with the Jack Ruby side of the equation, not Lee Harvey Oswald.

Immediately, Kilgallen secured a friendship with Belli. She had to know he represented mobster Mickey Cohen through national media coverage of Belli and Cohen's exploits.[1] In fact, Kilgallen had included Cohen in a September 26, 1958 "Voice of Broadway" column writing, "Mickey Cohen, the California gangster, is about to tour the nation lecturing on one of his favorite topics, 'Corruption in Politics.'"

Upon arriving at the Ruby trial, Kilgallen used her persuasive powers to full gain. It was likely that Belli, the lady's man married *six* times, was enamored with her. As Belli's longtime secretary Joyce Revilla told this

---

[1] As reported by the *New York Times*, during an American Bar Association convention, while conducting his "Belli Seminar," Belli introduced a "tax expert" as Professor Julian O'Brien of Harvard University. The professor proceeded to lecture the attendees with what Belli described as "an amusing pastiche" which ended with altogether fitting proportion, "My advice to you guys is, Pay your taxes." Duly impressed, the delegates to the convention began to discuss Professor O'Brien's speech that evening. They were shocked when they discovered that it was not a Harvard professor who had spoken to them but Meyer Harris "Mickey" Cohen, Belli's buddy and a Los Angeles mobster who had been charged with tax evasion.

author, "Belli chased everything with a skirt on." It was certainly possible that Belli was chasing the famous Kilgallen with hopes of bedding her.

The two certainly had much in common. Both enjoyed the spotlight, the fame, the publicity, the lavish parties, the power in their respective fields of interest. Like Kilgallen, Belli coveted media exposure through print, television and film. He certainly had a passion for acting. He had learned well in the courtroom as a skilled trial lawyer.

Joyce Revilla recalled that Belli went through "a phase when he wanted to be an actor" and sought roles on the big and little screen. Later, he would guest star in a *Star Trek* television episode "And the Children Shall Lead" as an avenging angel. When director Francis Ford Coppola was auditioning actors to play Don Corleone in the *Godfather* film, Belli read for the part. True to his Texas-sized ego, Belli pouted when Coppola chose Marlon Brando for the role.

Revilla believed it was possible Belli made a deal with Kilgallen. She agreed to boost his prospects with the plethora of entertainment contacts she had in Hollywood and New York. In return, he gave her access to the defense, to Ruby that no other journalist enjoyed.

By approving Kilgallen request to interview Ruby through co-counsel Joe Tonahill, Belli took the gamble she would learn too much from Oswald's killer. However, each interview lasted less than ten minutes. Besides, Belli was certain Kilgallen would believe Ruby was crazy. That meant she would pay little attention to what he said. Belli was wrong. He had underestimated Kilgallen just as so many others, especially men, had through the years.

Bonded by their respective celebrity statuses, Kilgallen and the flamboyant Belli, the most famous attorney in the world at the time spent time before and after court. Kilgallen attempted to learn as much inside information about Ruby's case as possible.

Belli was quite tight-lipped about his relationship with Kilgallen. This happened both during and after the Ruby trial. No one this author interviewed at his office recalls his even mentioning her name.

In Belli's 1964 book, *Dallas Justice*, only one page acknowledges the famous reporter. He wrote, "Ruby did say he got angry at his favorite columnist, Dorothy Kilgallen, when she wrote that he was a gangster...." Years later, in his autobiography *My Life On Trial*, Belli mentioned Kilgallen briefly on one page out of 351. He wrote, "Dorothy Kilgallen [was] in Dallas for most of the [Ruby] trial and a frequent lunch companion of mine."

Television footage of Kilgallen with Belli at the Ruby trial is viewable at TheReporterWhoKnewTooMuch.com. Confirming the close relationship she enjoyed with Belli and co-counsel Joe Tonahill, Kilgallen had at one point sat within a privileged foot or two of Belli during a Ruby trial news conference. Wearing a spotted leopard top, and holding an audio tape recorder in front of Belli, Kilgallen asked "How long does a person have to live in Dallas to be a prospective juror?" Belli and Tonahill both answered. Later footage showed Kilgallen whispering in Tonahill's ear. His face reflected a surprised look at whatever she told him.

That Belli never disclosed much about Kilgallen was consistent with his behavior through the years about the Ruby trial. From the 1960s to 1995, when he died, he very much respected the Mob's allegiance to the loyalty oath of Omertá, a code of silence.

Despite requests to do so on many occasions by family, friends, legal colleagues and the media, Belli was suspiciously silent when the Ruby case became a topic of conversation. Known for his loquacious nature, Belli avoided talking about the Ruby case. Belli's associate Kent Russell told this author, "I pumped him about it because I sensed something was wrong with his representation. But he wouldn't give any thought or consideration to a conspiracy. He just kept saying how bad Dallas was....He just totally shut the door about Ruby. He didn't want to go there. I never quite understood that."

In the mid-1980s, this author briefly practiced law with Belli in San Francisco and became friends to the extent that the famous attorney invited him to the major league baseball All-Star game at Candlestick Park where Belli's star power was witnessed firsthand. While writing Belli's biography, *Melvin Belli: King of the Courtroom*, it was apparent to me the famous attorney was quite secretive about certain aspects of his legal career, especially the Jack Ruby case.

Clues, never divulged, as to what Kilgallen learned from the Ruby interviews directly affecting his involvement in the assassinations, provided her impetus to continue digging into the twin assassinations. Kilgallen's friend, CBS producer Marlon Swing, was certain that the Ruby interviews paid off for the famous journalist: "Dorothy would have gotten a lot out of the Jack Ruby interviews because she had that investigative technique. She had stumbled onto something."

Meanwhile, Kilgallen's columns reflected a growing suspicion about what really happened in Dealey Plaza and the Dallas Police Department basement. This led to her early exposure of Jack Ruby's statements to the Warren Commission. Despite grilling by government agents for hours on end, Kilgallen refused to disclose her source. Recall the FBI file memo that read, "She stated that she was the only person who knew the identity of the source and that she 'would die' rather than reveal his identity."

During her investigation, Kilgallen collected information from the Ruby interviews and inside facts from Belli and Tonahill. Recall that Kilgallen had assisted the defense with exposure of Joe Tonahill's letter to the Warren Commission demanding more information about Oswald from the FBI and Justice Department. The commission and FBI refused to cooperate. The Justice Department only provided information about Oswald deemed "not relevant" to JFK's assassination. This refusal, in addition to the swell of information she had gathered, enhanced Kilgallen's curiosity.

Without doubt, it was Ruby's testimony at the Warren Commission perpetuating Kilgallen's fervor to discover who killed JFK. The *Journal-American* published the secret testimony on August 19, 1964, five months after the Ruby trial. One may only imagine how shocked this crack investigative reporter turned detective was when she learned that Ruby had said, "I have been used for a purpose," and "I won't be around for you to come and question me again."

Later in his testimony, Ruby continued to request a lie detector test. Chief Justice Warren promised him one. Ruby said, "Gentlemen, my life was in danger here," and then "I may not live tomorrow to give any further testimony."

To add to the intrigue, Ruby provided a statement outside his Warren Commission testimony that was most revealing. He spoke slowly and methodically as if scripted. Standing before what appeared to be a court railing, his arms gesturing as he spoke, Ruby said in an eerie tone:

> The world will never know the true facts of what occurred. My motives. I'm the only person in the background that knows the truth pertaining to everything relating to my circumstances. The people who have had so much to gain and have such an ulterior motive to put me in this position I'm in will never let the true facts come above board to the world.

Armed with this information, Kilgallen continued to attack the Warren Commission Report (she listed some 100 discrepancies to consider) and the overall investigations by the FBI and Justice Department. To those who wanted the assassinations investigation terminated, they were on notice Kilgallen was still on the job. Government agencies may have closed the door but Kilgallen did not. This must have caused concern that she would get too close to the truth.

Kilgallen's determination to expose the truth was dangerous. She was truly a huge threat as the months passed into late 1965. Kilgallen was not like other reporters. She had the bully pulpit, the national forum, the proven credentials. Her *Journal-American* column and investigative stories appeared in hundreds of newspapers across the country. The powerful Hearst media syndicate backed her. She had a solid reputation as a credible journalist. She was also a television star seen each week by millions of viewers.

At the lavish parties she and Richard hosted, attended by anyone and everyone who was important in the world, Kilgallen was the main attraction. When she spoke or wrote, people listened and read with interest because of her credibility. If Kilgallen would not quit, if she exposed damning evidence continuing to call into question the "Oswald Alone" proclamation, the chance of further investigation became a reality. This caused problems, big problems, for anyone with something to hide.

CHAPTER 25

For those fearing any follow-up investigations on the assassinations, the worst possible scenario would have been the convening of a grand jury. None happened in 1963/64. The explanation provided at the time was a simple one: J. Edgar Hoover proclaimed that unless evidence of a conspiracy was uncovered, no convening of a grand jury could happen.

The House Select Committee on Assassinations report[1] released in the late 1970s provides a new perspective. From the information gathered, it is clear that if Kilgallen exposed even the whisper of a conspiracy in November 1965 or thereafter, the course of history could have been significantly altered.

As the Committee began its investigation, noted syndicated columnist Liz Smith, one of Kilgallen's rivals in the 1960s, wrote a column entitled, "The Kilgallen Mystery." Released nationally on December 15, 1976, and featuring a large photo of Kilgallen, Smith's column revealed that both author Lee Israel, and Kilgallen's son, Kerry, had been attempting to "wrest from the FBI and CIA the pertinent papers concerning Kilgallen's involvement with the assassination of JFK."

Calling it the "Strange Case of Dorothy Kilgallen," Smith said that while Israel sought the papers for a book she was writing, Kerry wanted them because "he is mad, frustrated, and wants to find out what his mother

---

[1] The United States House of Representatives Select Committee on Assassinations (HSCA) was established in 1976. Its purpose was to investigate the assassinations of John F. Kennedy and Martin Luther King, Jr. by considering new evidence that had appeared since 1963. The HSCA completed its investigation in 1978. One year later, its final report was issued.

knew and how she really died." Smith added that Kerry, who must have suspected the official cause of death was suspect, was "proud of what he has learned of his mother, and wants the story of her prescience and courage in the matter of JFK's death made public."

Without providing a source, Smith swore, "The FBI has voluminous material" about Kilgallen. Regarding the CIA, Smith added, "What was this international agency doing investigating a gossip columnist? The CIA had 20 odd pages on Dorothy Kilgallen in its files. It contacted 51 CIA offices in her 'case!!!'" In closing, Smith stated, "With both the FBI and CIA in the shadows of suspicion and clouds of disgrace, one would think it would behoove them to act quickly and openly and make the Kilgallen dossiers available to her outraged son. But the cover-up continues." No evidence has revealed that either Lee Israel or Kerry Kollmar was successful in the attempts to retrieve government files about Kilgallen.

The CIA focus on Kilgallen causes suspicion it may have had something to do with her death. Recall that she had crossed paths with the agency as early as 1951 when she alleged Radio Free Europe was not "free." Kilgallen suspected subversive groups influenced it and the column triggered the agency's interest in her. A subsequent dossier documented Kilgallen's less than cooperative attitude when agents in search of a source for her column entry contacted the protective journalist. Criticisms of Kilgallen prevail throughout the report including, "[She] procrastinated until we lost all patience with her." Regarding the agent who hounded her for information, the report stated, "He [did] everything in his power to get Miss Kilgallen to change her mind [about revealing her source] [but] he despaired of any interest."

Despite the CIA's harsh words, Kilgallen's confrontation with it happened 14 years before her death. Connecting the agency as a strong suspect if in fact she was murdered, is less than viable unless new evidence surfaces.[2]

---

[2] Further evidence regarding whether the CIA, other governmental agencies, or individuals who could have harmed Kilgallen may be exposed in October 2017. This is the date the government releases more than 3000 documents relating to the JFK assassination as part of the 25th anniversary of the JFK Records Act since Congress mandated that all efforts be made to release everything in the government's possession unless an overriding case can be made for withholding them in the national interest. This author's examination of the pending document list indicates no specific reference to Kilgallen.

Regardless, when the HSCA report was finally released, it severely criticized the Justice Department having "largely abdicated what should have been important responsibilities in the continuing investigation." It then added, "Officials at Justice did not exercise any significant role in shaping, monitoring, or evaluating the FBI's investigation, despite the Bureau's organization status with the Department."

The report also said there was "little indication Justice Department officials moved to mount a sophisticated criminal investigation of the assassination, including its *conspiracy* [Emphasis added] implications." It added that the department failed to use its "power and capabilities of a federal grand jury, and the granting of immunity."

The Committee concluded federal jurisdiction *did* exist over the assassination because there *was* evidence of a conspiracy in 1963. In addition, the report stated Robert Kennedy's mental state "significantly affected the Government's handling of the investigation" while chastising him with failure to advance "a strong position" with FBI Director J. Edgar Hoover "on the course of the investigation."

While this conclusion appeared in the late 1970s, it blankets what would have occurred in 1963, 1964, or later if Kilgallen had rustled up enough evidence to suggest that a conspiracy existed. This, in turn, could have triggered the call for convening a grand jury investigation. It would have possessed "evidence-gathering tools as a grand jury" and "grants of immunity," as noted by the Committee.

To those negatively impacted by a grand jury probe, Dorothy Kilgallen was indeed a strong threat. By November 8, 1965, the day she died, Kilgallen had been pursuing new evidence for 18-plus months.

While considering Kilgallen's determination to push forward, a decision guaranteed to embroil her in controversy, it was apparent hairdresser Charles Simpson had a special affection for the gifted journalist. Marc Sinclaire had introduced them. Over time, Simpson became Kilgallen's trusted friend. He was most impressed with her humble manner. During the recorded interview in the late-1990s, Simpson said Kilgallen was "even gracious to the girls at the desk, all the small people," a reference to the popular Lily Daché's Midtown Manhattan Salon for Ladies. He added,

Charles Simpson was Kilgallen's hairdresser and make-up artist along with Marc Sinclaire.

"I've never known this woman [Dorothy] to be mean in any way." He also said "[Dorothy] had a rosary, a pearl rosary and she would take it out on the second floor of her townhouse, a five-story Georgian mansion and what she did was go out and there was a little hedge on there and she would lay the rosary out there when Marc or I flew anywhere and leave it there until we returned. And she told us she did this."

The recorded comments by Simpson are quite impressive. Wearing a bright golf shirt while chain-smoking, the balding and mustachioed Simpson spoke deliberately. He paused and reflected before answering questions about Kilgallen. When the interviewer attempted to get him to agree with a statement, and he did not, Simpson held his ground.

Specifically, the hairdresser, who also handled Kilgallen's make-up chores, recalled she was smart enough to "only go so far," and not "cross the line" when dishing criticism of celebrities and public figures. Simpson also said that "when it came to really big stuff," Kilgallen did "not pull any punches when necessary when there was someone who really needed to be exposed for something they were doing, government people, things like that she pulled no punches." He added, "It wasn't like today when if [celebrities] have fungus under [their] fingernails, [the media] exposes it. There was an unwritten law then and Dorothy knew the limitations."

Simpson, who stated, "I've never seen her in a Sunday night show when she wasn't alert and with it," remembered the days when "I fixed her hair every Sunday before *What's My Line*" He said he and Marc Sinclaire both had keys to Kilgallen's townhouse so they could wake her without "waking up the servants." Simpson said the "night she died, Marc had done her hair for the show and she was taking a plane to London the next day. This is why I find it very hard to believe that she committed suicide for the simple fact that she was looking forward to this trip to London the next morning. And Marc went over very, very early in order to get her ready for the plane trip to London and that's when he found her."

Regarding the JFK assassination, Simpson recalled that Kilgallen "never quit investigating, never quit." He said she, "dug up something about the assassination of President Kennedy that somebody didn't want her to know because she even told us of her own volition, 'I used to share things with you guys,' she said, as noted, 'but after I have found out NOW what I know, if the wrong people knew what I know, it would cost me my life' and she was dead about nine months later."

Regarding the Jack Ruby Warren Commission testimony, Simpson said, "She printed it on the front page of the *Journal-American* BEFORE the president received it and therein lies the tale. From then on we were stalked. Marc and me, our phones were tapped [since] they were trying to figure out where she got her information, that she could get this information before the president got it." This was because, Simpson said, "Actually, even though I didn't know anything about the assassination, these people, whoever they were, didn't know that, they didn't know what Dorothy may have told us. And, yes, I kept it to myself and denied everything until recent years." Asked if it was safe to talk about it at the time of the interview, Simpson paused and then replied, "No, uh, no."[3]

On one specific occasion, Simpson declared that someone followed Sinclaire and him. He said "four men in expensive suits" tried to force him

---

[3] During the audiotaped interview of John Broich, the interviewer told him, "Mark Sinclaire was very frightened when I contacted him. I had to calm him down." During another interview, the interviewer stated, "Sinclaire told me a very frightening story in which people threatened his life and he had to keep quiet."

into a room but "I refused." He added, "When I got back to my room [at the Pickwick Arms], someone "had gone through all my things" and that he and Sinclaire "joked that it was either the Mafia or CIA."

Marc Sinclaire, speaking carefully about Kilgallen and her intention to gather enough evidence exposing those involved in JFK's assassination, corroborated Simpson's account of Kilgallen's steadfast pursuit of the truth, a path fraught with danger since it was counter to the "Oswald Alone" theory perpetuated by the powerful J. Edgar Hoover and the Warren Commission. During his videotaped interview, Sinclaire was asked why he finally spoke about Kilgallen after several decades. He answered, "I was terrified to talk about this. When Lee Israel called and told me about her book, I wouldn't talk to her at all ten years after. I was still having problems." Asked why he decided to finally talk about his friend, Sinclaire, pausing to think before answering, stated, "Now everyone is dead or older than I am so I don't think it makes much difference." Commenting on why others had refused to question how and why Kilgallen died, he stated, "They wouldn't have because you could wind up dead."

At the outset of the interview, Sinclaire examined a newspaper front page featuring a headline touting Kilgallen's exposure of Jack Ruby's Warren Commission testimony and then commented, "That's when the heat really started. That's when my phones were bugged...people started following us [he and Simpson]...it wasn't very good after that." He also said, "Everything was done to discredit [Dorothy] after she wrote about the assassinations. To degrade her."

Sinclaire recalled, "Dorothy wouldn't stop [with the JFK assassination investigation]. She had it all. She told me about this. And Donnell [Simpson] was there too and he knew. We knew what she was doing." He added, "She said this was the case of a lifetime, a story of a lifetime. That she would prove...who assassinated the president." Regarding the Ruby Warren Commission testimony, Sinclaire said, "[What Dorothy did] was like slapping them [the government] in the face."

Citing the rumors swirling about JFK's assassination, Sinclaire stated, "People were saying there was more to this than meets the eye. Maybe the government did it [killed JFK]. Maybe [President] Johnson's people did it.

People would ask me questions because I knew Dorothy and they would want to know. Charlotte Ford [Henry Ford's daughter] wanted to know. Mr. Levitt [A famous developer, William Levitt was called "the father of modern American suburbia"] wanted to know. He would ask me questions when I went to do his wife's hair."

Sinclaire believed he was invited to people's homes, "…to try to pump me. Find out what they could find out from me. I wouldn't say anything about Dorothy and I knew Donnell wouldn't. We were very close-mouthed on it." Regarding Phyllis Cerf, Bennett's wife, Sinclaire added, "…I did her hair. I didn't like her very much. She was always asking me how Dorothy died." Asked what he said, Sinclaire replied, "I never told anyone until now. Not even Lee Israel."

Kilgallen's friend, Marlon Swing, agreed Kilgallen had learned a great deal from the Ruby testimony and was targeted for doing so. "That's when the phones were tapped," he said, "when they were trying to figure out how she had gotten her information."[4]

* * * * *

According to the two hairdressers, Kilgallen believed that the information she had learned placed her life in danger. And, according to what one man told another, she was right.

The person who corroborates Kilgallen's statement is surprising: Jack Ruby's attorney Melvin Belli. While researching my biography of Belli, Dr. Martin Schorr,[5] a good friend of Belli's, told me he spoke with him within days of Kilgallen's death. Dr. Schorr, a noted clinical psychologist on staff at several San Diego county hospitals, recalled Belli saying, "They've killed

---

[4] In an October 5, 1995 letter to researcher Kathryn Fauble's assistant from Walter Cronkite's assistant, Cronkite was quoted as saying, "I have known Marlon Swing for many years and am certain that he is highly credible and honest although I have never discussed with him and know nothing of his experiences or theories regarding the Kilgallen death."

[5] Dr. Martin Schorr was a controversial witness during the 1969 trial of Sirhan Sirhan for the murder of Robert F. Kennedy. Dr. Schorr testified for the defense regarding Sirhan's mental capacity at the time of the shooting.

Dorothy; now they'll go after Ruby." Dr. Schorr said he was shocked by the statement but did not follow up with any questions.

Fifteen months later, after Ruby died on January 3, 1967, Belli added to the intrigue of what he knew about the assassinations scenario. Office manager Carol Ann Lind told this author Belli said, "Something's not right. Maybe *they* injected Ruby with cancer cells." Others including Belli's law partner Seymour Ellison, told this author Belli said the same thing to him "many times." All wondered what Ruby's attorney knew that no one else did.

These two statements, never part of the mix into any evidentiary investigation of Kilgallen's death, shed new light on what happened to her in 1965. Questions abound such as whether the "they" Belli mentioned regarding "they've killed Dorothy," and "they injected Ruby," were the same "they" Robert Kennedy noted shortly after learning of JFK's death: "I thought *they* would get one of us: I thought it would be me." Or the "*They* should've killed me," part of the statement RFK made to presidential confidante Ken O'Donnell.

Who were the "they"? Who were those, or perhaps one person among them, who most benefited from Kilgallen's murder? Was it the same man, or men, who Kilgallen suspected may have masterminded the assassinations of JFK and Lee Harvey Oswald?

While assessing the plausibility of these men, or one in particular, being responsible for Kilgallen's death, her haunting words to friends and colleagues are important. Recall Kilgallen told her make-up assistant Carmen Gebbia that she was "all excited" about something. Knowing of her interest in the assassinations, Gebbia asked, "Is it Kennedy?" Kilgallen replied: "Yes, and it's very cloak and daggerish."

Asked by Gebbia to elaborate, Kilgallen said she was going to visit New Orleans.

There she was going to meet someone who was going to give her "information on the case." It would happen in a "designated area" where "she doesn't know the man but she'd recognize him." Gebbia also said Kilgallen explained several times, "If it's the last thing I do, I'm going to break this case."

Kilgallen made similar comments to close friends, the ones who called her "Dolly Mae" or "Dot." They included Johnnie Ray, *WML?* producer Bob Bach, and author Mark Lane. They realized Kilgallen had long ago discarded the "Oswald Alone" theory. Now she was on the last leg of her long journey toward discovering the truth. She expected to expose anyone who had thus far escaped responsibility for the murder of her beloved president.

Without doubt, "they" were watching her every move. Dorothy Kilgallen had put herself in peril. She exposed herself to danger from dangerous men, ones who gave no thought to eliminating the enemy. "They" had learned what Bennett Cerf proclaimed: "When Dorothy went after a story, nothing could get in her way."

CHAPTER 26

Without doubt, two men had stronger motive to see Dorothy Kilgallen eliminated than any of the suspects considered thus far.

Ironically, the men sharing this dubious bond operated on an opposite sides of the law: FBI Director J. Edgar Hoover and New Orleans Mafia Don Carlos Marcello. The common thread is the plausibility that both of them would have suffered if Kilgallen's investigation resulted in a grand jury probe of JFK and Lee Harvey Oswald's assassinations.

Regarding Hoover, there is no question he detested the feisty investigative reporter. He believed that Kilgallen illegally obtained, and then exposed, Jack Ruby's testimony at the Warren Commission before the official report's release. This action, Hoover might have called it betrayal, on Kilgallen's part embarrassed Hoover as he monitored the Commission's secret investigation. He was not one to be embarrassed.

To Hoover's way of thinking, Kilgallen had stolen government secrets, perhaps akin in modern day to Edward Snowden's leaking classified information from the United States National Security Agency. Hoover believed Kilgallen had betrayed her country and should be prosecuted to the fullest extent of the law. Why he did not file charges against the insubordinate reporter speaks volumes about why Hoover feared whatever evidence Kilgallen might disclose in her defense.

Worse, Hoover, despite the vast resources of the Bureau, could not discover the mole at the Warren Commission who leaked to Kilgallen Ruby's testimony. This added to his anger toward the famous columnist. Instead of being in prison where Hoover believed Kilgallen belonged, she was the star of the show. Instead of ridicule coming her way for the illegal actions, praise followed her "exclusive," one printed in newspapers not only in the U.S. but around the world through the Associated Press. On a daily basis, Hoover was bombarded with questions about how the leak happened. Congress even considered an investigation with Hoover as the potential scapegoat.

Brushing over the powerful, vindictive FBI director's fury would be a mistake. One may only imagine the anger Hoover exhibited. Kilgallen, the woman described in an FBI file as, "flighty and irresponsible" had outwitted him.

Kilgallen's refusal to name her source was bad enough but more important the famous journalist represented a threat if she discovered new evidence contrary to that collected by the Warren Commission. This was something Hoover could not permit to happen.

Why? From the moment of JFK's assassination, Hoover was the main advocate for the "Oswald Alone" theory. Recall his memos directing every investigation toward that end. Selling the theory to everyone including the public, the media, Dallas police investigators, and the Warren Commission was essential. Fortunately, the Commission bought Hoover's version of the facts and conclusions meaning the Bureau had no responsibility for Oswald, a lone "nut," having killed President Kennedy.

The sales pitch had worked across the board with one, and amazingly enough, only one notable exception among the hundreds of journalists covering the assassinations: Dorothy Kilgallen. Her friend Mark Lane may have been suspect of Hoover's proclamations, but the Director knew Kilgallen had been on the prowl for more than a year. Instead of calling it quits, it was full speed ahead. From Kilgallen's early columns to her revealing Ruby's Warren Commission testimony, Hoover knew she was a powerful force on all fronts.

In effect, Hoover was "all in" with the "Oswald Alone" theory. Proof of his intent comes from the Director's actions on November 25, 1963. First, he forced the Dallas Police Department to forward all files to the Bureau in Washington. This prevented any investigation on its part. Hoover also told

White House aide Walter Jenkins it was critical to have "something issued so we can convince the public that Oswald is the real assassin."

Recall that Hoover then instructed aide Clyde Tolson to write memo to the Attorney General setting out the evidence that Oswald was responsible for the shooting that killed the president. The order came despite there being little evidence of any credible motive on Oswald's part for assassinating JFK.

Hoover's reputation certainly was in jeopardy if Kilgallen caused trouble for him and the Bureau. He knew she was an immediate threat due to the "Oswald File Must Not Close" column the star reporter published on November 29, 1963. Recall several of her words clearly indicating she believed there was more to the assassinations than disclosed [bold print added].

> **If** Oswald was President Kennedy's assassin, the case was closed, was it? Well, I'd like to know how, in a big, smart town like Dallas, **a man like Jack Ruby—owner of a strip tease honky tonk—could stroll in and out of police headquarters as if it were a health club at a time when a small army of law enforcers was keeping a "tight security guard" on Oswald. Security!** What a word for it.
>
> ...so many people were saying there was **"something queer"** about the killing of Oswald, **something strange** about the way his case was handled, **a great deal missing in the official account of his crime**.
>
> The American people have just lost a beloved President. It was a dark chapter in our history, but **we have the right to read every word of it. It cannot be kept locked in a file in Dallas.**

Kilgallen's message certainly signaled her discord with the "Oswald Alone" theory butadding, "Justice is a big rug. When you pull it out from under one man, a lot of others fall too," must have caused Hoover sleepless night since the Director was on notice just seven days after JFK was killed, and only five days after Ruby murdered Oswald, that the famous crime reporter was on the job. Later, recall that that the incensed Hoover had taken the time to scribble "WRONG" in his handwriting on an FBI memo beside conclusions Kilgallen had reached based on secret Dallas Police Department records.

From the date of the "Oswald File Must Close" column release, it makes sense to believe Kilgallen was under FBI surveillance. This continued on through 1964 as her *Journal-American* columns and articles lambasted the assassinations investigation. Then she added the coup de grace, exposure of Ruby's Warren Commission testimony before its release date.

In fact, based on a Bureau memorandum dated September 30, 1964, there is no question the FBI was investigating Kilgallen. Agents, according to the memo, were acting, "In connection with our inquiry regarding Kilgallen specifically requested by the President's Commission to determine where she obtained the verbatim testimony of Jack Ruby's interview in Dallas." Proof Kilgallen knew the FBI represented the Commission is a given with a further post reading, "Kilgallen is fully aware that our inquiry is based on a specific Commission request."

Adding to Hoover's fury toward Kilgallen had to be the response she printed after being contacted in an attempt to disclose the source of the Warren Commission leak. As noted, Kilgallen wrote in a column entitled, "Maybe You Didn't Know," "I'm inclined to believe that the FBI might be more profitably employed in probing the facts of the case [JFK assassination] rather than how I got them which does seems a waste of

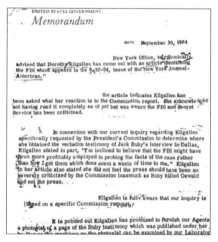

time to me." Again, one may only imagine the tough guy Hoover's toxic reaction to Kilgallen mocking his beloved Bureau.

Most disturbing is that Kilgallen had been under close surveillance *five years* earlier according to an FBI Memorandum to Hoover dated September 17, 1959 obtained by this author under the Freedom of Information Act. This was apparently a clandestine operation since an informant was assigned to infiltrate the lives of both Kilgallen and husband Richard. Regarding him, the memo stated, "DICK KOLLMAR operates the Left Bank Restaurant on West 50th Street. The informant advised [Kilgallen] goes there about once or twice a week and that KOLLMAR has been dating other women. He has his own private apartment on the third floor of the building..."

Further, the Memo stated, "KOLLMAR is or has been interested in both sexes" and that "KOLLMAR showed interest in the informant…Informant stated under the pretext of discussing the presentation of her art work [in the Left Bank], he induced her to go to his private room at the Left Bank and there, attempted to make intimate advances."

Concerning Kilgallen, the Memo stated, "DOROTHY KILGALLEN and her husband RICHARD KOLLMAR… have their own private lives" and "KILGALLEN is active in a group called the 'Science Club,' which meets on Mondays for luncheon at P. J. Clarke's Bar. The informant has attended several of these meetings...." Added was information the informant "advised that Miss KILGALLEN has been extremely attracted to the singer JOHNNY RAY...."

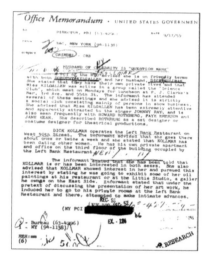

Whether Kilgallen knew the FBI had her in its sights is unknown but it makes sense to believe she did. Recall that she had told author Mark Lane, "Intelligence agencies will be watching us. We'll have to be very careful."

Through any surveillance, including that of the informant, Hoover and his operatives were knowledgeable of Kilgallen's drinking habits, and, arguably her drug habits as well. Weary of what she might uncover through her continuing investigation, is it plausible that the Director with his reputation at stake had a hand in Kilgallen's death? Had he assigned rogue agents to the task? And then had those agents stage the death scene to make it appear that she died accidently.

Under this theory, Hoover prevented the dogged reporter from any opportunity to cause the director damage from her disclosures, the fresh evidence she had uncovered that could destroy Hoover reputation and even topple him from power. If so, perhaps he was the one who ended up with Kilgallen's assassination file, destroyed at first chance.

Curiously, the FBI contacted Richard "Dickie" Kollmar, Dorothy's son, in 1975 searching for his mother's assassination file. Why this happened 10 years after her death is unknown.[1] What is known or at least suspected, is the potential there exists Kilgallen FBI files never revealed. Attempts by this author to discover the files has been unfruitful but perhaps in the future, a fresh investigation into Kilgallen's death will result in disclosure. If so, the question of whether J. Edgar Hoover, whose motive to eliminate Kilgallen cannot be underestimated, was complicit in his archenemy's tragic demise may be answered.

* * * * *

Aside from J. Edgar Hoover, there is one man who shared the risk her search for the truth could trigger a grand jury investigation. Arguably, he may have had a stronger motive to eliminate Kilgallen based on all of the facts and circumstances surrounding her mysterious death.

That man is New Orleans Don Carlos Marcello. While many in the Mafia had good reason to be afraid of what Kilgallen might uncover, Marcello had the most to lose.

To target Marcello as a suspect, a bit of history is required. It focuses on the actions of Robert Kennedy and Joseph Kennedy instead of JFK. It also asks the question: Why wasn't Bobby killed in 1963 instead of JFK?[2]

It is undisputed that well before the 1960 presidential election, RFK, a member of the McClellan Committee investigating organized crime, focused on several Mafioso's as targets for deportation or imprisonment. During the hearings, Bobby's anger roared when he confronted many of America's crime bosses. They included Sam Giancana, Carlos Marcello, Mickey Cohen[3] and Santo Trafficante. Each invoked the 5th Amendment. Frank Costello also appeared at the hearings.

---

[1] This author attempted to contact "Dickie" Kollmar through various means, including notifications on his Facebook page, to ask why, among other things, the FBI contacted him in 1975. Mr. Kollmar did not reply.

[2] A full account of this author's theories presented are featured in the book, *The Poison Patriarch: How the Betrayals of Joseph P. Kennedy Caused the Assassination of JFK* published in 2013.

[3] Mickey Cohen's FBI file, obtained through the Freedom of Information Act, featured the words, "COHEN HAD KILLED IN THE PAST AND SHOULD BE CONSIDERED ARMED AND DANGEROUS."

RFK particularly insulted Sam Giancana[4] but Carlos Marcello was also embarrassed during Bobby's intense questioning. It was clear Bobby hated the underworld figures with a passion. When he released his book, *The Enemy Within*, RFK wrote, "They have the look of [Al] Capone's men. They are sleek, often bilious and fat, or lean and cold and hard. They have the smooth faces and cruel eyes of gangsters; they wear the same rich clothes, the diamond ring, the jeweled watch, the strong, sickly-sweet-smelling perfume."

Ironically, a few years later when JFK was battling Vice-President Richard Nixon for the presidency, credible sources confirm Kennedy family patriarch Joe Kennedy realized an important fact: his son would lose the election unless he won West Virginia and Illinois. Without these state's electoral votes in JFK's column, the race was doomed.

To get help, Joe knew where to look. Chicago-based mobster Giancana and his underworld friends like Marcello had connections to the unions and politicians. Most important, millions in cash distributed by underworld emissaries produced votes.

Desperate, Joe recruited family friend Frank Sinatra, Kilgallen's foe. He became the intermediary to solicit the mobster's assistance[5] with money and power in West Virginia but especially in Chicago.

In his book, *My Way*, popular singer Paul Anka ("Diana," "Put Your Head on my Shoulder," "Puppy Love"), who crossed paths with Giancana, wrote, "Everybody knew the Mafia boss from Chicago was someone not to be messed with…he had a violent MO…the bottom line is, Sam was a murderer."

To gain Giancana's help despite his seedy reputation, (at one point the Mafia Don shared girlfriend Judith Campbell with JFK), the Kennedy

---

[4] At one point during the hearings, RFK made fun of Sam Giancana. After he erupted into a nervous laughter at one of Bobby's questions, RFK said, "I thought only little girls giggled, Mr. Giancana!"

[5] Tina, Sinatra's daughter, confirmed this account. She was interviewed on *60 Minutes* to promote her book *My Father's Daughter*. Tina stated, "[My father] got Chicago mob boss Sam Giancana to help John F. Kennedy win the presidency by asking [my dad] to talk to the Mafia about securing the labor union vote in the crucial West Virginia primary in 1960." An editorial on the Sinatra family website (sinatrafamily.com/forum/index.php, viewed November 2015) was written by daughter Nancy. She posted the quote, "Please keep in mind when reading or hearing stories about JFK, FS [Frank Sinatra], and Sam Giancana that it was Joseph Kennedy Sr. who approached Frank for help in contacting Sam Giancana because he knew Frank, like all others on the circuit, performed in nightclubs owned by mob bosses." Nancy Sinatra also told author Seymour Hersh, "Over lunch, Joe [Kennedy] said, 'I think that you can help me in West Virginia and Illinois with our friends. You understand, Frank, I can't go [see them.] They're my friends too but I can't approach them. But you can.' I know that gave Dad pause. But it still wasn't anything he felt he shouldn't do. So off to Sam Giancana he went."

patriarch promised something in return—if JFK became president, the new administration would tread lightly on any Mafia investigations.

Joe Kennedy's strategy worked. JFK won both West Virginia and Illinois, and was elected president. He beat Vice-President Richard Nixon by the slimmest of margins (112,827 votes out of 68 million-plus; 0.16%; 303 electoral votes to 219). Later, Evelyn Lincoln, JFK's secretary admitted, "They [the Kennedy's] stole the election."

When John Kennedy entered the White House, Giancana, Marcello, Cohen, Frank Costello and Trafficante expected Joe to keep his word. He did not.

According to Kennedy family confidante John Seigenthaler's disclosures to this author, Joe actually ordered JFK to appoint Bobby Attorney General.[6] Joe did so even though he knew, based on RFK's relentless pursuit of Mafia figures, including Marcello, during the McClellan racketeering hearings, Bobby would relentlessly pursue the mobsters. In the eyes of the dangerous underworld figures, Joe had double-crossed them.[7][8]

---

[6] Seigenthaler, later to become the founding editorial director of *USA Today* as well a stout defender of First Amendment rights, told this author he was present during the two days in 1960 when JFK made his decision. "The president first floated the balloon about Bobby becoming the attorney general during a Florida golf match with Bill Lawrence of *The New York Times*," Seigenthaler recalled. "Bobby told me 'that's dad,'" meaning Joe was insisting on the appointment and behind the hint to Lawrence." One evening, Seigenthaler said he ate dinner with RFK and Ethel at their Hickory Hill home. "They talked about how RFK could teach, write, and travel and what a great career he had in front of him. Bobby wasn't going to take the job, and he said, 'this will kill dad,' a reference to disappointing Joe. But the next morning, during breakfast of bacon and eggs with JFK at his Georgetown flat, the president responded to Bobby's initiating words, 'Now about my situation,' by telling his younger brother 'there is no one around I really know. I need someone who will be interested in my interests and I need you.'" During the 7 to 10-minute monologue, Seigenthaler told this author, "JFK made his case, brief and concise by saying that Bobby was best qualified to handle organized crime and so forth. JFK then poured them both some coffee before Bobby said, 'Well, I have some points to make.' But Jack had made up his mind and he said, 'let's just grab our balls and go.'"

[7] In the book, *Mob Lawyer*, Frank Ragano, attorney for Marcello, Trafficante and James Hoffa, quoted Giancana—described by author Evan Thomas as one who had "hung people on meat hooks"—as saying, "That rat bastard, son-of-a-bitch. We broke our balls for him [JFK] and gave him the election and he gets his brother [Bobby] to hound us to death." Sam's daughter, Antoinette Giancana, and co-authors John R. Hughes and Thomas H. Jobe, wrote in *Mafia Princess*, "When Sam learned that Robert F. Kennedy had been appointed attorney general, he felt it was a rabbit punch in the dark."

[8] Prior to JFK's assassination, Joe Kennedy had been warned by a crime family emissary that RFK needed to back off his pursuit of underworld figures based on Joe's promise. The Kennedy patriarch agreed to speak to Bobby but instead had JFK do so especially after an FBI wiretap indicated Giancana's displeasure with RFK's campaign to destroy the Mafia. Despite JFK's plea, Bobby refused to back off. A few days later, Joe Kennedy suffered a stroke from which he never fully recovered. He must have known his worst fears had been realized, that JFK had been killed by the Mafia based on revenge for Bobby's actions.

Predictably, Bobby began a crusade to prosecute the mobsters as early as April 1961. Without warning, unceremoniously, and arguably illegally, RFK and the Justice Department deported Marcello to Central America. After being thrown out of Guatemala, he wandered through the jungle nearly dying before surreptitiously re-entering the United States. One may one imagine the rage Marcello exhibited with revenge a certainty. As acclaimed author Nick Pileggi (*Wise Guy: Life in a Mafia Family* (movie *Goodfellas*) and *Casino: Love and Honor in Las Vegas*) told this author, "Marcello was Sicilian, but born in Tunisia and grew up with both Sicilian and Arabic vendetta tendencies. He was not a turn-the-other-cheek kind of guy. Fury and revenge were his credo."

While Giancana, Cohen, Costello, and Trafficante looked on, RFK's relentless pursuit of Marcello, who had embarrassed Bobby by re-entering the U.S. after being deported, continued. The Justice Department renewed deportation charges against the New Orleans Don. They also charged him with conspiracy to defraud the government in New Orleans Federal court.

As the fall of 1963 approached, Marcello's back was against the wall; he had exhausted every deportation appeal. He also faced the conspiracy charges trial. Considerable prison time was possible if convicted. Desperate with no way out, his freedom and multimillion-dollar empire at risk, the Don had no choice but to take action with the only question whether to eliminate Bobby, his chief nemesis, or the president.

Why kill John Kennedy instead of Bobby whom Marcello despised? Simple common sense dictates that the clever Mafioso knew if he eliminated Bobby, JFK would use all of the government's resources to come after him. However, if JFK was assassinated, then RFK would be rendered powerless.[9][10]

---

[9] Nancy Ragano, wife of Frank Ragano, attorney for Carlos Marcello, Santo Trafficante, and James Hoffa, told this author she watched Frank and Trafficante laugh, joke, and raise glasses of champagne high in the air. Each was toasting JFK's assassination at the International Inn, a five-star hotel in Tampa, Florida.

[10] In the House Select Committee on Assassinations Report, Marcello is quoted as telling an informant, "The President was the dog, the Attorney General Kennedy was its tail. If you cut off the tail, the dog will keep biting; but if you chop off the head, the dog will die, tail and all."

New Orleans Don Carlos Marcello being deported by U.S. Immigration under orders from Attorney General Robert F. Kennedy

Predictably, this was exactly what happened. Within a short time after JFK was dead, a victim of his father and brother's poisonous misdeeds not his own, RFK disbanded the Justice Department's organized crime division specifically intended to put mobsters like Marcello out of business."[11] Common sense indicates that Bobby must have realized that he was the real target of Marcello's vengeance, not his brother, the president.[12] This is what led to RFK's guilt, his readings of the Greek classics and the *Bible*, his mention of the Mafia and Marcello to colleagues, and his inability to function after the assassination. Bobby knew JFK should have never died, never have been assassinated, that the wrong man had paid the ultimate penalty.

---

[11] During November 1963, Carlos Marcello stood trial in New Orleans on the conspiracy charges. Shortly after noon CST on November 22 Marcello, during a break in the testimony, was tapped on the shoulder by one of his underlings, David Ferrie. He informed Marcello, "Our troubles are over. JFK is dead." After the jury retired to reach a verdict, Marcello was acquitted in an hour.

[12] During the summer 1967, RFK, in a rare moment of disclosure, told advisor and speechwriter Richard Goodwin, husband of noted historian Doris Kearns Goodwin, that he believed his brother was killed by "the guy from New Orleans," meaning Marcello.

If there remains any doubt regarding the ludicrous nature of the "Oswald Alone" theory Kilgallen questioned, it should have been dismissed once and for all after Robert Kennedy Jr. confirmed his father's suspicions during a January 2013 interview with PBS's Charlie Rose. RFK Jr. said his father told him he believed the Warren Commission report was "a shoddy piece of craftsmanship." RFK Jr. also stated, "[Dad] spent a year trying to come to grips with my uncle's death, reading the work of Greek philosophers, Catholic scholars, Henry David Thoreau, poets and others trying to figure out the existential implications of why a just God would allow injustice to happen of the magnitude he was seeing."

Regarding the mechanics of JFK's assassination, RFK Jr. said his father believed the evidence was "very, very convincing that it was not a lone gunman [who shot JFK]." When Rose asked if he believed that RFK "felt some sense of guilt because he thought there might have been a link between his very aggressive efforts against organized crime," RFK Jr. said his father, "had investigators do research into the assassination and found that phone records of Oswald and nightclub owner Jack Ruby...'were like an inventory' of Mafia leaders the government had been investigating." Common sense logic dictates this "inventory" must have included Carlos Marcello whom RFK had bird-dogged from the outset of his being named attorney general.

If RFK Jr. had learned of presidential confidante Kenneth O'Donnell's account, previously mentioned, Bobby's son would have realized that words from his own father's mouth regarding RFK's suspicions about Marcello, "the New Orleans capo to whom Jack Ruby had ties," to an unimpeachable source like O'Donnell confirmed what Bobby had told his son.

Continuing to explore the plausibility that Marcello orchestrated JFK's death, it follows that one of Marcello's soldiers, Mafia low-life Jack Ruby, an ally of Marcello's Dallas crime underlings Joe Civello[13] and Joe Campisi, became the assassin to eliminate Oswald, one of Marcello's operatives hired to kill the president. This was necessary since Oswald could not be trusted

---

[13] During a Chicago speech, Robert Kennedy branded Marcello and Civello a "malignant threat to society."

to keep his mouth shut. He was a loose end and Marcello could not afford loose ends.

With Oswald eliminated, Ruby had to be silenced, and killing him in a Dallas jail cell was out of the question. Next best was to threaten the seedy nightclub owner if he talked and thus the first visitor to his jail cell was Campisi.[14] To placate Ruby, Campisi informed Oswald's killer that help was on the way through an attorney that was the mob controlled.

Kilgallen's soon-to-be "friend," Melvin Belli, fit that bill since he certainly was "mob approved." Former Belli legal associate John O'Connor told this author, "Mel was tight with Mickey Cohen and talked about him all the time. He certainly was one with connections [to the underworld] and my understanding was that he was approved as 'okay' by the mob." Seymour Ellison, the former partner who accompanied Belli to Las Vegas on several occasions, told this author, "Mel loved the mob and they loved him." Another Belli associate who wishes to remain anonymous said, "Mel was intoxicated with the Mafia," he told this author. "He loved the power, the money, the irreverence they had for authority just like he did."

Based on his being "mob approved," Belli, Mickey Cohen's attorney, had been ordered at the behest of Marcello, through Cohen, to discredit and silence Ruby. Belli did so by employing the ludicrous "psychomotor epilepsy insanity defense." It made Ruby look crazy in the eyes of nearly anyone who later investigated the assassinations. Belli then prevented Ruby from testifying despite his client's requests to do so. Ruby was no longer a loose end of concern to Marcello. End of story with Belli having done his job.

Based on her columns and articles, one may certainly assume this same scenario must have occurred to Kilgallen who, through her two exclusive interview with Ruby, realized the insanity defense was a joke, a cruel joke that could have sent Ruby to the electric chair. She had realized at Ruby's trial that the famous attorney's representation of Ruby was a farce, a ruse as evidenced by his own admissions to friend and chauffer Milton Hunt that the Ruby case was "fixed…it's a whitewash."

---

[14] Author David E. Scheim: "Joseph Campisi was described by Ruby's sister Eva Grant as a close friend of Ruby. Ruby's roommate George Senator named 'a Mr. Campisi, who operated the Egyptian Lounge' as one of Ruby's three closest friends."

Curiously, according to Nancy Ragano (the wife of Frank Ragano, attorney for mobsters Marcello and Santo Trafficante and Teamsters boss James Hoffa), Frank and Belli were very close friends to the extent of Belli representing Frank when he sued *Time Magazine* for libel a few years after the JFK assassination. When Frank told Trafficante about his hiring Belli, the mobster said, "Listen, whatever you do, don't ask him about Jack Ruby. It's none of your business." Nancy said her husband never interrogated Belli fearing his client's wrath if he delved into Belli's representation of Ruby.

In effect, Marcello's clever plan prevented any investigation toward other suspects who were involved in the assassinations. With JFK eliminated, Bobby powerless, and the mob-friendly LBJ in the White House, the Mafia Don was safe from deportation. Only one problem existed: Dorothy Mae Kilgallen, who kept digging into JFK and Oswald's deaths. That Kilgallen called Ruby a "gangster" in one column lends credibility to her suspicions he was connected to the underworld. This, arguably, was the first clue Kilgallen had leading to her belief that what she had been calling a "conspiracy" surrounding the JFK and Oswald assassinations had all of the earmarks of a successful mob operation based on revenge.[15] [16]

Since Kilgallen was acquainted with mobsters, had covered mob trials, and thus knew of their ruthlessness, it is not a stretch to believe she suspected JFK had been "hit" based on mobster retaliation for Bobby Kennedy's obsession to eliminate organized crime figures, specifically Marcello. Then one of the "hitmen," Oswald, had been "hit" by Ruby and that "hitman's" mental state muddied and silenced by Belli when he employed the insanity defense at Ruby's trial.

Recall Belli, apparently confused during Ruby's trial, calling his client "Oswald" several times to the dismay of the judge, something Kilgallen

---

[15] Recall that during Kilgallen's era, Mafia influence flourished, gangsters were celebrities of sorts with powerful means of controlling politics, law enforcement and the courts. There was an atmosphere of corruption and little doubt exists Kilgallen knew of Marcello whose deportation had been condemned by *New York Times* articles.

[16] Another powerful woman, the then Speaker of the House of Representatives Nancy Pelosi agreed with Kilgallen's conclusions. In May 2011, she told author Larry J. Sabato, "As soon as I saw Jack Ruby shoot Oswald, I thought, 'Of course! That's what they do to someone who kills somebody—kill him so he can't talk.'"

would have noticed as well. No surprise there since when Belli learned Oswald had been shot, recall that he told friend J. Kelly Farris, "Well, since Oswald's dead, I'll have to defend Ruby," a telling remark that lends credence to believing Belli had been "on call" to defend anyone apprehended after JFK was killed. Whether the mob-connected Belli was aware of the plot to assassinate the president is unknown but his own words to Farris point in that direction.

Kilgallen's trial interviews with Jack Ruby are significant. Aside from the one column she wrote describing Ruby's emotions during his trial, Kilgallen never divulged the exact nature of what Oswald's killer told him. However, Joe Tonahill stated, in his videotaped interview, "[Jack] wasn't uttering nonsense because this interview with her was very significant in his classless life, you know and I think he enjoyed it very much and cooperated with Kilgallen in every way that he could and told her the truth as he understood it. And it was just a very agreeable conversation between them and I just can't understand people doubting the sincerity of that interview because to me, and I watched them, a very sincere discussion going back and forth."

Asked why Ruby had decided to speak to Kilgallen, Tonahill stated, "I don't think there was any doubt about it…Jack was highly impressed with Dorothy Kilgallen and he figured she was a very classy person, she had good programs, *What's My Line?* and she was a highly intelligent person and I think of all the writers that were down there during the Ruby trial…about 400 from all over the world…she probably was the one that, to him, was the most significant 'cause he was in the entertainment business. He had a strip joint and he looked upon her as someone who could be able to help him. And he was trying to get help from everybody he could that had any significant standing in the community or anywhere else. He was a name dropper, you know."

Common sense dictates Marcello saw Kilgallen as a second coming of Bobby Kennedy. Like RFK, Kilgallen's crusade was personal and not just business. JFK was her friend, the president who had been so kind to young Kerry.

Whatever Jack Ruby told Dorothy Kilgallen led her on a trail to only one city besides Dallas—New Orleans, home to Marcello's illegal operation.

There Marcello, who had to have known of Kilgallen's interview of Ruby, heard the footsteps of the one person still alive who could topple his multi-million-dollar empire[17] by connecting him to the assassinations.

Marcello, a cold-blooded killer,[18] could not let this happen. He thus had the strongest possible common sense motive to eliminate the abrasive reporter. Kilgallen, described as acting like a prosecutor on *What's My Line?* was writing a book with disclosures that could trigger an assassinations grand jury investigation leading to his doorstep. Motive was the basis of her theories. By not keeping her intention to write the book private and instead shouting that she was going to "crack the case wide open," she triggered danger knocking at her door.

As the HSCA Committee report in the late 1970s stated, "Carlos Marcello had the motive, means, and opportunity to have President John F. Kennedy assassinated though [we were] unable to establish direct evidence of Marcello's complicity." If the Committee had scoured the salient facts surrounding Kilgallen's death in tandem with the above statement, they arguably could have targeted Marcello with much more specificity.

---

[17] In *The Plot to Kill the President*, former HSCA counsel G. Robert Blakey and his co-author Richard Billings wrote, "By 1963, the mobster was grossing many millions annually, $500 million from illegal gambling, $100 million from illegal activities in over 1,500 syndicate-connected bars, $8 million from professional burglaries and holdups, $6 million from prostitution, and $400 million from diverse…'investments.' When he wanted to relax, Marcello could enjoy the benefits of the 22-million-dollar, 6,500-acre estate Churchill Farms he owned near New Orleans."

[18] In *Marcello*, a biography of Carlos Marcello, author Stefano Vaccara noted the New Orleans Don's propensity for violence. Stefano wrote that if anyone double-crossed Marcello, "the man ended up being strangled and his body thrown in a tub of caustic acid. The remains were then dumped into a swamp where the alligators would take care of the rest."

CHAPTER 27

Of important consideration regarding Carlos Marcello's plausible motive to eliminate Dorothy Kilgallen was her visit to New Orleans within a month of her death. Author Lee Israel, in a September 30, 1995 audiotaped interview, said, "[Kilgallen] was tracing [Jack] Ruby's past, his mob ties."

This New Orleans trip was the one prior to the trip she was planning when she died. Based on his credible research and inside information garnered from interviews with Johnnie Ray before he died, Ray's sole biographer Jonny Whiteside wrote:

> Dorothy was in high gear working on the Kennedy assassination, an investigation that demanded more and more of her time. To Johnnie, it all seemed quite mysterious. She mentioned a planned trip to New Orleans for further research into Lee Harvey Oswald's background and connections there (a daunting contradiction of his pro-Cuba street corner politics and incongruous associations with right-wing conservatives and the Carlos Marcello crime family.)

Israel and Whiteside's observations indicate two important points: 1) Kilgallen was not abandoning her JFK and Oswald assassinations investigation, and 2) she had somehow made the connection evidently linking Oswald to Marcello with interest in searching Ruby's past "mob-ties" to connect the three men. Kilgallen had already noted the potential connection of Ruby to Oswald in the "DA to Link Oswald to Ruby" February 1964 column since she would not have written that column unless she had some evidence linking the two men based either on her own research or information the District Attorney's office had passed along. [1] [2]

Recall Marc Sinclaire's eerie details about the New Orleans adventure. Kilgallen demanded that they take separate flights. After only one day in the city, Kilgallen scared Sinclaire when she told him to return to New York City and not tell anyone he accompanied her there. Kilgallen never reported on her visit. Whom she spoke to was unknown. Regardless, whatever Kilgallen discovered triggered the plans for a second visit, one that excited her. This led to statements to friends that her life was in danger, foreshadowing her death shortly thereafter.

Why the New Orleans-based Marcello had much to fear from the relentless reporter, and the book she was writing, is clear. If one examines closely the details about Kilgallen's assassinations investigation, all indications point to her mainly focusing on the assassination of Oswald by Ruby *not* Oswald's alleged assassination of the president. The savvy Kilgallen apparently realized what other competent researchers who fit facts to conclusions instead of the other way around, have during the years: Oswald was a puzzling/confusing character and attempts to decipher his role in the killing of JFK an absolute quagmire with few definitive answers available.

Instead, Kilgallen instincts triggered an ultimate focus on Jack Ruby. Why? Because she had not only observed him up close at trial on a daily basis but interviewed him twice providing great insight into Oswald's killer. In addition, Kilgallen could check not only his background but investigate discrepancies in statements he made to the Warren Commission since she was the first reporter to read them, and since Ruby was still alive, the potential existed to interview him again. This strategy was unique, far afield from that conducted by any reporter or investigative body consumed with

---

[1] The connection of Jack Ruby to Marcello was also noted in the HSCA report. FBI records indicated Ruby called Nofio Pecora, a "capo" working for Marcello, three weeks before November 22, 1963. Also, Ruby could not have operated a strip club in Dallas without Marcello's okay.

[2] At Ruby's trial, District Attorney Wade did not introduce witnesses connecting Ruby and Oswald. Kilgallen never provided any explanation for Wade's failure to do so in any of her subsequent Ruby trial columns.

targeting Oswald as the key to unlocking the mysteries of the JFK assassination when Kilgallen believed he was not.

In addition, after interviewing Ruby twice, Kilgallen had gained a soft spot for his plight, some sympathy for the man who shot Oswald. Whatever she heard during the twin interviews caused her to wonder if Ruby was a patsy, used and then discarded. Recall what she wrote after the second interview: "I went out into the almost empty lunchroom corridor wondering what I really believed about this man."

Kilgallen's actions while pursuing the investigation indicated she had taken on the task of defending Ruby herself. She was standing up for him, demanding justice, becoming his paladin. She wondered if he had fair treatment, if his constitutional rights to a fair trial were honored. Armed with this mindset, Kilgallen was in fighting mode determined to leave no avenue of interest unturned.

Kilgallen's siding with Ruby's defense team at his trial evidenced proof of Kilgallen's focus on Ruby. She also attempted to aid the defense by securing more information from the FBI about Oswald. Then Kilgallen exposed *only* Ruby's testimony at the Warren Commission before its intended release instead of the thousands of pages of pertinent information about others associated with the assassinations. It also appears likely she flew to New Orleans based on what he told her in the interviews. To put it mildly, Kilgallen was obsessed with Ruby. She was not about to give up on discovering the truth about why he killed Oswald. And, most important, who may have ordered Ruby to do so.[3]

There is cause to believe Kilgallen would have pursued interviewing Ruby again if she had lived longer. Remember that Dallas District Attorney Henry Wade had stated he was willing to recommend that Ruby's death sentence be reduced to life imprisonment since it was important because "

---

[3] In a September 7, 1976 *Washington Post* column, Jack Anderson wrote of interviewing mobster Johnny Rosselli regarding Ruby. Anderson said Roselli, connected to mobsters like Marcello, told him, "When Oswald was picked up, the underworld conspirators feared he would crack and disclose information that might lead them to them. This almost certainly would have brought a massive U.S. crackdown on the Mafia. So Jack Ruby was ordered to eliminate Oswald...."

...there are still a lot of unanswered questions." Wade did not elaborate and no follow-up article appeared.[4]

Without doubt, Kilgallen, tenacious like her father Jim, had a strong constitution and a willingness to forge ahead when others would have stopped. During her career, Kilgallen never backed away from a challenge, never letting being a woman stand in the way of challenging men or women when she believed in the cause. She broke the "glass ceiling" before the term was fashionable as she advanced from a one-week trial at her father's newspaper to a full-time reporter to the only female columnist on Broadway to a famous columnist syndicated to 200 newspapers across the country. Regardless of the obstacle, she succeeded during an era when it was definitely a man's world.

Kilgallen had set the tone when she wrote, "I'm a reporter who likes danger and excitement" in her published book after challenging the two men during the around the world race. Jim Kilgallen was right when he said his daughter was courageous. Close friend Maggie McNelli also expressed Kilgallen's strong will. She said, "Dorothy had a tremendous will to win.... As a matter of fact, she'd kill you to win."

With this in mind, specifically recalling Kilgallen's investigative trail from early 1964 in sequence to November 1965, is possible. Doing so makes what she wrote in her September 3, 1965 *Journal-American* column, approximately two months before the day she died, especially relevant. It read in part, "This story [JFK assassination] is not going to die as long as there's a real reporter alive—and there are a lot of them."

Unfortunately, for history's sake, there were not "a lot of them." Only one—Dorothy Kilgallen.

---

[4] On October 5th, 1966. The Texas Court of Criminal Appeals ruled, among other matters, that Judge Joe Brown's denial of the change of Ruby's venue motion was reversible error. They ordered a new trial be held away from Dallas. Judge W. T. McDonald, after discussing the emotions seething in Dallas after JFK's murder, wrote, "Against such a background of unusual and extraordinary invasions of the expected neutral mental processes of a citizenry from which a jury is to be chosen, the Dallas County climate was one of such strong feeling that it was not humanly possible to give Ruby a fair and impartial trial which is the hallmark of American due process of law."

CHAPTER 28

In all likelihood, the timing of Dorothy Kilgallen's death cannot be a coincidence. The fact is that it occurred within days of telling friends she possessed evidence pointing toward who killed JFK and why. This provides good cause to believe that plans were in place to murder her on the very weekend her body was discovered.

Inside information fed to those who feared Kilgallen caused a realization: she was too close to the truth. Whoever snitched on her, whoever betrayed her trust, must have triggered a call to action. Result: Kilgallen's second New Orleans trip must never happen.

Examining that proposed trip warrants consideration. During the prior visit, something occurred, based on Marc Sinclaire's account, to spook Kilgallen but it was not enough to make her stop the investigation. Instead, the courageous journalist was forging ahead and even excited about it. Whatever it was she expected to learn in New Orleans may have been the grand finale, the key to uncovering the truth about the assassinations.

Recall that in the "DA to Link Ruby to Oswald" column,[1] Kilgallen suggested that Oswald may have actually worked in Ruby's nightclub. In the days and months that followed, it appears she had somehow further

---

[1] To date, no publication of any kind or any investigation report has ever mentioned this column. It appears to have been missed by any and all so-called JFK assassination experts despite its historical importance.

connected them,[2] and if, through a second trip to New Orleans as Johnny Whiteside's column intimates, she was able to solidify the link between Oswald and Marcello, then the risk of traveling to New Orleans was worth it. Why? Because that link fit perfectly in view of the connection she had established between Marcello and Ruby, perhaps through the interview with Ruby, providing the smoking gun evidence she would present in articles or her upcoming book. Kilgallen, if she could obtain the final proof she needed to connect all three men with Marcello masterminding the mob operation to kill JFK from the "source [whom I do not know but will recognize] who is going to give me information about the case" she mentioned to *What's My Line?* make-up man Carmen Gebbia, would indeed have "the scoop of the century," as she once boasted.

However, there was a snitch in the mix, a Judas. That person had told someone the status of Kilgallen's investigation. The famous reporter, like John F. Kennedy, Lee Harvey Oswald, and Jack Ruby, was doomed. She just did not know it yet.

* * * * *

Before attempting to pinpoint who may have been the traitor within Kilgallen's inner circle, it is important to consider the means by which she died. This helps provide a plausible explanation for identifying the snitch's identity, the one who, in all likelihood, set Kilgallen up for the kill, or was the killer.

Unlike the ability to target Marcello as the one who had the strongest motive to orchestrate the murder of Kilgallen, proving *how* she was murdered is more difficult. This is because no follow-up investigation commenced. Nevertheless, the *means* by which Kilgallen was killed is connected to the *opportunity* to commit the crime. The first place to consider both is by revisiting the death scene at her townhouse.

The most credible eyewitness is Kilgallen's main hairdresser Marc Sinclaire. In the videotaped interview conducted by investigative reporter

---

[2] If Kilgallen did indeed have proof that Oswald and Ruby knew each other before the JFK assassination, or Henry Wade had the same proof but never displayed it at trial as Kilgallen predicted, then it's plausible to believe that Oswald did register a glimmer of recognition of Ruby before Oswald was shot.

Kathryn Fauble's associate during the 1990s (Excerpts available at TheReporterWhoKnewTooMuch.com), Sinclaire recalled entering Kilgallen's home on the morning of November 8. She had asked him to fix her hair for an appointment she had at Kerry's school.

Sinclaire said he headed for a small dressing room on the townhouse's third floor where Kilgallen normally had her hair done. This room was next to her main clothes closet leading directly to Kilgallen's master bath. Sinclaire recalled, "When I entered…she was not in that room but the air conditioning was on and it was cold outside.[3] So I turned on my curling irons and I walked into the [adjacent] bedroom, not thinking she would be there."

That bedroom was the Master. It was adjacent to the "Black Room" where the couple entertained guests. The couple had not slept in the Master for some time. Sinclaire, in a separate audiotaped interview, said Kilgallen "…was lonely, really lonely…and she proceeded to tell me the situation that occurred in the [Master] bedroom she no longer slept in, which I had often asked why she didn't use that bedroom since it was so much more convenient." Sinclaire, when asked if this was the bedroom where she caught Richard with one of his paramours, apparently a "business partner," agreed, stating "and that was another ironic thing I thought was that Dorothy would have never slept there let alone committed suicide there or even have a fatal overdose there. She hated that bedroom and we only used it because of the dressing room. Or we would have never used it at all."

Sinclaire explained that Kilgallen normally slept in her private office, the "Cloop," on the fifth floor. Richard slept in a bedroom on the fourth floor. Sinclaire further described what he discovered:

> She was sitting up in bed, and I walked over to the bed and touched her, and I knew she was dead right away. The bed was spotless. She was dressed very peculiarly. I've never seen her dressed like that before. She always [was] in pajamas and old socks and her make-up was off and her hairpiece was off and everything. She was completely dressed like she was going out, the hair was in place, the make-up was on, the false eyelashes were on.

---

[3] Temperatures in New York City in November 1965 hovered near the freezing point. In those days there was no central air conditioning; each room had a wall or window unit.

Sinclaire added:

The matching peignoir and robe, a book laid out on thebed, a drink on the table, the light was on, the air conditioning was on though you didn't need an air conditioner you would have had the heat on. And she was always cold. And why she had the air conditioning on I don't know.[4]

Sinclaire, who explained that perhaps someone had turned on the air conditioner "to keep the body a certain temperature," said the glass[5] was "on the right hand side, way away, way over, and the book was turned upside down it wasn't in the right position where if you'd been reading you'd lay it down and it was laid down so perfectly."

Sinclaire continued to describe the scene:

Rigor mortis had set in on one hand, the right hand and it had drawn up the covers a little bit. And there was lipstick on the [left] sleeve of the Bolero jacket…and the light was on and she was sitting up.

I went back in the dressing room, picked up the intercom, and rang for James [the butler]. I said, "James, I am unable to wake Miss Kilgallen. Could you please come up?" He RAN up the stairs. I could hear him. He came up the front stairs and he ran like he was very excited and of course the door was locked. But I had come in from the back door. I don't think they expected me, no one knew I was coming. And this was before 9:30 in the morning, nine, five after nine.[6]

So I opened the door to the bedroom and James came in, and at that time I noticed a sheet of paper laying on the floor that had been pushed under the door. And James came in and he was very flustered. He wasn't himself at all.[7]

---

[4] The book was *The Honey Badger* by Robert Ruark, a journalist, author, world traveler and big game hunter. He was the same Ruark who wrote a column criticizing Frank Sinatra. He said the crooner had frolicked with mobsters during a trip to Havana in 1947.

[5] Sinclaire's recollection conflicts with that of Dr. Umberger who collected two glasses from Kilgallen's night table brought to the NYC Medical Examiner's Office. It may be that Sinclaire was mistaken since John Broich confirmed Dr. Umberger's account of there being two glasses.

[6] In a 1978 interview, tutor Ibne Hassan confirms Sinclaire's statement regarding when he found Kilgallen's body. Asked about the accuracy of official reports that the discovery happened at 12:30 pm, Hassan said, "That is not correct. Her body was found quite early. I would say in the vicinity of nine o'clock."

[7] Author Lee Israel quoted Evelyn Clement, butler James Clement's wife, as saying Kilgallen "was lying there with her earrings on." This account does not appear in the ME documents or elsewhere in any report.

Sinclaire's statement regarding Kilgallen wearing a blue robe with her hair, makeup, and false eyelashes in place with the covers pulled up matched the descriptions in the NYC medical examiner's documents, providing credibility for his account. He added, "And I was very upset so I turned to [James] and I said, 'I'm going home. You can reach me there if you want to' and I left the building." Sinclaire then added, "When I got downstairs and went out the front door, there was a police car sitting in front of the house…There were two officers in it. Sitting right dead in front of the house. They didn't pay any attention to me when I came out…. I find it very strange that they were sitting there dead in front of the house and Dorothy was dead upstairs. Yes, I find it very strange."

Asked about being interviewed, Sinclaire said, "They called me that night. My then press agent Jan, I can't remember her last name, anyway, she called me, and asked me to come to Romla Metzler's house and I did. And the two of them interrogated me basically trying to find out what I knew about Dorothy's death. And I didn't have very much to tell them." He added, "But why would they call me? Metzler was a [*Journal-American*] fashion writer."

Shown a newspaper story reporting the maid having discovered the body, Sinclaire said, "They mixed that all up. But I don't think I was the first one to find Dorothy. I've never thought that."

According to tutor and family companion Ibne Hassan, who described Kilgallen as "articulate, very sociable, polite and elegant in dress and manner," Sinclaire was right. During a November 2015 interview with this author, Dr. Hassan, who enjoyed a stellar career in international politics after earning several PhD's, said, "Before I went to class at Columbia around 9:00 a.m. that Monday [November 8], I saw all of the servants rushing around the lobby as I was leaving. I asked James what happened. He said, 'Dorothy died. She may have drank too much.' Then I left for class." Hassan also stated he did not recall seeing a police car outside Kilgallen's townhouse lending credence to his having left for class before Sinclaire arrived.

Hassan attended Kilgallen's funeral but Sinclaire did not. He stated, "Her sister Eleanor called me and asked if I would do Dorothy's hair and makeup because no one knew how to fix her as well as I did…I went to the funeral home, Abby Funeral Home…I didn't like the funeral director because he was very rude about Dorothy's death." Sinclaire added that he went ahead but then the power failed (there was a total blackout of NYC) and he had to return the next night and finish.

Sinclaire said he did not attend Kilgallen's funeral because "I did not like the way they were behaving. I didn't like the way the family was behaving. I didn't like the way the press was behaving. I didn't like any of it. I knew more than they did and I didn't want to be a party to it."

Charles Simpson, Kilgallen's alternate hairdresser, confirmed Sinclaire's eyewitness account in a videotaped interview by investigative reporter Kathryn Fauble's associate (TheReporterWhoKnewTooMuch.com). He recalled that Sinclaire, "called me on the phone and told me that he had found her dead. And he said, 'When I tell you the bed she was found in, and how I found her,' he said, 'you're going to know she was murdered.' And when he told me, I knew." Simpson added, "When Marc told me that day and then we got back together and he talked to me and told me where he found her, and how, it was abnormal, the whole thing was abnormal. It was just abnormal. The woman didn't sleep in that bed much less the room and if she still were sharing that room with Richard, that was Richard's bed. That's the one he set fire to. It wasn't her bed."

This referred to an earlier incident on December 15, 1953. A drunken Kollmer had accidently set his bed on fire with a lighted cigarette after falling asleep. His screams alerted Kilgallen. She rushed to save him.[8]

One important note regarding Sinclaire's story is the time factor. His recollection (and for that matter, Hassan's) that he entered Kilgallen's townhouse between 9:00 a.m. and 9:30 and then discovered Kilgallen's body is completely at odds with various newspaper accounts.[9]

* * * * *

---

[8] Harold Gold, the fireman who extinguished the fire appeared on *What's My Line?* on November 14, 1954. Kilgallen did not guess his identity.

[9] Neither Sinclaire nor Simpson knew of the other's interview questions and answers before they were interviewed.

Explanations for the death scene irregularities noted by Marc Sinclaire lead to several plausible scenarios. Each must be considered when determining how Kilgallen may have died.

The first, as noted, involves the potential Kilgallen's husband Richard was the culprit, either by accidently or intentionally providing his Tuinal to his wife, causing her to be rendered unconscious and ultimately die when the Tuinal mixed with the other drugs and alcohol. Either way, remorseful over his actions when he discovered she was dead, Richard could have decided to make his dead wife presentable so that when her body was discovered she looked as beautiful in death as she had in life. Richard may have then staged the death scene, first stripping Kilgallen of the dress she wore to *What's My Line?* and replacing it with nightclothes from her closet. He could have decided to leave on her hairpiece, makeup and false eyelashes so any photographs would capture her beauty.

Having undressed and dressed her, probably in the bedroom, Richard could have placed her under the covers, and positioned the *Honey Badger* book on her lap. To make certain her body was preserved, he may have turned on the air conditioner.

To cover his tracks, and point any investigation toward accidental death or even suicide, Richard could have positioned the empty Seconal drug vial on the night table while forgetting to position her reading glasses there. This may have been an oversight.

Since it has been determined Kilgallen's body was discovered several hours before the police were notified, why did Richard wait to inform them? No one knows for sure, but perhaps he began drinking and in his diminished state, was unable to make a decision. Certainly by the time the police, other officials, and friends arrived, he was drunk.

A second possibility regarding the death scene irregularities deals with another person being responsible for her death who was in the townhouse with Kilgallen when she died. Who such person was and how he ended up there is subject to further study. However, if someone intended to murder Kilgallen, presumably he also needed to make her death look like an accident. This person could have altered the death scene to lead any investigation in the direction of accidental death thereby dismissing any possibility of foul play.

If there was staging of the death scene, it is important to consider how the killer may have accompanied Kilgallen into the townhouse. This could have happened once she arrived home from the Regency Hotel bar. No one can say for sure since the police investigation, as noted, was *no* investigation of Kilgallen's death. Sadly, it was as if the attitudes of Dallas Police Chief Jesse Curry and J. Edgar Hoover following JFK's assassination prevailed. There was no need for any investigation because the evidence was seemingly solid that Oswald alone killed the president. Here, the cause of death was quickly determined to be accidental and no need for an investigation of any kind was ever considered.

To reconstruct Kilgallen's movements on the evening of November 7, 1965 and the early morning hours of November 8, it is necessary to break down the events in her life. This involves understanding what happened from the time she readied herself for the *What's My Line?* appearance to when her body was found. These events are:

- Preparation for her final *What's My Line?* show

- Appearance on the program

- The time spent with Bob Bach at P. J. Clarke's directly after the program

- The stop at the Regency Hotel bar with a companion author Lee Israel called the "mystery man"

- The time between leaving the bar and arriving home

- Entrance into the townhouse

- Entrance on the third floor and the Master bedroom

- Body being discovered

Regarding Kilgallen's final program preparation, hairdresser Marc Sinclaire, at Kilgallen's townhouse to fix her hair, said in his videotaped interview, "She was subdued but no more than usual. She was tired." Asked why this was true, he replied, "She was out the night before." Clarifying

Kilgallen's state of mind as she readied herself for the program, Sinclaire explained that Kilgallen was "going home afterwards but obviously she didn't because she went to the Regency."

According to Sinclaire, Kilgallen planned to wear "a long, white silk file evening gown" on the program. He told her she had worn it the week before. When she said it didn't matter, Sinclaire told her "okay" and helped her into it. He added, "She wanted to wear that dress. [It] was cumbersome because that dress took up the back seat [of the limo]. We always discussed clothes ahead of time, because…if it was an evening dress, I would do [her hairstyle] more elaborate, than I would do…for a shorter cocktail dress."

Sinclaire had woven fake flowers collected from a vase in the townhouse entrance hall into Kilgallen's hair believing the flowers would go well with the dress she had chosen. He called it a "very formal dress…"

Sinclaire recalled being shocked when he watched *What's My Line?* that evening. He immediately noticed Kilgallen had apparently changed her mind before the show. She had, he stated, discarded the silk-file dress[10] for a "low-cut, wing-sleeve chiffon dress by designer Anne Fogarty."

A stickler for detail, Sinclaire believed the short dress did not mesh well with the flowers in her hair. "She couldn't take the flowers out because they were woven into the hairpiece," Sinclaire said adding "Obviously there was something to make her change that dress at the last minute…after I left I think she got a phone call [at home] from somebody, and she agreed to meet whoever it was at the Regency.[11] That's my belief because she wasn't going to Clarke's (P.J. Clarke's)." He continued, "She'd asked me if I wanted to meet her [later] because she did not have anybody she was going to meet with, and she was not dressing for a 'date date.'" Told that Kilgallen did go to Clarke's, Sinclaire said, "We'll maybe but not long. She might have done that and then gone home but it wouldn't have been an evening like she had."

---

[10] In an audiotaped interview, Sinclaire stated, "When I came in the bedroom that morning from the dressing room and found [Kilgallen's] body, that white silk-file dress was hanging up.… "

[11] In his videotaped interview, Sinclaire said he visited the Regency Hotel cocktail lounge many times stating, "I had clients who stayed there so I'd go by there and do their hair, especially people from out of town like Princess Margaret."

Asked why he didn't go out with Kilgallen that night, Sinclaire said, "I was tired myself. She had done something every day that week and she had more appointments for me the following week. And I didn't want to see her anymore. I wanted to go home."

Concerning the famous television star's final *WML?* performance (www .youtube.com/watch?v=6gn6jS1UK78), there was no apparent change from her usual program demeanor. Before the show, director Franklin Heller chatted with Kilgallen in her dressing room. He said she was "quite normally composed in every way." He added that the two talked about her "travel abroad." This may have alluded to Charles Simpson's belief that Kilgallen planned a trip to London.

Recall that moderator John Charles Daly said, "Dorothy was just full of beans last night. She was in great spirits." Viewing the taped show confirms this observation. With sharp questioning, she guessed the identity of a woman who sold dynamite. She later teased Bennett Cerf about his comments to the woman who was a football writer. When a man who owned the Hollywood Wax Museum appeared and stumped the panel, Kilgallen quipped, "This is [our] own wax museum." She referred to the advanced age of her and fellow panelists. Following the program, Kilgallen showed Cerf the *Murder One* preface. He was impressed.

By all accounts, Kilgallen's and Bob Bach's stop at P. J. Clarke's was a brief one. The twosome elbowed their way through the packed house before being seated by Frankie Ribando, Table 36's maître d'. A favorite waiter, Patty Blue, brought Kilgallen a drink, apparently vodka and tonic. At some point, Kilgallen told Bach, as noted, that she had a "late date."[12] The two then left separately sometime past midnight.

More about the famous journalist's time spent at the Regency Hotel bar is important but connected directly to a man she met there. Discussing him will follow but for now, it is important to examine the time between when Kilgallen left that bar, when she arrived at the townhouse entrance,

---

[12] Bob Bach's wife Jean said, "I knew she had drinks with Bob. They'd been at P.J. Clarke's. She told him to just drop her off at the Regency Hotel since she was having a late date that night."

when she entered the townhouse, when she finally ended up in the Master bedroom, when she died, and when her body was discovered.

Kilgallen's townhouse was located at 45 East 68th Street between Madison Avenue and Central Park. There was a front entrance door. Kerry Kollmar's tutor and family companion Ibne Hassan told this author no door attendant was present to screen tenants and guests in November 1965. No surveillance cameras were present. None appeared in the United States until 1969.

Witnesses saw Kilgallen at the Regency Hotel, located six blocks from Kilgallen's townhouse, at 2:00 a.m. Recall Western Union manager Dave Spiegel swore Kilgallen called him at 2:20 a.m. This account appears credible and assists with estimating the time Kilgallen died.

It seems logical to believe Kilgallen placed the call to Spiegel from a hotel pay telephone located near the bar or perhaps a phone brought to her table by the bartender. If so, this means she did not leave the Regency until at least 2:25 a.m. or a bit after. She would not have arrived home, either by walking (highly unlikely), by taxi, limousine, or perhaps in a car, until 2:30 or a bit later if the short trip was delayed.[13]

It is important to recall Marc Sinclaire stating that rigor mortis had set in when he discovered her body at a bit after 9:00 a.m. Medical evidence suggests rigor mortis begins two to six hours after someone dies. This means Kilgallen had to have died sometime before 7:00 a.m. since at least two hours had to pass before Sinclaire discovered the body. Recall Dr. Luke concluded that Kilgallen died "between 2 and 4:00 a.m.," the estimate the Junior medical examiner provided to a newspaper the day after Kilgallen's death. This could be accurate and if so, then Kilgallen's blood alcohol content, listed as 0.15 in the autopsy eprort, had to have been much higher when she actually died leading to the conclusion she drank heavily either at the Regency Hotel bar or at the townhouse.

---

[13] No one to date has reported how Kilgallen left the Regency Hotel bar or with whom. In his DVD interview, Marc Sinclaire said that Kilgallen "visited the Regency Hotel bar many times" and that "she liked it because there were three entrances, through the lobby and down some stairs, the street entrance, and through a back entrance."

When asked about Kilgallen's time of death, Marc Sinclaire stated in his videotaped interview, "I don't know what time she died." Regardless, when Kilgallen arrived at the townhouse, she could gain entrance either through the front, or rear door, which led to a garden. Each had old-fashioned locks with the keyhole in the knob. Since the rear entrance was rarely used, Kilgallen most likely entered through the front door.

There was no parking garage; parking was on the street. Outside the front door was the metal box where Kilgallen apparently left here newspaper columns for pick-up. Somehow, the messenger found the column and delivered it to the *Journal-American* offices. Recall the afternoon edition of November 8 included it with the notation Kilgallen wrote the column during the early hours. Whether this was true or whether Kilgallen had written the column earlier or later on November 7 for delivery early the next morning is impossible to determine.

The entrance hall inside the townhouse front door led to the flight of the back stairs and elevator. Next to this room was a poorly lit area where bicycles and sleds were stored.

Adjacent to the stairs was a doorway leading to the servant's quarters. A sewing room was next to a long hallway leading to the servant's small living room. This room included the door to the back yard. Across the way was another door leading to the second floor kitchen. The home staff consisted of James and Evelyn Clement, and Ellen O'Hara, "a stooped, yet dynamically energetic elderly Irish woman." Kerry Kollmar described her as "the kindest, warmest person in the household of my childhood."

Kilgallen's townhouse directly faced 68th Street second from the corner. From various reports, those at home in the townhouse at the time Kilgallen died included husband Richard, 11-year-old son Kerry, and Ibne Hassan.

Who may have had keys to the Kilgallen townhouse is anyone's guess. Both Marc Sinclaire and Charles Simpson had keys. Predictably, the servants did as well as Richard. Whether anyone else had spare keys, no one knows. Ibne Hassan told this author there was a buzzer outside the front door. It rang a bell in the townhouse to alert the presence of a visitor. Whether the buzzer was working during the early morning hours of November 8 is unknown.

The question remains whether Kilgallen entered the townhouse alone or with a companion who was not a family member, tutor or servant. Several alternatives exist: she left the hotel with someone who then accompanied her into the townhouse before she entered; someone forced her to let him in after she opened the door; or someone was lying in wait inside the townhouse and surprised her when she entered. The latter suggests this person either had a key to the townhouse or picked the lock.

Two plausible explanations, besides Richard being involved with the possibility of an accidental or accidently on purpose overdose, exist as to how Dorothy Kilgallen's life ended at the young age of 52. The first is that the barbiturates described by John Broich and Drs. Baden and Hoffman were injected against Kilgallen's will. The second is that someone forced her to ingest a heavy dose of capsules and perhaps even the vodka causing heart failure due to the dangerous combination of the two.

Kilgallen was not knifed, strangled, beaten or shot to death, since the medical examiner's office report stated there was no trauma. There was also no evidence surfacing that an autopsy indicated the presence of piercing of her skin. This would have indicated that injection of drugs was possible.

This was not to say that during the haphazard post-death analysis of the body by the medical examiner's office those involved missed this forensic evidence. However, to date, no facts have surfaced pointing toward injection of the drugs being a possibility.

If drug injection makes no sense, ingestion of the drugs makes the most sense as the means regarding cause of death. If she did not willingly swallow them, then what means of force are likely?

At least two possibilities appear. The first is that whoever was intent on causing her harm could have threatened her with physical harm if she did not ingest the capsules and drink the vodka. The assailant may also have threatened Kilgallen's family members with harm if she did not follow orders. Afraid to scream and call for help, Kilgallen acquiesced to the demand and followed orders by swallowing the capsules while drinking the vodka.

A second alternative involves excessive force. When she refused to cooperate, a gun or knife became the threatening weapon. Then the assailant physically forced the capsules into her open mouth. The terrified Kilgallen swallowed them after which the assailant forced her to drink the rest of the vodka. After the drug overdose and alcohol took effect and Kilgallen passed out, the assailant could have fled with Kilgallen's JFK assassination file in hand.

* * * * *

Having considered how Kilgallen died if someone intending to harm her was in the townhouse, it is then necessary to return to the question as to how that person arranged the death scene.

Staging it meant there was placement of the body in the wrong bed in the wrong bedroom while she still had on her makeup, false eyelashes and hairpiece. However, the assailant, in all likelihood, did not know it was the wrong bed in the wrong bedroom. They also may not have cared about the makeup, false eyelashes and hairpiece.

One problem with this scenario is confusion regarding the nightclothes Kilgallen was wearing when her body was discovered. Marc Sinclaire described her outfit as both a blue peignoir and a Bolero blouse. Lee Israel wrote that Kilgallen was wearing a "blue robe." The latter matched the NYC medical documents with no mention of any Bolero blouse.

According to Sinclaire, either would have been completely uncharacteristic or "peculiar." During his videotaped interview, he said Kilgallen never wore these nightclothes to bed instead opting for her favorite pajamas and old socks.

Also of interest is the ME's notation that Kilgallen, while wearing the blue robe, wore "nothing else." No account was provided as to whether a bra or panties was discovered either in the bedroom or her nearby dressing room.

This said, could the killer have undressed Kilgallen? After doing so, did he toss away the Chiffon dress she was wearing when she left the Regency Hotel bar? There is no account of that dress's whereabouts on the day of her death. Regardless, to conclude that the assailant would have had the inclination to remove the dress, remove any undergarments, and replace them with the odd nightclothes seems unlikely.

Regardless, the peculiar nature of the death scene clues should have triggered "Investigate! Investigate! Investigate!" However, those called to duty—police, ME staff, Kilgallen's fellow journalists, even her close friends and family—despite confusion about conflicting facts, brushed off Kilgallen's death as accidental. This was reprehensible since those responsible for murdering one of the most powerful female voices in America escaped arrest and punishment.

Unfortunately, without benefit of a fresh investigation, logic fails when considering the reasons for the death scene existing as it did in the early morning hours of November 8, 1965. That is, unless there is a third possibility as to how Kilgallen became the victim of a homicide. This involves targeting the one person with easy access to the gifted reporter just prior to her death.

CHAPTER 29

Evidence of Dorothy Kilgallen's fear of harm from those who feared her comes from a variety of sources.

Kilgallen's close friend Bill Franklin, Johnnie Ray's manager for years, said, "Dorothy was very disturbed by the whole thing [the JFK assassination]…[she] was sure there was some kind of a conspiracy. She said she was close to breaking the whole thing open, and also that she felt threatened, life-threatened, as a result of her work."

Upon learning of Kilgallen's death, Franklin said Ray was overwhelmed with grief. "[He] started crying like a baby." Regarding how she died, Franklin added, "John didn't believe she died of natural causes. He said, 'I ain't gonna tell you everything that I know about what Dorothy knows [about the JFK assassination] but I don't believe that she laid down and went to sleep like that.' He didn't tell me the whole story, though. Never would. I ask him that day and he just said 'It's dangerous to know what Dorothy knows.'"

During one interview, Johnnie Ray said, "Beyond question…I believe Dorothy was murdered. I just couldn't prove it." Speaking with television host Joe Franklin, Ray, asked if the reason for Kilgallen's death was "defined," answered, "Beyond question" without elaborating on what "defined" meant.

Ray's subsequent manager Alan Eichler told this author "Johnnie knew Dorothy was killed. He knew who the killer was and how it was done and who did it. But he couldn't prove it." Eichler added, "He was convinced she was murdered. He said Dorothy had extensive assassination files and she was certain she knew the truth about who killed JFK. Johnnie believed that's why she was killed."

Kilgallen's friend Steve Rossi, a stand-up comedian of note and Marty Allen's partner, later added, "They alleged that [Kilgallen] died from an overdose of barbiturates, but I know for a fact that she wasn't taking anything at the time.... Once she started writing the book on the Kennedy assassination, I think somebody came in there and poisoned her." Syndicated columnist Liz Smith believed, "[Dorothy] did know too much. Her murder was very mysterious." Kilgallen's friend Jean Bach said, "If enough people believed Dorothy had the scoop on what really happened [in the JFK assassination] that would impel them into some sort of violent action."

Even Earl Ruby, Jack's brother, while denying Jack was involved in any conspiracy, admitted Kilgallen's death was "suspicious." He did so during a September 30, 1995 audiotaped interview. Sam Giancana's girlfriend, singer Phyllis McGuire, was quoted in a *Vanity Fair* article written by Dominick Dunne. She said she considered Kilgallen's death to be "suspicious" and that "she knew something about it."

Liz Smith's conclusion that Kilgallen's death was "mysterious" and Earl Ruby and Phyllis McGuire's belief that it was "suspicious," are correct. As expected, plausible conclusions center on circumstantial evidence. If one agrees Richard Kollmar wasn't responsible for Kilgallen's death and Carlos Marcello, or any others in positions of such power, ordered her killed, then one thing is certain: this person would never have been directly involved with the actual murder. Instead, there was the recruitment of one or more trusted operatives to set up, or in fact, eliminate Kilgallen.

There appears little question that stealing and then destroying Kilgallen's JFK thick investigation file must have been part of any murder plot. To date, no one has ever acknowledged reading the file. Based on his extensive research and inside information from Johnnie Ray, biographer Jonny Whiteside[1] wrote: "The fruit of an eighteen-month investigatory work load, [the file] was described by contemporaries as a bulging sheaf of documents,

---

[1] Following the release of his book, *Cry*, Johnnie Ray's biography, Whiteside reported being stalked regarding the information he wrote about Kilgallen. Ray would not divulge to this author the names of those who harassed him.

notes, research, interview transcriptions, contacts, photographs and clippings. She had personally guarded the material, kept it either by her side or under lock and key."

Regarding the veracity of Kilgallen's investigation, Whiteside opined:

Unlike most of the crackpots and paranoids who swiftly joined the chorus, Dorothy's suspicions were grounded on apparent fact and backed up by intense research. Her coverage of the case, before and after the Warren report, was the most aggressive and in-depth being done. Kilgallen not only anticipated many of the theories since endlessly propounded, she was able to explore and attempt to verify specifics at a time when the trail was still fresh. Dorothy's political and underworld contacts were unrivaled within the Fourth Estate, if any reporter had the capability to follow a chain of conspiratorial evidence to its end, it was Dorothy.

* * * * *

As noted, the two men with the most to lose if Kilgallen's investigation triggered a grand jury investigation are J. Edgar Hoover and Carlos Marcello. Since Kilgallen focused her attention on New Orleans, Marcello's home turf, he is suspect number one.

If logic based on motive prevails, the question then arises as to how the desperate Marcello reached his tentacles into New York City through an operative. This operative needed to be in a position of trust. That way Kilgallen could share with him the status of her JFK and Oswald assassination investigation.

This person had to become a member of Kilgallen's circle of close friends. He had to be on the inside. He could then report to Marcello or, more likely one of his associates or underlings whom Kilgallen suspected. The man had to know where the investigation was headed as November 1965 approached.

This person also had to be trusted enough to meet Kilgallen during the early morning hours on the day of her plotted murder. Most likely, it was the same man who met her at the Regency Hotel bar. Who else could it have been unless a person or persons tricked or forced Kilgallen to let them in the townhouse or was lying in wait inside?

If it was Marcello gunning for Kilgallen in November 1965, who would he have used to monitor Kilgallen's investigation? Marcello operated out of New Orleans with his empire stretching to Dallas. He would have needed a New York connection to have access to anyone close to the famous journalist.

One suspect Marcello could have contacted was his mentor and friend, New York City Don Frank Costello. A little-known fact about Kilgallen is that she was actually friends with the dangerous Mafioso, born in 1891 as Francesco Castiglia in Calabria, a province in the toe of Italy.

Few people to date have realized the extent of the relationship between Kilgallen and Costello. A clue to its nature springs from an April 28, 1960 *New York Post Daily Magazine* article uncovered by this author. It was part of the ten-part series called "Dorothy Kilgallen Story: A Post Portrait" published April 20-29 of that year.[2]

Much of the article's content dealt with Kilgallen's *Journal-American* "Voice of Broadway" column, her investigative reporting skills and the radio and television stardom. Featured also was background information about her early days and family and her immense popularity. The writers explained that she was a true media icon whose empire stretched into the various folds of American life through the Hearst syndicated columns and articles in *Cosmopolitan* and *Good Housekeeping* magazines. New York City area residents, the writers noted, could easily find Kilgallen since her investigative reporting on famous trials or other fascinating events appeared on page one of the *Journal-American* and her "Voice of Broadway" column appeared on page five. Those wanting to hear her voice could tune in to *Breakfast with Dorothy and Dick* on the radio and, of course, *What's My Line?* was broadcast on CBS every Sunday night.

The articles also focused on Kilgallen's society life and how she balanced her career with motherhood. It chronicled her friendships with everyone

---

[2] That Kilgallen was featured in a ten-part series by the *Post Daily Magazine* only enhances the celebrity status she enjoyed at the time. Checking the *Post's* articles in the 1960s reveals no indication any other public figure, let alone a woman, was given such widespread coverage.

from Queen Elizabeth II and Prince Phillip to the Duke and Duchess of Windsor to Aldous Huxley to Truman Capote to Elizabeth Taylor and Richard Burton.

Sherman Billingsley, a Costello associate and a former bootlegger who was the founder of New York City's Stork Club, was also quoted. He called Kilgallen "just about the biggest female celebrity around...she was Miss New York." The *Post Daily Magazine* writers spoke of her lofty status, writing, "Wherever Dorothy Kilgallen goes fame precedes her, envy follows her and a crowd looks on. She is one of the communication marvels of the age."

In Part XIII of the series, the *Post* writers noted, "A couple of years ago Kilgallen and a few of her male friends had what they like to call the 'Weekly Science Club.' It meets every Monday afternoon in a reserved alcove of a well-known Third Ave bar for the avowed purpose of discussing new ideas and driving away the Monday blues." The article then named a few of the regulars including Bob Bach, Kilgallen's friend and a *What's My Line?* associate producer.

To complete its coverage of the "Weekly Science Club," the writers revealed that each of the regulars could bring a "mystery guest" to the bar[3] from time to time. The next sentence read, "Dorothy had brought along Tony Perkins [*Psycho*], Sugar Ray Robinson [famous boxer] and Frank Costello, among others." This is apparently the same "Science Club" previously mentioned in the FBI's 1959 memorandum detailing how a female Bureau informant had infiltrated the club. Who this woman was is not identified in the memo nor is any reason given as to why Kilgallen was under surveillance but the fact remains that the Bureau had decided to spy on the famous journalist without her knowledge, arguably a violation of the famous journalist's civil rights.

Regardless, through the years, several authors erroneously summarized the *Post* writers' text. They stated, in essence, "Kilgallen was chummy with [Frank] Costello." This characterization is clearly misleading, blunting the true meaning of what the relationship was between Kilgallen and Costello.

---

[3] The *Post* writers apparently did not want to expose P.J. Clarke's on 3rd Avenue and 55th Street as the bar. There is no question that it was the one they alluded to in the stories.

Her inviting the notorious Costello to her weekly club meant more than them being just "chummy." Instead, it indicated she knew Costello well enough to bring him into her close group of friends as a special guest.[4] Recall also that Johnnie Ray biographer Jonny Whiteside wrote Costello had "occasionally joined [Kilgallen's] table at P.J. Clarke's."

Kilgallen hairdresser Marc Sinclaire confirmed her friendship with the mobster. During his videotaped interview, he said, "At a little Italian restaurant in [Little Italy], we went down there one night, and [Costello] was there and he bought us drinks and was very nice to us. She later told me who he was, I did not know who he was. Maybe we were there just to see him. I'm sure Mr. Costello gave her information but she would never tell me that he did…She knew organized crime figures. She knew a lot of them."

Adding proof to the strong friendship with Costello, Sinclaire stated, "He gave her a diamond cross and she said, 'I can't wear [it] since it is so huge' and so we broke it up and made it into earrings. She wore them a lot."

To understand how dangerous a man Costello was, singer Paul Anka, who knew the mobster from performing at New York City's Copacabana, wrote of him, "He was something: very tough-looking guy, heavy-set, bull-doggish face with greased-back hair and a big cigar…he was the epitome of that whole Mafia thing. Everyone was scared shitless of him."

Why Costello, who made billions for the mob before he retired after being shot in 1957, was a friend of Kilgallen's is a mystery. No information is available clarifying why the friendship existed and exactly when it started. Regardless, Kilgallen must have known of Costello's lofty Mafia affiliation. She either disregarded it or, to give her the benefit of the doubt, used the

---

[4] Besides the friendship between Kilgallen and Costello, the Mafia Don enjoyed a relationship with J. Edgar Hoover. Reports, including one from respected columnist Westbrook Pegler, confirmed that Costello and Hoover met frequently in New York City's Central Park where Costello gave the Director horse racing tips based on the races being fixed. The two men also frequented the Stork Club and one report from Hoover's friend and presidential crony George Allen said that once Hoover and Costello met in a Waldorf barbershop with Hoover telling the gangster, "You stay out of my bailiwick and I'll stay out of yours." Whether Hoover could have made a deal with Costello to silence Kilgallen for both of their benefit, or for just Hoover's, is possible, but no evidence currently exists pointing in that direction. If a deal was made, Hoover could have promised to turn a blind eye toward a criminal allegation against Marcello in return.

relationship to discover information for her column or articles no other source could provide.

For a woman of such high ethical standards, associating with the Mafia Don to the extent of inviting him into her circle of close friends is puzzling. Nevertheless, the friendship existed. Inspecting how it may have affected her death provides some clarity as to why she died, and how.

* * * * *

There certainly was some fascination, some glamour, attached to Mafia figures, including Costello, during Kilgallen's era. In *Five Families*, author Selwyn Raab wrote, "Judges, important politicians, congressman, authors, and New York society and café figures had no qualms about attending soirees that Frank Costello frequently hosted in his penthouse at the Majestic Apartments overlooking Central Park. Tastefully decorated in art deco style, the only ostentatious notes in the apartment were a gold-plated piano and several slot machines."

Noted author Nick Pileggi told this author that gangsters like Costello were called "sportsmen" or simply "gamblers" notwithstanding their underworld connections. That makes it easy to disregard how dangerous a man Costello really was. This was especially true after he seized control of the lethal Charles "Lucky" Luciano crime family in New York City. That family was involved in robbery, theft, gambling and murder.

Costello's power (he commanded 300 soldiers) extended to New Orleans where Carlos Marcello ruled. During the 1940s, Kilgallen's friend Costello expanded his illegal slot machine empire to New Orleans after, Pileggi said, "New York City Mayor Fiorello La Guardia banned slots from the city." All the while, Costello continued to be involved in illegal gambling in Florida and Cuba with notorious crime boss Meyer Lansky. Costello also shared illicit revenues from illegal race wires with Bugsy Siegel in Los Angeles. After he was murdered, Costello's partner was Melvin Belli's client Mickey Cohen.[5]

---

[5] Mickey Cohen was quoted in his FBI file as saying, "With respect to the notorious Frank Costello, Cohen says he considers Costello to be a 'fine gentleman.' He added, 'Frank is a really beautiful and kind human being; really a good man.'" Another entry stated, "Costello was in LA for secret meetings with underworld figures including Mickey Cohen."

NYC Mafia Don Frank "The Prime Minister" Costello.

Costello, a handsome, dashing figure who boasted of bootlegging with Joseph P. Kennedy, had the nickname "The Prime Minister." This was due to his acumen for "fixing" disagreements between the underworld crime families. He enjoyed more political influence with judges and politicians than any other mobster in the country while paying off police to ignore his gambling operations.

Ralph F. Salerno, a New York detective during that era and an expert on organized crime, said of Costello, "A lot of politicians and judges owed their elections and positions to him." Including NYC Judge Thomas Aurelio. Recall that he had faced disbarment charges due to his "friendship" with Costello, his promise to fix cases in return for the mobster's support.

Costello was smart enough to portray a legitimate side. He had his fingers in a poultry company and a chain of "MeatMarts." According to sources, the Mafia Don was a silent partner in the popular Copacabana nightclub Kilgallen frequented. Another source declared that Costello actually was "the owner" of the Copa while using his friend Jack Entratter as the "front."

Splitting hairs over what relationship Kilgallen had with Mickey Cohen's partner and Carlos Marcello's mentor Frank Costello is not as important as is the fact that she obviously *knew him and he knew her*. It is certainly plausible to believe that if Carlos Marcello and his band of thugs needed to orchestrate the death of the famous columnist, Costello, a Marcello loyalist who never hesitated to eliminate anyone threatening him or his friends, was the man to do it. He had access to vital information: where Kilgallen lived, her daily habits, and her close friends.

Bottom line: logic dictates that if Marcello, or Hoover persuaded Costello that Kilgallen needed to be eliminated and her JFK assassination file confiscated and destroyed, Costello, Kilgallen's friend or not, could have set it up.

Critics of this scenario may argue that all of this was simply coincidence. They would say that Marcello's friend Mickey Cohen's lawyer Melvin Belli *just happened* to become Jack Ruby's attorney, that Kilgallen and Belli *just happened* to become fast friends during the Ruby trial, and that Kilgallen *just happened* to be the only reporter who interviewed Jack Ruby during his trial. They would add that she *just happened* to be the one who exposed the Ruby Warren Commission report testimony before it was officially released, and that Kilgallen *just happened* to be the "only serious journalist," to quote Mark Lane, still working on solving the JFK assassination.

Skeptics may also argue that Kilgallen *just happened* to possess a thick file full of 18 months' worth of credible evidence from reliable sources, and that she *just happened* to tell friends days before her death that her life was in danger and "she would crack the case wide open." They'd argue that Kilgallen *just happened* to be a close friend of mobster Frank Costello, that she *just happened* to visit New Orleans with Marc Sinclaire within a month of her death where she scared him with comments about their safety, that Kilgallen *just happened* to be making plans to visit New Orleans which *just happened* to be Marcello's backyard so as to confirm her having connected Marcello, Oswald and Ruby.

These critics may also suggest that Costello *just happened* to be Marcello's mentor and good friend, Costello *just happened* to be connected to Mickey Cohen and Frank Sinatra, Kilgallen's mortal enemy as well as

Mickey Cohen, Belli's client, and that it *just happened* that the very same JFK assassination file disappeared forever. They would suggest that Belli *just happened* to tell his friend Dr. Martin Schorr shortly after he learned of Kilgallen's death "They've killed Dorothy; now they would go after Ruby" to which Belli *just happened* to mention later to secretary Carol Lind upon learning of Ruby's death, "Maybe they injected him with cancer cells." Most revealing is that Kilgallen *just happened* to die within days or arguably, months, of cracking the JFK and Oswald assassination cases wide open.

Either coincidence or reality exists with common sense pointing toward the latter. This conclusion, based on motive, makes sense due to the proven links between Kilgallen and Ruby, Kilgallen and Belli, Kilgallen and Costello, Ruby and Marcello, Ruby and Belli, Belli and Cohen, and Cohen to Marcello and Costello. Those who feared Kilgallen and her JFK assassination file knew what Kilgallen's friend Marlon Swing knew, "[Kilgallen] was a very powerful woman—people don't have any idea of the contacts and power she had…Dorothy had favors she could call in from people all over the world."

Kilgallen, in effect, advertised she was on the brink of solving the JFK and Oswald assassinations based, it seems clear, on the realization she had uncovered a true Mafia hit operation using the word "conspiracy" to describe it. Recall Marc Sinclaire's comment, "I did know from Dorothy finally that there was a conspiracy [to kill JFK]. That it was a group of people, not one. She told me." If Kilgallen told Sinclaire, and boasted to others, as mentioned, that she "was going to crack the case wide open," she imprinted a bullseye on her back as a likely target by those threatened with exposure due to her JFK and Oswald assassinations investigation. Certainly Marc Sinclaire knew of the danger. When investigative reporter Kathryn Fauble's associate told him those at Goodson-Todman productions, producers of *What's My Line?*, refused to discuss Kilgallen's death, Sinclaire wasn't surprised, stating in his videotaped interview, "You could wind up dead."

Maybe Kilgallen believed she was invincible. She was certain that because of her high-profile status, of her star power, that no one could touch her. In her syndicated column of December 15, 1976 entitled "The

Kilgallen Mystery," Kilgallen's rival Liz Smith wrote that Kilgallen told Mark Lane, "I'm going to break this case." When Lane asked her whether she was afraid, she said, "That's all inconsequential. They killed the President of the United States. The government's not prepared to tell us how it happened or who did it. And I'm going to do everything I can to find out what happened."

Wile she soft-pedaled threats, it seems clear that at some point as the tragic weekend in November approached, Kilgallen changed her mind. Recall that she had told Marc Sinclaire and Charles Simpson, "...after I have found out now what I know, if the wrong people knew what I know, it would cost me my life."

Kilgallen was right since the "wrong people" apparently did find out what she knew arguably from someone close to her, possibly a "plant" who leaked confidential information. Identifying the person who may have been responsible requires returning to the "wrong" bed in the "wrong" bedroom where Kilgallen was found wearing false eyelashes, a hairpiece and makeup she never wore to bed, to examine whether she was alone and or in the company of someone intending to harm her.

CHAPTER 30

Based on hairdresser Marc Sinclaire's eyewitness observations about Dorothy Kilgallen's death scene, it is tempting to believe that someone with evil intentions had to be with her in the townhouse's third floor Master bedroom. However, this does not necessarily have to be true. She could have been alone.

Examining which theory makes more sense requires consideration of eyewitness accounts of Kilgallen's time at the Regency Hotel bar. As noted, it was located just six blocks from her townhouse. The key is to focus on a "mystery man" she met during the wee hours of November 8, the day she died.

Several people saw the "mystery man." However, since Kilgallen sat in a dark corner booth with the man, descriptions are for the most part incomplete.

Fortunately, a firsthand account is preserved on videotape by an associate of investigative reporter Kathryn Fauble. The eyewitness is Katherine Stone, a contestant on Kilgallen's final *What's My Line?* program.

The attractive Stone, wearing a low-cut black dress and sporting a pixie haircut, attempted to stump the panel but Kilgallen was too sharp for her. After Tony Randall, Arlene Francis and Bennett Cerf were baffled, Kilgallen guessed that Stone's occupation was selling dynamite. (www.youtube .com/watch?v=PSTgYIABk6w).

Stone, who resided in Madisonville, Kentucky, was asked to join the *What's My Line?* staff at the Regency Hotel piano bar located on a lower level. She recalled in the 1999 videotaped interview that Kilgallen had left

Katherine Stone, a *What's My Line?* contestant and one of the last people to see Kilgallen alive, points to the booth at the Regency Hotel Bar where Kilgallen was engaged in conversation with the "mystery man."

the television studio alone in a CBS limousine before Stone and her friends were transported to the Regency in another limousine.

Commenting on what happened when she entered the cocktail lounge, Stone said, "When we walked in, there was this big beautiful, long baby grand piano, it was over there on the left, and then over to the right, way back in the corner was sort of like a curved booth." Pointing to that area in a photograph, Stone said, "This is where [Dorothy] was, definitely in that corner, right there." (Excerpts from Stone's interview may be viewed at TheReporterWhoKnewTooMuch.com)

Continuing, Stone added, "And the man was sitting right next to her and I mean close because they were talkin' where they didn't want anybody to hear or what, you know. I could see they both had a drink. There wasn't any laughing, people jokin', this and that and the other. They were talkin' and the reason I know this is for the fact I kept an eye on her 'cause I wanted to talk to her afterwards to tell her, you know, that I enjoyed being there, happy she guessed my line, so on and so forth. In other words, you wouldn't have felt like going up there. I knew they were talking business, serious business of some kind. I had that feeling."

Stone admitted she was standing in a group with others and that these people "were enjoying their cocktails" but "I had my eye on Dorothy. I'd look over and what to see what was going on 'cause I wanted to talk to her. So that's the reason I was paying so much attention and I wasn't having many cocktails, you know."

Stone believed Kilgallen was wearing the same clothes in the bar she wore on the *WML?* program "since she wouldn't have had time to go home and change." Stone said she was told the piano player was a favorite of Kilgallen's stating, "she liked his playing but when he finished a song she never clapped. The way she was acting, it was strictly business with her that night; no giggling or laughing."

Asked during the interview if she could identify the man, Stone, unfamiliar with Kilgallen's private life, said she did not know. However, she "had the impression he was younger than Kilgallen."[1]

Once the famous television star's death was reported to be a drug overdose, Stone said, "people wanted to know if I thought she killed herself from drugs and pills and I told them I didn't believe she overdosed. She was as sharp as could be on the program and looked normal at the cocktail lounge. I thought maybe this man might have done something to her, that he might have killed her." Stone agreed that maybe "the man gave her something, got her out of there."

---

[1] Stone's comment that the man was "younger" than Kilgallen causes suspicion that it could have been Johnnie Ray. But no evidence has ever surfaced that it was based on his admissions, or anyone in the bar stating that it was him. During her interview, Stone was not asked specifically if the man talking to Kilgallen was Ray, but since he was such a celebrity, it makes sense to believe that she would have identified Ray if he had been sitting next to Kilgallen.

Asked by the interviewer if perhaps Kilgallen had been "slipped a Mickey Finn," [drugging a drink to render someone senseless], Stone agreed, stating, "This could have happened."[2]

Press agent Harvey Daniels, whose clients included the Regency Hotel, corroborated Stone's recollections of Kilgallen being with a man in the Regency Hotel bar at 1:00 a.m. He saw Kilgallen and said she was "bright, cheery and a little high." When Daniels left a half hour later, he assumed Kilgallen was still sitting in the dark corner with the man. Apparently, Kurt Maier, the piano player in the bar also confirmed the presence of a man with Kilgallen. Neither Daniels nor Maier provided any description of the man.

If a "Mickey Finn" was not the instrument of poison used to end Kilgallen's life, then one must turn to the two barbiturates discovered by Dr. Luke (Seconal and Tuinal) and the three barbiturates that were discovered in her blood stream by Broich—Seconal, Nembutal, and Tuinal. These drugs may serve as guideposts for analyzing what caused Kilgallen's death, and how administration of the drugs may have happened. A question also exists as to why Broich found traces of Nembutal on one of the glasses positioned on the nightstand by Kilgallen's deathbed.

The starting point is to examine the composition of the three drugs in more detail. Each is designated today as a Schedule II narcotic requiring a prescription. All three are barbiturates, among the most frequently employed of the hypnotic and sedative drugs used at the time.

Secobarbital sodium, Seconal, also known as a "Redbirds," "Reds," and "Red Devils," due to having been marketed in red capsules, is a white, odorless, hygroscopic powder. It possesses a bitter taste. The drug is very soluble in water and in alcohol. It is a "short-acting" barbiturate. This means the drug is activated within a person's blood stream in 40 minutes or so dependent on one's weight. Without doubt, the effects of Seconal, commonly

---

[2] While it is certainly possible that a powerful "Mickey Finn," a drink laced with a psychoactive drug or incapacitating agent (especially *chloral hydrate*) was spiked in Kilgallen's drink either at the Regency Hotel bar or perhaps even in her townhouse, a main objection arises concerning this theory. This concern stems from there being no evidence of chloral hydrate noted in Dr. James Luke's autopsy report or in the follow-up analysis by the chemist, John Broich. The ineptness of Dr. Luke's examination may mean negligence occurred but Broich's testing appears to have been professional in nature.

known as sleeping pills are very safe if taken in the proper dosages. When alcohol is mixed with the drug, the Seconal is metabolized more quickly.

How dangerous is Seconal if taken in stronger dosages? The medication is now prescribed in the states of Oregon, Washington, Vermont, Montana and New Mexico for physician-assisted death. This happens through "Death with Dignity" laws.

A step-up on the danger ladder of barbiturates is pentobarbital sodium, Nembutal. It was called "Yellow Birds" or "Yellow Jackets" when marketed on the street as yellow capsules. The drug is white, odorless, crystalline granules or a white powder with a slight bitter taste. It is very soluble in water and alcohol. The latter accelerates its effect below the normal 40-minute range of Seconal.

Nembutal's powerful effects in high doses have led to its use in executions. Both Missouri and Texas have employed the drug for euthanasia purposes. Regarding the risks of a Nembutal overdose, San Francisco clinical pharmacologist Randall Boris told this author, "The problem with Nembutal is that there is a very thin line between taking the right amount and just a bit too much. There's a true low threshold of safety there."

The third drug discovered in Kilgallen's blood stream was Tuinal, "Blue Birds" since it has been marketed in blue capsules. As noted, Tuinal is a combination of the two barbiturates, secobarbital sodium and amobarital sodium. It is a mixture of equal parts. The drug is a white, crystalline, tasteless odorless powder soluble in water and alcohol. Mixed with the latter accelerates its normal effect of 40 minutes or so. Tuinal can cause specific side effects, including headache; dizziness or loss of balance; difficulties with breathing; slow, shallow breathing (respiratory depression) and confusion. Most importantly, recall Tuinal can be very dangerous when abused. Death may result if even a small amount is taken in excess of the prescribed amount.

Regarding the effect of any combination of the three, Seconal, Nembutal, and Tuinal, Boris stated, "That would be quite lethal, shutting down the brain within a short period of time, as short as an hour or less."

Boris also pointed out that each of the three drugs is normally contained in very small capsules. He stated, "It's quite easy to break them apart if someone chooses to do so and then empty the contents into a glass of water or an alcoholic drink. Any mixture with alcohol is very dangerous and speeds up the effect considerably. Basically, what happens is that the person just stops breathing."

Asked by this author to comment on the traces of Nembutal on one glass confiscated by Dr. Charles Umberger and analyzed by chemist John Broich, Boris said "The sodium, salt, in the Nembutal could leave a telltale sign on the rim of a glass." Boris added, "This would happen if the person taking the drug drank from the glass shortly after consuming the Nembutal. That would not happen if the drug had completely dissolved."

Since both Seconal and Nembutal leave some evidence of a bitter taste in any alcoholic drink, it is necessary to mask that taste. Adding quinine is the answer. It is a central ingredient into any combination for example, of gin or vodka, and tonic water. If a 10-ounce glass is used, it could be four parts tonic that includes the quinine, and six parts vodka.

Curious is the absence of any notation of quinine being present in Kilgallen's system in Dr. James Luke's medical examiner documents. Unfortunately, John Broich was never asked about this matter during his audiotaped interview. Neither, in all likelihood, would have known Kilgallen's favorite drink of choice was vodka and tonic.

* * * * *

With this information in mind, if the "mystery man," presumably a "hit man," decided to end Kilgallen's life during the early morning hours of November 8, 1965, he could have spiked her drink with the deadly combination of the three barbiturates. The ticking clock leading up to her death could have started with the two drinking at the Regency Hotel bar.

Regarding the amount of alcohol, arguably vodka, Kilgallen drank, the medical examiner's report provided the only data. It listed the blood alcohol content as 0.15 but, as noted, this was the level mid-afternoon of the 8th, meaning that level was much higher hours earlier when she presumably died. Recall in the ME report the notation that Kilgallen's liver was "fatty," but not "cirrhotic."[3]

---

[3] The medical examiner's conclusion Kilgallen's liver was not damaged should put to rest any speculation she was an alcoholic. This rumor ran rampant at the time and still exists today but is without merit.

Any conclusion as to how much alcohol Kilgallen actually drank is nearly impossible to determine due to their being no follow-up investigation. This confuses any chance of understanding how the three barbiturates in Kilgallen's system could accelerate because of the presence of any alcohol.

Recall that eyewitness press agent Harvey Daniels said that Kilgallen was a "little high." This observation apparently meant that he somehow noticed the effects of the alcohol she had consumed. In this state, the tipsy Kilgallen could have asked the "mystery man" to accompany her back to her townhouse. In the alternative, if she knew him well, perhaps they had planned for him to go there with her all along. Whatever reason, the drum roll to Kilgallen's death would have begun with drinking the vodka setting her up for the drug overdose shortly thereafter.

It is a virtual certainty that Dorothy Kilgallen drank vodka at the Regency Hotel bar based on past habits. However, the possibility that her drink was spiked with a deadly dose of barbiturates at the bar is more difficult to prove. Hairdresser Marc Sinclaire was curious about this aspect of Kilgallen's death, stating, "She was given it [the pills] somehow. I don't know if it had been injected, given in the back of the car, done in a drink. I don't know that and I don't know if she left under her own power from the Regency Hotel."

During his 2015 interviews with this author, former NYC medical examiner's office toxicologist Dr. Donald Hoffman said Kilgallen's drink having been spiked was certainly "possible" but that a "sophisticated drinker would detect the bitter taste of the barbiturates." He said that quinine could have been used to mask the bitterness and that "anyone who was really intoxicated might not notice the bitterness since their mental state would be cloudy."

If, in fact, Kilgallen's drink was spiked, then she may have begun to experience a few signs of the effects of the drugs. This included confusion, unsteadiness, drowsiness, wobbly legs and a possible partial loss of faculties.

Whether anyone besides Harvey Daniels noticed anything unusual about Kilgallen's behavior is impossible to ascertain. Author Lee Israel was apparently banned from speaking to anyone at the Regency Hotel regarding Kilgallen's appearance at the bar. No reason was provided by Israel.

Any of those who saw Kilgallen, if she was unsteady, may have believed she was drunk, or "high" as Daniels stated. Nevertheless, if the "mystery man" had sneaked the drugs into her vodka and tonic while she was in the bathroom or making a telephone call, perhaps to the Western Union manager at 2:00 a.m., then she would have asked him to help her get home. Alternatively, as noted, perhaps the two had planned for an early morning tryst in the townhouse. Either way, Lee Israel concluded from her research that the appearance of the death scene indicated that of a "lover being present." Apparently, Kilgallen having left on her makeup, hairpiece and false eyelashes may have permitted this conclusion, one pointing to Kilgallen having been with someone she knew well, certainly not a stranger but arguably the "late date" she mentioned to Bob Bach.

Conceivably, at Kilgallen's invitation, the "mystery man" could have escorted Kilgallen out of the hotel either through the front door, a side door or a back entrance. Then he would have accompanied her to her townhouse just a few blocks away probably by taxi or in his car. During this time, her unsteadiness most likely increased. Unfortunately, there is no one to provide an account of her mental or physical state from the hotel to her townhouse.

At this point, the question as to whether the "mystery man" entered the townhouse with Kilgallen is important. First, consider the possibility that he did not do so but instead helped her unlock the front door and then vanished into the night.

If this happened, then the "mystery man" with evil intent in his heart, believed whatever barbiturate dosage he spiked into Kilgallen's drink at the bar along with vodka was strong enough to kill her. To sync this with the death scene, Kilgallen, unaware that she had ingested a lethal dose of dangerous drugs, could have wobbled into the elevator. Her destination may have been the "Cloop." As noted, it was located on the fifth floor, the home office where she slept.

Likely, though, Kilgallen would have stopped at the third floor where her pink bathroom, clothes closet and dressing room were located. If the barbiturates were spiked into her drink at the hotel, then she may have felt nauseous. This was a common side effect of the drugs. If this happened, Kilgallen could have decided to seek relief. This would account for her entering her bathroom and swallowing a couple of teaspoons of Pepto Bismal, "pink fluid" discovered in her stomach.

Unsteady and perhaps a bit confused about the lack of mental faculties, Kilgallen, instead of fiddling with the usual bedclothes, may have just shucked the Chiffon dress. She then grabbed the strange nightclothes (Bolero blouse and blue peignoir, or blue robe) from the clothes closet and put them/it on.

According to this plausible scenario, Kilgallen then hobbled back toward the elevator. However, she decided she could not make it to the fifth floor. The logical place to collapse was the nearby Master bedroom. She would have entered and fallen on the bed.

This account, of course, does not answer several questions besides why her makeup, false eyelashes and hairpiece (all noted in the NYC ME documents) were still in place. Among them: How did Kilgallen end up so perfectly positioned in the middle of the "spotless" bed (Sinclaire account, not in ME documents) with covers from neck to toe? (noted in the ME documents) Why was the Robert Ruark *Honey Badger* book she had already read present? (also in ME documents) Why was the nightstand lamp and the air conditioning turned on? (not noted in the ME documents) Why was the empty vial of Seconal pills on the nightstand? (Detective Doyle account; not in ME documents) Why was there a glass, one of two, that had contained alcohol, probably vodka, as suggested by Dr. Charles Umberger, on that same nightstand? (not in ME documents)

If this account appears unlikely, and Kilgallen was indeed murdered, then the possibility exists that the "mystery man" was in the townhouse with her. At one point, she had entertained her lover Johnnie Ray since Richard had caught them leading to his threatening to kill the singer. This means inviting the "mystery man" inside the townhouse could have happened.

Under this scenario, and without any commotion, the two could have quietly entered. Because Kilgallen knew the servants would not return until early morning, there was no worry to wake them on the lower floors.

Richard, Kerry and the tutor were all sleeping on floors above the third. The "mystery man" was thus safe to accompany her as the two entered the elevator. Then they headed toward her bathroom, the clothes closet and her dressing room adjacent to the Master bedroom on the third floor.

Kilgallen, either from the drinking or food she had eaten during the evening, had an upset stomach. While she was gone, the "mystery man" could have offered to fix them both a drink accounting for the two glasses noted by Dr. Umberger.

Following this theory, while Kilgallen was in the bathroom taking the Pepto Bismal, the "mystery man" could have poured vodka into Kilgallen's glass. In all likelihood, this is when he could have broken the barbiturate capsules in two and sifted the deadly powder into her drink. This would account for the barbiturate residue being on one of the glasses.

When Kilgallen reappeared from the bathroom, still feeling woozy, she simply took off her Chiffon dress. She could have then grabbed the strange nightclothes from the closet. Recall that there was an indication, according to Marc Sinclaire, that a lipstick smear was evident on the Bolero blouse. This could have happened after Kilgallen clumsily removed the Chiffon dress and put on the strange nightclothes.

At this point, Kilgallen had not removed her makeup, false eyelashes and hairpiece. Perhaps she still wanted to look good for the "mystery man."

As the minutes passed toward a half hour or so, Kilgallen, after sipping from her drink as she conversed with the "mystery man," could have begun to sink into a state of uneasiness. She may have experienced more confusion while wondering why the drinking was affecting her ability to think straight. Kilgallen, in all likelihood, had trouble keeping her eyes open. It was then that her companion could have helped her into the middle of the bed and covered her up. Slowly, as he watched her die, she was suddenly warm. She could have asked him to turn on the air conditioner.

Within forty-minutes or less dependent on how the combination of Seconal, Nembutal and Tuinal affected her, Kilgallen would have, in all likelihood, experienced bradycardia. This was a slow heart rate accompanied by dizziness and fainting. Try as she may, the famous journalist and television star could not fight back against the poisonous drugs accelerating through her system. At some point, they combined with the vodka to stop her brain from functioning.

If the "mystery man" was responsible for spiking Kilgallen's drink, how did the empty vial of Seconal pills end up on the nightstand? One possibility is that he could have retrieved the vial from her purse or perhaps from the bathroom medicine cabinet. He could have emptied it if it wasn't already empty, and then carefully placed it on the nightstand. When discovered, it served exactly the purpose intended: to throw the authorities, including the medical examiner, off track by immediately heading them in the direction of accidental death.

His mission nearly complete, the "mystery man" could have then left the bedroom but not before he collected Kilgallen's assassinations file, the one that never left her sight. This was another reason to believe he could have been in the townhouse with her. Absconding with the file, as noted, was an important part of his directive.

The "mystery man" then could have quietly exited the townhouse probably using the stairs. Whether he left a fingerprint or two or any other incriminating evidence behind is unknown. There was no follow up search of any of the townhouse rooms by forensic experts.

What bolsters the assumption that the extremely heavy dose of dangerous drugs mentioned above were in Kilgallen's system is the later analysis by Drs. Baden and Hoffman. Based on "the raw data in Dr. Luke's report," the two doctors concluded, "the percentage of barbiturates found in [Kilgallen's] brain and liver indicated that the body reposited the equivalent of fifteen to twenty 100-milligrams of Seconal capsules."

Notice that Drs. Baden and Hoffman did not specify that the capsules *were* in Kilgallen's system. Instead, they opined there was "the *equivalent*"[4] of those capsules. Certainly, the combination of Seconal, Nembutal, or

---

[4] As a point of comparison, when actress Judy Garland of *The Wizard of Oz* fame died in 1969, her blood stream contained the equivalent of ten Seconal capsules. Also, Marilyn Monroe's toxicology report indicated high levels of Nembutal (38–66 capsules) and chloral hydrate (14–23 tablets) in the actress's blood stream. Similarities between the confusion surrounding Monroe's death and that of Kilgallen are obvious based on clues at the death scene with neither woman permitted any proper investigation of their deaths.

Tuinal indicates at least the "equivalent" of the Seconal capsules the two doctors suggested. In fact, what other reason is there for this diagnosis?

Based on this theory, the perfect opportunity had presented itself to kill Kilgallen through the "mystery man." However, the exact means by which she died through ingestion of the three deadly barbiturates is clearly speculation. There was no investigation pinpointing how the drugs entered her body. However, an undeniable fact remains—the three barbiturates *were* in her bloodstream

With this in mind, the analysis by Dr. Donald Hoffman, the toxicologist who viewed the medical examiner's raw data following Dr. Michael Baden's analysis, was correct. Recall that he said of Kilgallen's death, "the formal data indicate that it was acute poisoning due to alcohol and barbiturates *and that [the] barbiturates alone could possibly have killed her.*" [Emphasis added].

Most interestingly, based on the clear presence of the three barbiturates, NYC medical examiner Dr. James Luke had accurately reported the cause of death. It stated that she died of a "combination of barbiturates and alcohol." However, the "circumstances undetermined" words included in the report may now plausibly be determined. There is little doubt Kilgallen died of a combination of the Seconal, Nembutal and Tuinal with the vodka as accelerant. Bottom line: Dorothy Kilgallen was most likely murdered either by the "mystery man" or through his efforts as an accessory. Who was he and did he have any connection to those benefiting from Kilgallen's death?

CHAPTER 31

Targeting the logical suspect who betrayed Dorothy Kilgallen by leaking details of her JFK and Lee Harvey Oswald assassination investigation to those fearing disclosure requires close attention to her inner circle.

This Judas needed to earn Kilgallen's trust in order to learn secrets about both her private life and her professional career. Since she was not one to confide in too many people, it had to be a special relationship, one built over time. The relationship had to be genuine since Kilgallen was an expert at spotting phonies.

As November 1965 appeared, those in Kilgallen's inner circle were few. They included husband Richard, hairdressers Marc Sinclaire and Charles Simpson, family companion and tutor Ibne Hassan, friends Bob and Jean Bach and Marlon Swing, actress Joan Crawford, and Johnnie Ray. Kilgallen's fellow panelists on *What's My Line?* were certainly friends, as was host John Charles Daly, but they were not considered close friends she shared secrets with on a regular basis.

Curiously, the only new member of Kilgallen's inner circle appeared shortly after she covered the Jack Ruby trial. He was also her companion as she continued her JFK and Oswald assassination investigations. His name was Ron Pataky, the new love in the famous journalist's life a year and a half before her death. As of the printing of this book, he is still alive but retired from the newspaper business.

Pataky, by all accounts, was Kilgallen's second major extramarital affair after Johnnie Ray. During his videotaped interview, Marc Sinclaire did not try to excuse Kilgallen's having affairs with both. The only mention of this matter was when Sinclaire stated, "[Dorothy] was lonely, really lonely," an apparent reference to the discord in her marriage with Richard including the absence of any sexual relations. Recall Johnnie Ray biographer Jonny Whiteside writing that shortly after Kilgallen and Ray met, "They found themselves in bed—a cascade of violent release and deep passion...."

Twelve years her junior when he met Kilgallen (51) in June 1964, three months after the Ruby trial, Ron Pataky (39) had a murky past. Consensus appears to be that the two met during a 20th Century Fox European press junket for three upcoming films: *The Sound of Music*, *The Agony & The Ecstasy*, and *Those Magnificent Men in Their Flying Machines*.[12]

During that June, Kilgallen wrote in her *Journal-American* column about the terrific reception she had received in London: "Since I've been in Europe for four days, not keeping up with the newspapers at all, I don't know how things were going at the United Nations, but I could testify that as of this minute in London, British-U.S. relations seem to be better than ever in history. The sun was smiling on England when I landed at London Airport, and the Londoners were smiling on the Americans." She then added three examples of how well the trip was progressing. The first: "At the airport, Ron Pataky, the *Columbus Citizen-Journal* columnist, invited me to ride into town with him. He said to the cab driver: 'I haven't any pounds with me, would you take American money?' The hackie grinned. 'Hop in governor,' he said. 'It's the best money in the world.'"

When author Lee Israel conducted the first extensive interview with Pataky regarding his relationship with Kilgallen in the 1970s, he provided varying versions of when they first met and what transpired from 1964 until Kilgallen died some 17 months later. According to Pataky, the first

---

[1] The cover for the July 6, 1964 issue of *Box Office* magazine featured a Lufthansa Airlines photograph of media invited on the junket. The text read, "The working press section on the tri-roadshow flight which took 110 newsmen to three location sites in Europe." Inside, the list of "junketeers" was posted. Included were the names of Dorothy Kilgallen and Ron Pataky along with Army Archard of *Variety* and Herb Dorfman of ABC-TV.

[2] Louis Sobel wrote in the *Journal-American* that Kilgallen attracted as much attention as the movie stars did during the junket. They included Charlton Heston and Julie Andrews. Sobel said Kilgallen called Heston "Chuckles"; he called her "Dottie."

encounter happened in Salzburg, Austria, not London, on the set of *Sound of Music*. Pataky said Kilgallen tripped while entering a bus and he caught her whereupon she acted "flirtatiously" leading to their having drinks at a local restaurant.[3]

Pataky covered entertainment for his newspaper. His sturdy build and good looks had already captured the hearts of celebrity women. They included Frank Sinatra's future wife, Mia Farrow and Italian operatic singer and sultry actress, Anna Maria Alberghetti. At one point, Alberghetti and Pataky were engaged to be married.

Midwest Today publisher Larry Jordan asked Pataky during a mid-2000s audio-recorded interview why he was attracted to Kilgallen, a woman so many years his senior. He replied, "For all of her brashness in print, she was very poetic…[Dorothy] was a dyed-in-the-wool romantic, to be sure. A very soft person. I never saw her angry. I don't think, other than strictly business, something like discussing the Jack Ruby thing, Dorothy and I ever had a serious conversation…. She was a sweet lady, my best friend in the whole world."

Pataky, who told Jordan he introduced Kilgallen to his mother, swore the year-and-a-half affair was platonic in nature. He said, "[We'd] shuck the rest of these phonies and go off and do our thing. And we made trips together. We went to Florence together, we went to London together…We'd kiss hello on the cheek if I was coming to town [New York City]. But there was no goodnight kiss when I dropped her off, and I dropped her off a lot of times. Because it wasn't that kind of relationship. Never. I had my girlfriends. She knew about them…we never, ever spent any time in a hotel room."

Pataky's blanket denial appears dubious. The couple had traveled to Rome and Florence in October 1964. No proof exists that they shared a hotel room or spent time in one together but author Lee Israel, based on her extensive research, noted, "In her girlish fiction, Dorothy Mae could

---

[3] A Canadian broadcasting network crew from the program *This Hour Has Seven Days* joined the junket and seven months later, on January 10, 1965, it aired a segment including interviews with several of the three film's stars including Julie Andrews, Rex Harrison, Charleton Heston and Sarah Miles. Kilgallen is on-camera several times and also interviewed regarding time spent with Heston. Lurking in the background is Ron Pataky as he takes photos of Julie Andrews. Video available at www.TheReporterWhoKnewTooMuch.com.

not have fantasized a more romantic ambiance for a love affair" adding that the two walked the streets of Florence enjoying each other's company as they surveyed the historical landscape.

Kilgallen's hairdresser Marc Sinclaire disagreed with Pataky's version of his relationship with the famous columnist. In early 1965, Sinclaire recalled, daughter Jill, married at the time, visited the townhouse. Pinpointing minute details, the hairdresser stated in his videotaped interview, "It was chilly because Jill had a sweater on and she was very angry. I was doing Dorothy's hair when she walked in from the service entrance and stood in the corner. She leaned against the dresser and stared at Dorothy. She and I were surprised the way [Jill] stormed into the room with venom in her voice and eyes."

According to Sinclaire, Jill confronted her mother. The hairdresser said Jill, "was very angry. She mentioned Pataky by name and said she was highly infuriated because her mother was going out with this man and sleeping with him all over town." Jill added, according to Sinclaire, "It's just too embarrassing to be seen in public with you."

When Jill left, Sinclaire said Kilgallen cried. Then she said, "I don't know why Jill wants to behave this way. She knows about her father and his indiscretions. I've told her. And she knows a lot of other things. I will never see Jill again in public." "And she never did," Sinclaire added." They were never able to patch things up before she died."[4]

Sinclaire recalled that the argument was so ugly he walked away from fixing Kilgallen's hair. He stood to the side while anger prevailed. Kilgallen's friend Marlon Swing also was aware of the argument. How Jill learned of the affair her mother was having with Pataky is unknown.[5]

In his videotaped interview, Sinclaire, who said Pataky wanted to "keep the affair very quiet," speculated on where the couple may have

---

[4] In an audiotaped interview, Sinclaire explained the Kilgallen/Jill confrontation nearly verbatim to the videotaped version of the story. He added, among other details, that the confrontation had taken place "a week or three or four weeks before [Kilgallen] died before all this [with Pataky] started to bubble over."

[5] Efforts by this author to extensively interview Jill during fall 2014 and 2015 proved unsuccessful. Before one brief conversation ended, this author asked whether she knew Ron Pataky and recalled the argument. Jill replied, "I never heard of him."

rendezvoused. He said, "[There] were several places [Kilgallen] could have [gone] with Pataky. One was my apartment, and there was [interior designer] Howard Rothberg's house. She could have gone to either. She had a key to [my apartment] and she had a key to his [Rothberg's]. When Sinclaire asked Kilgallen "Why are you going to a hotel?" the hairdresser said Kilgallen told him, "He [Pataky] wants to.'"

These hotels included the Regency where Pataky, who had Kilgallen's unlisted "Cloop" telephone number,[6] resided when he was in New York City. According to a woman who handled room assignments, Kilgallen had booked the room for Pataky, stating, "The keys were given to her." Sinclaire confirmed this fact in his interview "I know she met Ron there. They kept a room upstairs that she would go to. They often met there. Dorothy liked that place because you could go in two, three different entrances, the lobby and go. into the bar, you could go off the street and go in the bar, and you could go through the back entrance around to it."

The 2007 *Midwest Today* article mentioned a note discovered from Kilgallen to Pataky. Romantically themed, it mentioned "our little room on the 19th floor." By all accounts, it was at the Regency, now the Loews Regency at 540 Park Avenue in New York City.[7]

Asked in his videotaped interview whether Pataky had a "romantic streak," Marc Sinclaire said, "[Pataky gave her] notes and cards. I don't know about flowers. Once he sent her some cut-out valentines. And they all strung apart. Which she showed me."

Kilgallen's friend Marlon Swing disagreed with Pataky's assessment of the relationship stating, "She was like a little girl after her first date, going on about how they'd met, how marvelous he was, the moonlight and the clouds and the poetry he had recited to her. It was obvious that he had become very important."

---

[6] In his videotaped interview, Marc Sinclaire recalled Kilgallen calling Pataky from the "Cloop." When asked if Kilgallen's phones were tapped, he replied, "I think they were tapped but I don't know how much she was using them for [her investigation]. I think she was using her phones to talk to Ron Pataky but that was the phone up in the Cloop. She slept there and she spent a lot of time there. She was alone there. She didn't let anyone near her."

[7] In late 2015, this author visited the Loews Regency hoping to view the same surroundings Kilgallen experienced in the 1960s. Various remodeling efforts through the years made this impossible.

Dorothy Kilgallen's Ron Pataky romance raises issues with his complicity in her death.

Pataky's feelings for Kilgallen apparently were conflicted. "Ron swore to me he had never had intimate relations with Dorothy," Larry Jordan told this author, "and spoke of the mere idea as being repugnant to him due to her unattractiveness. But yet he heaped praise on her and called her his best friend."

During their interview, Larry Jordan confronted Pataky with the love note from Kilgallen to him. He also mentioned the romantic relationship between the two, something "her hairdressers confirmed." Jordan said "Pataky was still so insistent he was not sexually involved with Dorothy."

Kilgallen's letters to Pataky appear to say otherwise. Each has the sense of being from a woman interested in much more than a "friendship." One, signed in Kilgallen's handwriting, reads:

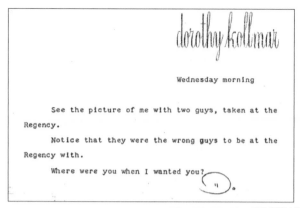

Interpretation of what Kilgallen meant by "I wanted you" is subject to conjecture but suggests Kilgallen had intimacy on her mind. At the least, the letter points to a previous rendezvous between the couple at the Regency Hotel.

A second letter, written September 22, 1965, is more revealing. Written within a short time before Kilgallen died, but after, as Marc Sinclaire noted, her trip to Switzerland, it reads

Use of the words "Sweetie" and "Kisses" and her admitting, "I miss you," again portend of more than the simple friendship Pataky swears he had with Kilgallen before she died. When shown the letters, he dismissed

any noting of intimacy telling author Israel there was no reference to "his body" or any sexual relationship.

* * * * *

Focusing on Kilgallen's death and curious as to whether Pataky may have been involved, Larry Jordan asked the columnist his whereabouts on the day she died. Pataky defended himself stating, "…I was in Columbus, Ohio—in my office—at eight in the morning. That's where I was horrified to receive the news of Dorothy's death…with a newspaper city room utterly jammed with witnesses all of whom knew Dorothy from her visits to my office. Moreover, phone records, from Columbus—placed me here until well past midnight that night."

Pataky's "alibi" conflicts with other accounts. Investigative reporter Kathryn Fauble revealed to this author that one of the main "alibi witnesses" Pataky mentioned did not back up his story.

Pataky said that "a fashion editor named Jane Horrocks" read the sad news of Kilgallen's death from the newspaper newswire to him. Fauble contacted Horrocks who wrote Fauble a 1998 letter this author has read. In it, Horrocks, whose byline in 1965 was Jane Kehrer before she changed it to Jane Kehrer Horrocks following a marriage, wrote, "I most certainly remember Ron Pataky. We shared an office at the *Citizen-Journal*…Ron was one of the busiest on the paper and was of necessity frequently out of the office…So it was that I took a number of telephone calls for him and Dorothy Kilgallen was frequently among those who called." Recalling November 1965, Horrocks added, "At the time of her death I was covering fashion showings in California so I cannot furnish any details."

Larry Jordan confronted Pataky with his suspicions that the journalist was being less than truthful about his whereabouts on the weekend of Kilgallen's death. Jordan said Pataky became belligerent. He then stated, "The next day [Monday] I had been in my office [in Columbus, Ohio] from 8 o'clock on," before asking, "What did I do…hire my own jet, fly [to New York], kill her, and then fly back in a hurry?," a response that surprised

Jordan who had not accused Pataky of any wrongdoing or even brought up the subject.

Also countering Pataky's claim that he was in Columbus was Kilgallen's friend Bob Bach, the *What's My Line?* associate producer. He was the same person who met Kilgallen at P. J. Clarke's for a short time immediately after her *WML?* appearance on the night of November 7th. Recall that Bach said Kilgallen told him she had a "late date" but later explained that he "was under the impression the date was with Ron Pataky." The reason: there was no one else at that time that she would have called a "date." That the "late date" was at the Regency Hotel where Pataky stayed adds credence to Bach's assumption.

Pataky's refusal to admit he was in New York City on November 7th or 8th included his resistance to admit he was at the Regency Hotel Bar that weekend. Lee Israel had apparently located three people who believed Kilgallen was meeting Pataky after going to P.J. Clarke's. He continued to deny this happened while stating that his mother had told him about Kilgallen's death in Columbus. He also stated he did not recall being in New York City for two to three weeks after she died.

Pataky never acknowledged a visit to New York City to rendezvous with Kilgallen between September 22 and November 8. He did admit, to author Israel, to speaking to Kilgallen on the telephone at 12:30 a.m. early morning Monday, November 8. Pataky said he could not recall the exact substance of the conversation but that it wasn't memorable. Based on eyewitness accounts, Kilgallen would have been in the Regency Hotel bar at the time.

In a mid-2000s interview, this time with an associate of investigative reporter Kathryn Fauble, Pataky varied his story a bit. He said it was his "best memory that we talked the night before Dorothy died" since "we usually called on the weekends." While telling Fauble that he could not recall what the two talked about, Pataky then stated, "the last time we spoke she was in great spirits. When you lose someone close to you, you remember that. She was alright with the world." Closing the interview, Pataky recalled that he heard about Kilgallen's death "while sitting in the office. It [Kilgallen's death] was on the wire. All hell broke loose."

Regarding the 12:30 a.m. telephone call with Kilgallen, Pataky also mentioned it during his interview with Larry Jordan. He swore she was not suicidal, that "she was just normal. She always called herself my New York secretary and Suzie Creamcheese." Pataky also admitted, according to Jordan, "to circulating in the underworld, to knowing mobsters including Sam Giancana." Asked to be more specific, Pataky said, "I knew Sam Giancana[8] through [singer] Phyllis McGuire.[9] Drunk one night, I tried to put the make on her. That didn't work...."[10] Jordan said Pataky, "bragged he knew all those guys [in the underworld]. He also knew mobsters who were involved with Hollywood. He knew a lot of people."

Like author Lee Israel, Larry Jordan had reservations about Pataky's credibility. Jordan suspected that Pataky was almost "too helpful" during his interview. One journalist who requested anonymity while speaking to this author went a step further. She said of Pataky, "He was either a nice guy who had gotten a bad rap through the years from the media or a pathological liar."[11]

To Larry Jordan's surprise, Pataky telephoned Jordan in September 2014 after they had not spoken for many years. Among the revelations Pataky told Jordan was that New York City police interviewed him after Kilgallen's death. Asked how the authorities would have known about him, Pataky said they discovered a note with his name on it on the nightstand in the bedroom where the authorities found Kilgallen's body. This story

---

[8] In his book, *My Way*, singer Paul Anka wrote, "[Giancana] was seen around town [Las Vegas] with one of the McGuire sisters, Phyllis, a beautiful all-American looker with a lot of hit records."

[9] On September 16, 1964, Ron Pataky, in his Columbus newspaper column. lauded the theatrical production of "Little Me" starring Phyllis McGuire. He wrote, "You'll love Phyllis McGuire. Young Belle's transparent innocence [comes across] perfectly and [McGuire is] singing her numbers beautifully. I can truthfully say that I enjoyed ' Little Me' more than any Kenley production of the entire summer."

[10] In a CIA file entitled "CIA Inspector General's Report on Plots to Assassinate Fidel Castro," there is the notation that Kilgallen was friendly with Phyllis McGuire. According to this account, the two were seen at the Copacabana. The notation reads, "Johnny Roselli [Mafia associate of Sam Giancana] found himself facing a table at "ringside" at which Phyllis McGuire was sitting with Dorothy Kilgallen and Liberace for the opening night of singer Rosemary Clooney."

[11] Most curious regarding Pataky's mental state was his later career change after he was fired by the Columbus newspaper in 1980. He attended Jerry Falwell's Liberty University where he earned a Master's degree in Christian Counseling. This was followed by further education through a Ph.D. in Christian Counseling from Trinity Theological Seminary.

appears dubious since no mention of any note or the police contacting Pataky appeared in any report. Recall that Detective John Doyle never told Lee Israel of the note or any knowledge of Pataky even existing in Kilgallen's life let alone contacting him.

Pataky also never mentioned either the note or the police contacting him before in any of the many interviews he has given. This included the one with an associate of investigative reporter Kathryn Fauble.

More revealing is that Pataky disclosed to Larry Jordan, "Dorothy lived in a lavish townhouse but I never set foot in it." He also suggested that she could have died of an overdose since "she was a boozer and pill popper." Pataky then admitted, "I saw her take pills, many times. I saw them in her medicine cabinet."

Most curious was Ron Pataky's failure to attend Kilgallen's funeral despite their lengthy relationship. He did not explain why to Lee Israel or Larry Jordan.

CHAPTER 32

To date, no one has positively identified Kilgallen's companion, "the mystery man," at the Regency Hotel bar during the early morning hours of November 8, 1965. Pataky swore it was not him but his inconsistent/conflicting statements blemish the account of his having been several hundred miles away in Ohio.

One incident in particular causes confusion. This happened following Kilgallen's most recent trip to New Orleans on October 24, 1965, 15 days before she died. Marc Sinclaire said in his videotaped interview that just before a *What's My Line?* program began, "Dorothy told me that they announced over a loudspeaker connected to the dressing room that she had a phone call from Ron Pataky that he was leaving the key for her from the Regency Hotel and it would be at the desk. And she was very upset about it." Asked why Kilgallen was upset, Sinclaire answered, "Because everybody in the studio knew she was gonna meet a man at the Regency Hotel." Sinclaire said some of her colleagues may have known about Pataky but "not all, not the whole shebang." Told Ron Pataky didn't want to draw attention to himself, Sinclaire explained, "Dorothy didn't want [their affair] known either, I don't think, not like that. She was still a married lady."

According to Sinclaire, it "rattled Dorothy" to the extent that "she was so shaken up that as the show began and the panelists were introduced, Dorothy sat down too soon, and then quickly got up again, the only time that happened since the panelists started showing off their Sunday formal wear in 1954."

Pataky told Larry Jordan the incident "seems odd...I remember that story. They weren't my keys. I was not there then." Pataky later changed his mind, telling Jordan, "I was there...sitting in the audience...Dorothy liked me to attend the show and I did several times."[1]

This statement also connects with the recollection from Mark Sinclaire of speaking to Kilgallen Saturday, November 6, two days before her death. In the 1990s videotape interview, Sinclaire elaborated on the call:

> We talked for about an hour. Her life had been threatened. Finally, I said, "the only new person in your life is Beau Pataky. Why don't you ask him if all this information that is slipping out about you is coming from him?" [Because] she was concerned where people were getting the information from. After finally, after exhausting me over what was going on, I'm the one that suggested that she confront Beau Pataky with it. I called him "Beau" because that's what she called him. And she was dead after that. Two days later.

In a separate audiotaped interview, Sinclaire said, "Dorothy was worried about dying." Asked if this was when she was considering buying the gun, Sinclaire replied, "Yeah, that was two weeks before she died and then the Saturday before the Sunday, the Monday she died and we discussed it for hours on the phone and that's when I said, 'Well, what about Beau?' You know we'd narrowed it down to just about everyone we could think of that was harassing and threatening her. That's the only time I took her seriously [about dying.] and of course, it was much too late. Up until then I didn't think anyone could touch her."

Sinclaire recalled that Kilgallen had also said, "You know, I have had threats on my life," and when he asked, "by whom?" she simply replied, "People," the only time Kilgallen ever specifically referred to those who were threatening her. After they discussed who might have been leaking her JFK investigation information, and Sinclaire mentioned Pataky, Sinclaire said, "There was a long pause and then Dorothy said, 'maybe.'"

---

[1] During an audio interview with researcher Kathryn Fauble, Pataky asked "Was *What's My Line?* on the weekends? When the interviewer said "Yes, on Sunday nights," Pataky appeared surprised as if he had no idea despite admitting he watched the show, one that aired on Sunday's for fifteen years.

Sinclaire, who stated he saw Pataky "at a distance" once at P.J. Clarke's but never met him, said, "Strange things were afoot after the New Orleans trip." Commenting on that trip, Charles Simpson declared, as noted, "She had obviously dug up something about the JFK assassination that someone didn't want her to know."

Pataky denied Sinclaire's account that Kilgallen had confided in him about her JFK assassination investigation. He told Larry Jordan, "...there's a lot that Dorothy didn't tell me. Clearly, she didn't want to worry me. She danced around problems. She did not want to tell me, for example, that she'd had death threats." [This comment triggers the question as to how Pataky knew of the death threats if Kilgallen did not share them with him.]

Concerning Kilgallen's frame of mind about Pataky, who was an aspiring songwriter, as November 8 neared, Marc Sinclaire had a definite opinion. In his interview, he said, "I would imagine that she was upset about Beau [Pataky]. I think he was the snitch, she was telling him so much [about the JFK assassination investigation], and that's that."

If Pataky was indeed the "mystery man" seen with Kilgallen during the final few hours of her life, his connection to Sam Giancana "and all those guys in the underworld" including "mobsters who were involved with Hollywood," appears relevant. As noted, Giancana was linked to Melvin Belli's client Mickey Cohen, and to Marcello and Frank Costello. Pataky certainly could have been a logical choice if any of the underworld figures, most likely Marcello, needed to eliminate Kilgallen. Under orders to shadow[2] Kilgallen by any of these dangerous men, or on his own accord, Pataky could have reported every move she was making toward her "cracking the [assassination] case wide open."

If this happened, if Pataky was monitoring Kilgallen, he knew she was too close to the fire, too close to exposure of those who feared her fresh evidence. He also could have known that she planned another trip to New Orleans in November to collect further evidence important to her continuing investigation. Perhaps she told him, as Jonny Whiteside mentioned,

---

[2] Kilgallen's friend CBS producer Marlon Swing was suspicious of Pataky stating, "Here was a new man in her life, one suddenly romancing her and prompted by somebody not necessarily himself but by some faction."

that she was connecting Oswald and Ruby, and, in addition, both men to Carlos Marcello. If he divulged this secret to the dangerous people who had recruited him to watch Kilgallen, a plan to eliminate her could have been set in motion.

Targeting Ron Pataky as the one most likely to be the mysterious man Kilgallen met during the early morning hours in the Regency Hotel bar seems quite plausible. Logically speaking, who else can it be that Kilgallen was sitting "close to" as described by Katherine Stone? Pataky was the only one she was dating, the only love interest in her life at the time since she and husband Richard were at odds and Johnnie Ray was a past romance. Those closest to her, including Marc Sinclaire, Charles Simpson and Bob Bach never mentioned her interest in another man aside from Pataky.

Perhaps most telling is that during the years following Kilgallen's death no one has ever come forward to disclose he was the one who met her within a few hours of her death. There would have been no risk in doing so *unless* the "mystery man" was instrumental in causing her death.

The potential that Pataky was the "mystery man," the one betraying her, recalls Marc Sinclaire's statement that he suspected Pataky was responsible for "strange events" happening during the few weeks prior to her death. If Kilgallen took Sinclaire's advice to "confront" Pataky regarding these strange events, then it is logical Kilgallen contacted Pataky and voiced her concerns. He, in turn, may very well have telephoned her before she appeared on her final *What's My Line?* program. This would confirm Sinclaire's suspicions that Kilgallen received a call after he left the townhouse. It would also provide a reason for Kilgallen changing dresses from the long, flowing one to a more comfortable dress in anticipation of her "late date."

If Pataky telephoned Kilgallen after she "confronted" him, the two could have agreed to meet later. This could have given him an opportunity to dissuade her from believing he had been leaking information about her JFK assassination investigation. Perhaps the early morning hour "date" was due to Pataky flying to New York City for the rendezvous. Or perhaps he was already in the city staying at the Regency.

* * * * *

The Ron Pataky that Kilgallen loved at the time was not simply a mild-mannered entertainment reporter and columnist from Ohio. Instead, he was a man with a propensity for violence. The first instance happened, according to a front-page story in the *Columbus Evening Dispatch* on December 5, 1963, less than two weeks after the JFK and Oswald assassinations and seven months before Kilgallen began an affair with the journalist.

The headline read, "Pataky Arrested; Slugged He Says: Party With Anna Maria Alberghetti at Friend's Home Ends Roughly." Beside the article appeared a photograph of the two holding hands.

The article's opening paragraph read, "Ronald A. (Ron) Pataky, 28, theater and movie critic for the *Columbus Citizen-Journal*, claimed Friday he was beaten and manhandled by police officers after he accidently cut his head at a friend's home Thursday morning after a drinking party." The reporter added, "Miss Alberghetti confirmed Pataky's story of the events leading to his arrest under charges of drunkenness and resisting arrest."

According to the report, the melee happened at the Columbus home of jazz bandleader Alvin F. Waslohn. Pataky was quoted as saying, "As we [he and Alberghetti] were leaving, I slipped on a rug. I hit the glass on the door. It broke and I cut my head." Concerning the allegation that he was "beaten and manhandled," Pataky said he entered the police vehicle quietly "as an injured man being taken to the hospital for treatment."

Police officer Charles West disagreed, telling the reporter he and a fellow officer had to "subdue Pataky" and that West gave him "a black eye" after Pataky "threatened him and used foul language." The report also quoted a duty patrol sergeant. He stated, "I was called to Riverside Hospital because Pataky was raising hell with the doctors and wouldn't lie down so they could examine him." Asked whether Pataky appeared to be intoxicated, the officer said, "Oh brother." Officer West added that Pataky had apologized explaining that he "was emotionally upset because of some disagreement with Miss Alberghetti."

Author Lee Israel provided a different account of the disturbing episode. She noted Pataky was an attractive man who had relationships with several young actresses, but they were short-lived when they realized he had a drinking problem. Israel also recounted one disturbing encounter when

Pataky, apparently inebriated, picked up a table and threw it across a room. The police were called with the actress, who asked not to be named, stating, "Something in Ron's brain clicked when he drank and he went bananas," while adding that Pataky admitted previous instances like that one including his having rammed his car into five others leading to the relationship ending.

Israel did not identify the woman in her book but in a 1992 letter she forwarded to investigative reporter Kathryn Fauble, the author indicated the "Italian beauty" was Anna Maria Alberghetti. She told Israel she recalled Pataky being intoxicated and "violent and nutsy" while confirming he had thrown a table causing the police to arrive.

Years later, in April 1971, according to a front-page article in the *Columbus Dispatch*, Pataky was involved in a bizarre incident in Ohio. The victim was National Football League running back Jim Otis. This happened during a time when Pataky was attempting to handle public relations for the Columbus Police Department.

On its front page, the *Dispatch* reported:

> Suburban Upper Arlington Police are continuing their investigation of conflicting stories in a shooting incident involving a theater editor, Ronald Pataky of the *Columbus Citizen-Journal*, and James Otis, former Ohio State University and Celina High School football star. Police reported that no one was hurt in the shooting and that no charges have been filed. Several shots had been fired at Pataky's residence early Tuesday.
>
> Pataky reported to Police that he and Otis had become involved in an argument. Otis, now a Columbus restaurant owner and member of the Kansas City Chiefs professional football team, told Police that Pataky threatened him with a blackjack and that four shots were fired at him as he left the editor's house. Pataky also told Police that Otis had fired a shot at him.

A follow-up article sported the headline "Pataky Faces Pistol Charge." It read, in part:

> Ronald Pataky, *Citizen-Journal* theater editor. was charged with discharging a firearm Tuesday after he admittedly fired four shots after a ruckus with former Ohio State football star Jim Otis. No charges were filed against Otis, 22, of 5026 Dierker Rd.

Otis left the house with a blackjack which he said hetook from Pataky. As he drove off, Pataky fired a .38-caliber pistol four times… Although Pataky told policeOtis fired once at him, police did not find a weapon in Otis' possession…. Neighbors reported hearing four shots.

At the time, Pataky was carrying an Auxiliary Police badge permitting him to arrest people while his appointment to handle public relations for the police department was pending. Because of the Otis incident, police officials revoked his temporary badge. He did not become the police department's PR representative.

Pataky's possession of a blackjack is quite alarming. However, his having attempted to kill Otis is quite another matter. From the official account of the incident, it also appears Pataky lied about Otis having shot at Pataky.

Without doubt, Ron Pataky wanted to be important, wanted to be a star like Kilgallen. He was ambitious, a social climber, a namedropper. In October 2014, he suddenly posted a photograph of himself and Robert Redford on Larry Jordan's Facebook page. One of Pataky and Kilgallen is posted on Pataky's website.

To his credit, Pataky was an attractive man who wooed famous women like Dorothy Kilgallen. He took it a step further, boasting to Larry Jordan that he had "dated half the women in Hollywood."

CHAPTER 33

Through the years since Dorothy Kilgallen's death, Ron Pataky agreed to several interviews. The first happened when author Lee Israel spoke to him at his home in Columbus, Ohio in the 1970s. She kept his identity secret, calling him the "Out-of-Towner," but it was clearly Pataky.

Kilgallen's "last love" then permitted an interview in 1992 with an associate of investigative reporter Kathryn Fauble mentioned before. Pataky also spoke to *Midwest Today* publisher Larry Jordan as previously mentioned. This happened during the mid-2000s and again in early fall 2014.

On October 22, 2014, this author telephoned Pataky in Columbus. After gaining permission to audiotape the interview, the conversation lasted for more than an hour. By design, the important aspects of his relationship with Kilgallen became the focus. This included specific subjects he had discussed with previous interviewers.

Pataky was quite friendly. He pronounced himself in good health. He complained about the rising costs of health care but otherwise claimed life was pleasant. Point by point, he then answered questions displaying a sharp mind while not displaying too much emotion. That is, until this author pressed him on certain inconsistencies in the statements he had given since Kilgallen's death. Then Pataky appeared to lecture, to become defensive while attempting to ingratiate himself with cute quips. They included, "you sound like a nice guy" revealing a charming manner that seemed a bit excessive.[1] [2]

Questioned about where he met Kilgallen in 1964, Pataky insisted it was in Salzburg, Austria during the 20th Century Fox press junket for three films. Instead of elaborating, he quickly added, "I never read *Kilgallen* [Lee Israel's book]; Israel was such a fool" and "a real piece of work." Pataky said people had told him "bits and pieces" about the book. This statement conflicts with a previous Pataky audiotaped interview where he mentioned, "what Israel said" in her book impossible unless he had read at least parts of the book.

His voice increasing in volume, Pataky then chastised those who believed he had something to do with the killing of Kilgallen as "Fools. someone with a 'Bigfoot' mentality." Pataky emphasized, "I am telling you the truth about what I've said."

Pataky called Kilgallen a "wonderful, wonderful friend," and said, "We talked nearly every day." He added that Kilgallen wanted more of a romantic relationship. However, he said, "This was about the time I got engaged to Anna Maria Alberghetti. I'd drop Dorothy off and go to P. J. Clarke's or the Plaza and she'd ask, 'can I go with you?' and I'd say 'no,' you've got to do a column and it's one o'clock in the morning."

The former Columbus newspaperman acknowledged, "Kilgallen liked to write romantic-sounding things, little notes," but "I stayed away from that." He then said Lee Israel interviewed him at his Ohio home and that she appeared "angry." He stated he felt Israel "was a dyke who had a crush

---

[1] On the day after the October 22, 2014 interview, Mr. Pataky called this author. It was clear that he had researched my background and credentials. He alluded to people I had written about whom he knew from his newspaper days. He was quite friendly and promised to send me a book he thought I would enjoy. He also provided me with his Website address (nembula-series.us). It references "Ron Pataky's Internationally-Acclaimed Photographic Art Form." Mr. Pataky asked if I knew that his artwork had been praised by many celebrities including four ex-presidents. Among the celebrities mentioned are Sir Laurence Oliver, Vincent Price, George Lucas, John Glenn, and Diane Feinstein.

[2] On October 27, this author sent Pataky an email through the address Pataky had provided. Several follow-up questions were asked including how the police knew how to contact him, if they did, following Kilgallen's death and why they wanted to talk to others at the newspaper as to whether he was in the office on the morning of Nov. 9, 1965. Pataky was also asked to comment on another poem displayed on the internet that was attributed to him that appeared to be directly connected to Kilgallen. Pataky did not respond to that email. On November 5, 2014, a copy of Pataky's self-published book, *Behold: The Funniest Funnies Ever*, arrived at my San Francisco office. He also sent a copy of a brochure promoting "The Nebula Series Photographs: An American Art Form."

on Kilgallen." Pataky said Israel, whom he called "mentally-shorthanded" in another audiotaped interview, seemed surprised "that a Midwesterner like me would be so close to [Dorothy]."

When asked whether he could understand why people might suspect that he was involved in Kilgallen's death, Pataky replied boldly, "WHY DO I GIVE A DAMN? [These people] need to get a life." Regarding Marc Sinclaire, Pataky said, "He was a pain in the ass." Asked why he believed this true, he answered, "Dorothy told me. He had every fault in the world for a hairdresser."

Pataky, informed that Sinclaire stated Kilgallen had shared with him the romantic nature of the relationship, commented, "Dorothy would never; Dorothy would never have said that. Mark Sinclaire is a hairdresser. I rest my case."

Asked if Kilgallen had confided in him about the JFK assassination, Pataky first admitted meeting Melvin Belli with Kilgallen "a couple of times in New York City." He then acknowledged that she did confide in him, stating, "Sure, we worked on it. I think she was probably 50% researched on that. She was getting close, I can tell you...if you have 50% of your project finished, it's all downhill from there. The other 50% is filling in the blanks, you know."

Asked how he learned of Kilgallen's death on November 8, 1965, Pataky insisted, "Stories that have been published have varied. I don't have any use for gossip. And I became a center of gossip. Never did like gossips."

Departing from his calm demeanor, Pataky's voice level elevated when confronted with stories his mother Daisy in Columbus had told him about Kilgallen's death. Raising his voice, he told this author, "THAT'S THE STUPIDEST THING I EVER HEARD OF. WHY WOULD I EVER SAY ANYTHING AS OUTRAGEOUSLY UNTRUE AS THAT?"

In a departure from when the true time of Kilgallen's death was announced, mid-to-late afternoon of November 8, Pataky said he had heard about it "earlier in the day," impossible since no announcement was made then. He said his mother called later. "It was a terrible event for her as well," he said, "Dorothy had bought her gifts, small gifts, and we'd gone out to eat...[Mom] was very upset."

Pataky complained about "half truths" that had been spoken through the years. Asked about Jane Horricks, the newspaper fashion editor, he confirmed that he shared a "glass cubicle" with her and a "third person named Ben Hayes, a columnist." Pataky said he was alone in the office space since Hayes and Horricks had not arrived yet "that morning." He added, "one of the copy kids came in and said, 'Ron, is Dorothy Kilgallen dead?' I said, 'no,' and about ten minutes later it came over the wire."

After discounting "what has been said about me," Pataky told this author, "I'm a very easy going guy. My nickname for 25 years was 'The Happy Hungarian.' I'm a very laid back guy. People asked, 'Don't you ever stop smiling?'"

Pataky was asked whether he was the "late date" Bob Bach believed Kilgallen had at the Regency Hotel bar a few hours before her death. Pataky emphasized, "I wasn't there. I don't have the luxury of knowing what he thought. You follow me?" He then added, "As well as I knew Dorothy and keep in mind, I knew her better and more intimately, without sex, than anyone we are discussing, and I can't conceive of her even trying to give that impression [of me being the late date] although she did write little cute notes all the time that would lead anyone who read them to think something was going on. But that's just the way she was; she was flirtatious in a non-sexual way."

Queried about whether he had ever been in Kilgallen's townhouse, Pataky said, "No, it was not my place to go there. I'd drop her off in a cab and she'd go right in the street level entrance." He asserted that he "had no part of the [New York City] social life. I was single all those years and there were a lot of women, you know. [One time], producer Joe Levine called and said, 'I'm giving a banquet at the Four Seasons in your honor. You are my new Jesus." Pataky then laughed before adding, "The New York crowd was fine. Some of them were nice people but I'm just not a society person."

Questioned about a nasty column he wrote about New Yorkers shortly after Kilgallen died, Pataky said, "Keep in mind, I was very hurt by [Dorothy's] death. I was destroyed by it." He then panned the so-called "sophisticated New York audience." He alleged, "Eighty percent of them are from Dubuque [Iowa]."

When asked about Mafia Don Sam Giancana, Pataky replied, "I met him. He came to Columbus, Ohio to hear [girlfriend] Phyllis [McGuire] sing one night. I almost put my head in a noose. I was bird-dogging her. She was willing to play, you know. Dorothy got into the picture. But there was no romance between Phyllis and myself as it turned out."[3]

Made aware of toxicology reports about the extent of the drugs in Kilgallen's system by John Broich, and Drs. Baden and Hoffman after she died, Pataky emphatically denounced such analysis. He stated, "Number one, I've never heard about that until right now. Number two, I don't believe one word of it. I have seen the truth run down, turned over and broken by fools. [You] shouldn't follow the words of these fools." Asked if Dorothy could have been the victim of foul play, he added, "No, I don't believe there was foul play at all. I do not know if she took those pills. My first awareness of anything medical was that the doctors had found enough of this or that but not enough to kill her. But mixed with alcohol it could have stopped her heart."

In a separate audiotaped interview, Pataky had provided a somewhat different explanation for Kilgallen's death. After explaining that to believe anything Lee Israel had written was to believe that "police were crooked or stupid, the New York medical examiner's office was either crooked or stupid, Dorothy's own newspaper was either crooked or stupid, and that Kilgallen's TV production company was either crooked or stupid," Pataky provided his own insight. He said, "As a cold-hard fact, I would have to assume she committed suicide. I think that's a fair assumption. Oh, no, I don't mean committed suicide. I was thinking of other than murder. My strongest inclination is that if I think about it at all, is that she OD'd. Took a little too many pills. Just a little too much whiskey…she was small…it would not take a lot to just quiet her down to where [her heart] stopped."

Asked whether Pataky's comments were "strange," Marc Sinclaire, in his videotaped interview, answered, "Strange, but understandable…

---

[3] In late February 2016, this author corresponded with Phyllis McGuire through respective letters. Ms. McGuire was cordial but did not answer questions regarding any relationship with Ron Pataky, the encounter where he and Sam Giancana met in Ohio or her quote in *Vanity Fair* regarding facts she knew about Kilgallen's death.

Accident, maybe, but it doesn't look like an accident (drug overdose). The thing he mentions about the corrupt police department, well, from my own experience, let me give it to you this way. They didn't report Dorothy's death until the afternoon. Then they said her body was discovered around noon. How is that so when I'm at the house between 8:30 a.m. and nine? How is that so?"

Continuing his interview with this author, Pataky then mentioned with no question being asked, "I was a policeman for six years and I'm very careful about things that are written. Like a source said this and that." Pataky then returned to the subject of whether he met Kilgallen at the Regency Hotel bar during the early hours before her death. "What does 'I had a feeling' mean?" he asked referring to Bob Bach's being "under the impression" that Kilgallen was going to meet Pataky. He then said, "Put yourself in my shoes. I was in Columbus, Ohio, dozens of people knew it; it was a newspaper office for Christ's sake. When I read that Marc Sinclaire said something, if he said it, and I know it not to be true, I get angry."

Asked whether New York City police contacted him after Kilgallen's death, Pataky replied, "I had calls from New York. So did a few other people at the paper. The obviousness of it all was that they said, '[Ron] was in Columbus. Are you crazy?'"

Regarding his not attending Kilgallen's funeral, Pataky said, "I could not have gone; no, I couldn't have gone. The most important thing in my life had been removed." He added:

> Keep in mind. We spoke nearly every day. And at length. I helped her with many projects and she helped me. She'd call and say "Let me read something to you." [One was] the lead to the Jack Ruby story. And she said, "I don't like [the lead] very well. What do you think?" And I said, well, it's a little dry. Why don't you try to make it a little mysterious? [Like] two unidentified men sat in a nightclub talking in hushed tones. She had told me this is what happened, part of the [Jack Ruby story]. One was Jack Ruby talking in a nightclub but she didn't make it sinister enough given the nature of the story. I just rattled that off and she said, "let me get that down."

When asked about how Kilgallen felt about Jack Ruby, whether she got "angry" when speaking about him, Pataky ignored the question. He said, "[We] had a warm and wonderful relationship. Easily the best friend I have ever had." Confronted with the allegation that he had had a violent altercation with Anna Maria Alberghetti, Pataky denied it asking, "Where was this alleged to have happened?…There was never, ever a problem there." He did acknowledge the incident with NFL football player Ron Otis in Columbus stating, "Oh, yeah, that happened. It was a twenty-five dollar fine [by the court]."

Asked once again if the New York City authorities had contacted him, Pataky said loudly, "They talked to me…to some other people to confirm that I was in Columbus and I WAS. EVERYONE KNEW IT." Pataky also confirmed again that he talked to Kilgallen nearly every day. When confronted again with his being at the Regency Hotel bar with her during the early morning hours of November 8, he stated, "I don't care what people say. Let's deal with fact. [And] I'm not sure that there was a guy [with her.]" When told that several other people had seen the man, he said, "She went from P.J. Clarke's to the Regency? Are you convinced of that? Let me give you an old man's wisdom. Some people say things like that to get themselves into the limelight."

Pataky, called by Kilgallen's friend, record producer Dee Anthony, "a smooth talking guy," admitted he had been to the Regency Hotel bar "more than twenty times" with Kilgallen. "I'd always said 'hi' to the bartender," he explained, "[I'd have thought] someone would talk to him. He's sort of the hairdresser of the booze business. They know everything."

CHAPTER 34

Considering Ron Pataky's statements during the several interviews provided through the years points to less than candid responses about important facts regarding his relationship with Kilgallen and her death. Kilgallen's hairdresser Marc Sinclaire certainly suspected Pataky of being involved in the hairdresser's death stating during his videotaped interview, "Yes, I think Pataky knows [who killed Kilgallen] I don't think he did the actual work, but whoever his employers were did [kill her]."

Sinclaire's suspicions as to Pataky's culpability in Kilgallen's death ring true when considering the newspaperman's behavior after she died. In addition to not attending the funeral for a woman he called "his best friend" who had been "removed" from his life without specifying who "removed" her, just five days after that funeral on Thursday, November 11, 1965, instead of mourning her loss or having attended the funeral, Pataky was partying in New York City. The proof comes from nationally syndicated columnist Earl Wilson's November 17 column. It detailed actress Mia Farrow's appearance a day earlier, the 16th, at Arthur, a new nightclub in NYC owned by Richard Burton's former wife Sybil. She was there to watch a CBS documentary featuring Frank Sinatra. Earlier, Kilgallen had reported the budding romance between Farrow and Sinatra.

Wilson wrote, "Mia proceeded to Arthur with Sheila MacRae, Jack Carter, Jack E. Leonard, drama critic Ron Petaky [sic], [and] her mother Maureen O'Sullivan, and broke out and danced." This meant Pataky, while he deliberately avoided attending the funeral of the "most important person

255

Ron Pataky in
late 2005.

in my life," was in New York City days after Kilgallen's death and funeral
enjoying the New York City nightlife.

In addition, despite calling Kilgallen his "best friend," one whom he
admitted talking to on a constant basis, and seeing frequently when he was
in New York City, the one with whom he had traveled abroad with, the one
who confided in him during her JFK assassination investigation, and the
one whom he invited to visit him in his hometown of Columbus, Ohio to
the extent of meeting his mother, Pataky never wrote a "tribute" column
about Kilgallen. In fact, he never wrote any column about her shortly after
she died or anytime in the future.

Curiously, instead of doing so, he landed in New York City in party
mode and then, instead of basking in the glow of the evening he spent
with stars abounding all around him, and relishing mention of Wilson's
prestigious column, Ron Pataky wrote a seething column entitled "Arthur
– (Heaven Help Us) – Another 'In' Dump of Dumps." The *Columbus Citizen-
Journal* published it on the 17th, the same date Wilson's column ran
nationally.

In the column, Pataky called Arthur a place where "real New York mingles with unshaven, unkempt girls and their frowzy-haired dates." He said the bar was "a dump" where "you can find stars (there to be seen), columnists (there to see), and the scum of the city (there to say they've been there)." He then attacked patrons calling them "cancer this decade calls culture," while adding, "In truth, New York audiences are the stupidest collection of dull clods ever to set foot in a club or theater." He ended the article by criticizing "BIG people" who lure "idiotic phonies" to places like Arthur's.

One may only speculate on why Pataky visited New York City shortly after Kilgallen's death, but the viciousness of his column points to continuing disdain for New Yorkers, and "BIG people" columnists like Kilgallen. Not only had Pataky avoided writing a column about Kilgallen and her remarkable life, but instead chose to write the scathing column. Instead of displaying feelings of sorrow about the loss, he struck back at her and her kind, the "BIG people," many of whom had syndicated columns, a stature he never achieved.

Pataky's inconsistent statements and ones conflicting with uncontroverted evidence to the contrary indicate he may know more about Kilgallen's death than he is willing to admit. But it is two poems Pataky wrote in his own hand many years after Kilgallen died that appear to signal his complicity since each points to the words being about Kilgallen and certain matters involving her death.

The first is called *Never Trust A Stiff At A Typewriter*. It included the stanza:

There's a way to quench a gossip's stench
That never fails
One cannot write if zippered "tight"
Somebody who's dead could "tell no tales."

Is the "stiff" at the typewriter Kilgallen? Is the "gossip" with the "stench" the famous columnist? Is the way to "quench" the "stench" to kill her so that she was "zippered tight" and could "tell no tales"? Most curious, if the poem wasn't about Kilgallen, why the reference to the "gossip's" typewriter when, by the time this poem was written, computers were the call of the day?

A second poem from Pataky's hand, *Vodka Roulette Seen As Relief Possibility* adds to the intrigue. Typed alongside a color image of what appears to be a bartender mixing drinks, it reads:

While I'm spilling my guts
She's driving me nuts
Please fetch us two drinks
    On the run.

Just skip all the noise'n
Make one of 'em poison
And don't even tell me
    Which one!

Is this poem a confessional of sorts, a subconscious attempt at cleansing for Ron Pataky? Was he attempting to admit guilt, to display his guilty conscience, to admit that he played "Vodka Roulette," that he somehow doctored Dorothy Kilgallen's drink with "poison" (Seconal, Tuinal and Nembutal) as part of a plan to kill her? Are the words, "While I'm spilling my guts" a reference to Pataky informing on Kilgallen? Does this mean he was leaking critical information to those who feared her getting too close to the truth and triggering a grand jury investigation?

Are the words, "She is driving me nuts," a reference to Kilgallen finally realizing that Pataky was the one responsible for the "strange events" in her life just before she died? Does Pataky mean by these words that Kilgallen was threatening to expose him for being the "snitch," the one who leaked her JFK assassination investigation evidence?

Regarding "Please fetch us two drinks on the run," do the words "on the run" mean Pataky asked the Regency Hotel bartender for "to go" cups. Then he and Kilgallen could have taken the drinks with them when they left. If so, might the words, "Just skip all the noise'n" and "Make one of 'em poison" refer to Pataky poisoning her drink after which he would have accompanied her to the townhouse to make sure the barbiturates did their job? This would have eliminated Kilgallen's threat to expose him as a snitch as referenced in the first poem when he wrote, "tell no tales."

Certainly the words "Make one of 'em poison and don't even tell me Which One!" appear to indicate the plausibility that somehow, some way, Pataky could have poisoned Kilgallen's drink. If this happened, only he knows—unless he confided in someone who has never come forward—the truth as to how the spiking took place.

CHAPTER 35

During this author's October 22, 2014 interview with Ron Pataky, he acknowledged writing the poem "Never Trust a Stiff at a Typewriter."

Pataky, clearly irritated, said, "I didn't write that until, the bulk of the material I wrote, until after about 1998. It wouldn't be to reflect back, [about] one person, even Dorothy at that late date when I'm writing thousands. You know there are over 3000 poems in my books." Asked if he understood why the lyrics compelled people to believe the poem was about Kilgallen, Pataky replied, "Well, no, I can't. I can see why a certain breed of people would, but it would never occur to me to have it associated with Dorothy."

Pataky was then asked about the poem "Vodka Roulette Seen As Relief Possibility." Before this author could mention that of all the drinks he could have written about, Pataky had chosen vodka, Kilgallen's drink of choice mixed with tonic water, he asked, "Is that the one that begins, 'Just skip all the noise'n, make one of 'em poison and don't even tell me which one?'" Assured that it was, Pataky was silent for a few moments. When told that certain people believe the poem is about Kilgallen and the possible cause of her death, Pataky replied, "Do you understand how silly that sounds to me? The friends I have known throughout my life would put no more stock in anything we've discussed today or Lee Israel than flying a kite to the moon."

Asked again if Pataky understood why others might still feel the poems related to Kilgallen's death due to the mention of "poison," he became quite agitated. "TWO SHORT POEMS OUT OF 3000," he said, "and you're trying to hatch an egg. I THINK STUPID PEOPLE SHOULD HAVE TO WEAR SIGNS THOUGH IT MIGHT BE A TURN-OFF TO CUBANS." Pataky answered the follow-up question, "Well, then what inspired the poems?" by saying, "I don't get inspired to write a poem. It is work. I do it for a living."

Continuing to avoid direct questions about whether the two poems focused on Kilgallen, Pataky roared, "IT'S SILLY. HOW WOULD THEY, WHOEVER 'THEY' IS, FIND THOSE TWO POEMS OUT OF 3000?" Regarding the artwork of the bartender serving drinks posted with the "Vodka Roulette" poem, Pataky said it was from a "service" and that the poem was "about alcoholic drinks."

Asked directly if he had any direct involvement in Kilgallen's death, Pataky replied, "Absolutely nothing." Then he said, "Listen, I'm going to make a statement. Only a damn fool would read either of the poems you pointed out and think they had something to do with Dorothy's death. Number one, they were done 40 years later or more [after her death], and they make no hint of Dorothy. One is about poison...40 years later. You're on the wrong track in my book. I cannot conceive of a kind of mind that would take those two out of thousands and put that [connecting Kilgallen] together."

When this author suggested that Kilgallen was too close to the truth concerning solving the JFK and Oswald assassinations, and had to be stopped, Pataky paused before speaking. He then said, "Of course, it's plausible. She HAD enemies. She HAD enemies. Is it plausible one of them wanted her dead?" Pataky then added, "One or more? She was a brash writer. She made a lot of enemies. Not everyone adored Dorothy." Asked about danger to Kilgallen's life, Pataky stated, "She told me. She said, 'I get threats.' I said, 'anything we can talk about?' She said 'no.'"

Most curious is why Pataky, while discounting the importance of the "Vodka Roulette Seen as Relief Possibility" poem, could recite the few stanzas verbatim, one that featured "vodka," Kilgallen's drink of choice instead a multitude of other choices. He did this without any hesitation by blurting them out the moment this author mentioned the name of the poem. Had he indeed experienced "relief" once Kilgallen was dead? She was certainly unable to soil his reputation by circulating to the entertainment world and to friends that he could not be trusted, that in fact, Pataky was a snitch.

That Pataky might have been the "mystery man" who was somehow involved in Kilgallen's death is subject to conjecture; but there is no question that Kilgallen ended up being "somebody who's dead" who "could 'tell no tales."

* * * * *

If Ron Pataky was indeed the "mystery man" who met Kilgallen on the weekend of her death, what is the rest of the story?

Did those who feared Kilgallen order Pataky to monitor the famous journalist, and then report the evidence she had discovered? When it became apparent she was too close to the truth, did those threatened inform Pataky Kilgallen must be stopped? Did Pataky, somehow vulnerable due to a threat on his own life of some sort, or perhaps money considerations, agree to betray Kilgallen through complicity in her death?

While Pataky's motive to eliminate Kilgallen is subject to conjecture, there is no question that he was not a stranger to violence. Recall he told this author he was "laid back," had the nickname "The Happy Hungarian." This is the side of his personality that he apparently showcased for the entertainment industry. However, there was a dark side to this outsider, trapped in Columbus, Ohio, far from the bright lights of New York City, the Pataky involved in violent altercations with Anna Maria Alberghetti and the NFL football player Jim Otis. Recall Alberghetti noted Pataky being "violent and nutsy."

If Pataky was indeed the "mystery man" and somehow was involved in Kilgallen's death or knows who was, his motive will always be a question mark. In addition, it is difficult with a cold case 50 years old to determine exactly how Pataky may have carried out Kilgallen's elimination. If Kilgallen "confronted" him as Marc Sinclaire had suggested during a phone call before she left for the *What's My Line?* program, and he agreed to meet at the Regency, then the nature of the serious conversation eyewitness Katherine Stone described between Kilgallen and the "mystery man" in the corner booth makes sense. During that conversation, the decision could have been made for Pataky to accompany Kilgallen back to her townhouse.

If Pataky had indeed poisoned her vodka and tonic at the bar, then he could have escorted her to the townhouse front entrance and left her to die from the overdose. Or, more likely, since confiscating the JFK assassination file would have been a priority, he could have accompanied her inside the townhouse to the third floor as she experienced dizziness and an unsteady gait. When Kilgallen finally collapsed, he could have carried her to the bedroom not knowing she never slept in it and left her to be found by Richard or Marie, the maid.

Before leaving the townhouse, Pataky, who arguably knew more about her JFK assassination investigation than anyone else, could have then taken her file and either destroyed it or gave it to those who, for their own reasons, wanted her dead. If so, Pataky—who had conveniently entered Kilgallen's life closely following her investigative work during the Jack Ruby trial—would have fulfilled any promise he may have made to those who had orchestrated his being a "plant" in Kilgallen's life. He had also eliminated any possibility that she could ruin his life through her poison pen.

If Pataky, on the other hand, merely set up Kilgallen for the kill, then any accomplices, the "employer's" Marc Sinclaire mentioned, could have awaited her at the townhouse entrance and forced Kilgallen to let them in with her. Poisoning her drink could then have happened, as previously described, with capture of the assassination investigation file as the priority.

Whatever the motive, whatever the means, Dorothy Kilgallen was indeed "zippered tight." The courageous journalist's typewriter had been silenced forever.

CHAPTER 36

In an attempt to provide Ron Pataky with a fair opportunity to clear up inconsistent statements through the years, this author interviewed the former newspaper columnist during the early days of September 2015.

After a preliminary discussion about his being the one person still living who knew Kilgallen best during the months before she died, he answered several questions dealing with his potential involvement in her death. During the course of the back and forth discussion, he continued to **deny**:

- Any romantic relationship with Kilgallen during their two-year relationship. ("…I don't believe I ever kissed her [on the mouth]; just on the cheek. And there was love. There was a deep love. A friendship love but we were just never sexually involved at all.")

- That Kilgallen told anyone, including her best friends, she was in love with him or had a sexual relationship. ("I don't believe that for one second. With her pride, she would have never said that. If we were hot and heavy for ten years, she would never say that to anyone including the hairdressers who she did not trust. She was a married woman with children.")

- That he never sent Kilgallen valentines "cut-outs." ("I don't believe I've ever sent a valentine in my life. I'm not a valentine kind of guy.")

- That he was in NYC on the weekend of Kilgallen's death. ("I was in Columbus…that was established by [NYC] police, investigators and the reason they contacted me was that I was very prominent in her life at the time.") (Note: as mentioned, there is no evidence in any report of investigations that police ever contacted Pataky.)

- Leaking any information about Kilgallen's JFK and Oswald assassination investigation to anyone. ("She told me someone had leaked information but she didn't know who it was, never never gave me any names.")

- That either of the two poems he wrote had anything to do with Kilgallen. ("The first book of rhymes was over 800 pages…for [people] to pick out some silly ass rhymes and try to make something real out it is just asinine, beyond my comprehension…it's just silliness, it's just humor.")

- That the poems were in any way a subconscious effort to cleanse a guilty conscience regarding his involvement in her death. ("The bottom line is I am utterly…my conscience is clear. I have no part in anything involving Dorothy's death.")

- Accusations by "those people" who suspect him of being involved in Kilgallen's death. ("You've got a bunch of people out there who started all of this, these are the same people who believe in Bigfoot…they just get a hint of a rumor and they run with it with no thought as to the outcome.")

- That he knew anything about her death. ("I still believe she died of an overdose and drinking.")

- The need to respond to "those people" accusing him of wrongdoing. ("I don't want to lower myself to deal with despicable people.")

Regarding new information Pataky provided, the following were of interest:

- Concerning Kilgallen's husband, he said, "[Richard] was a terrible mess."

- When he spoke to Kilgallen the night before she died, "There was no hint of depression."

- Kilgallen never knew Ruby before the assassinations: "I am quite sure she did not know him."

- Kilgallen "told me she was afraid" of those who feared her JFK and Oswald investigation and her writing a book but she "never gave me any names, never told me whom."

- He did not attend Kilgallen's funeral because "I didn't like the people [in NYC] and most of them didn't like me. They felt I had taken over a lot of Dorothy's life and social life."

- Regarding Kilgallen's trip to New Orleans shortly before she died and who she may have intended to meet there, he said, "I remember Dorothy mentioning the name of Jim Garrison. She must have told me that."[1]

- Concerning Jack Ruby's testimony before the Warren Commission, he stated, "Do you know what, for about six months I had the second copy of [his testimony] before it was released [publically]. She sent it to me."

- Asked "why" Kilgallen sent it to him, he said, "I don't know. She probably sent along a note and asked, 'what do you think of this? There was nothing sinister about it. It's hard for me in any way to be sinister about Dorothy."

- Regarding NYC gangster Frank Costello, he said, "I knew who he was. I met him a couple of times."

As the interview ended, this author attempted to persuade Pataky to divulge any further important information about Kilgallen's JFK and Oswald investigation, or her death. I noted Kilgallen's love for him and my intention to restore her reputation following no real investigation of her death resulting in the conclusion that she had died of a drug overdose combined with alcohol. I also told Pataky that based on my research,

---

[1] It may be recalled that Garrison was the New Orleans district attorney who investigated the JFK and Oswald assassinations to the extent of indicting Clay Shaw who was found not guilty by a jury. During his investigation, staffers advised Garrison to investigate Carlos Marcello but he declined to do so.

Kilgallen did not die accidentally or by suicide, but that given fresh facts and an apparent cover-up by the NYC medical examiner's office, foul play was apparent. "I've never heard that before," he roared and then returned to his belief that she did, in fact, die by accident. He exhibited no shock, no anger, no emotion whatsoever about Kilgallen having potentially been murdered.

Pataky then refused to provide any new information about Kilgallen's death based on faulty memory and his intention to stick with the accounts provided to this author and the other interviewers despite the conflicts. Of special interest was Pataky's first mention of Kilgallen having trusted him with a "the second copy" of the Jack Ruby Warren Commission testimony before it was released to the public. When asked why she did this, he quickly answered, "I don't know," before realizing he had admitted Kilgallen did in fact share vital information about her investigations once again conflicting previous statements about the matter.

Nevertheless, fifty years after Dorothy Kilgallen died, despite possessing motive, there is no conclusive proof she was murdered by Pataky on his own or as an operative of underworld figures. Only Pataky knows whether he is responsible for her death. To give him the benefit of the doubt, his inconsistent statements may be perfectly reasonable since the events he was questioned about happened in the 1960s, nearly 15 years separated from the Lee Israel interview, and four decades from interviews with Larry Jordan and Kathryn Fauble's associate. This author's interviews happened 50+ years after Kilgallen died.[2] Memory fades and Pataky's recollections may simply be faulty as to many aspects of his relationship with Kilgallen and the circumstances surrounding her death. This means he was not

---

[2] On February 19, 2016, this author forwarded an email to Pataky providing him with another opportunity to speak about Kilgallen. It read: "If there is any further information you wish to provide that can assist in the investigation of her death, or any matters you want to clear up regarding the information you gave me, please let me know." Pataky responded by avoiding the request and instead wrote, "As you know, I have always leaned toward believing that her death was a natural one, although I have no more solid reason for believing that than do those who believe she was murdered," before closing his email by stating, "I continue to miss the gal terribly, still very much aware at my present age of eighty (eighty one in May) that knowing her was one of the absolute most joyous highlights of what has been a fascinating life for me."

lying to protect himself but merely mistaken about what he told the various interviewers, including me.

In addition, Pataky's incidents of violence, as disturbing as they are, do not prove he was capable of murder. Moreover, while he disputes any true love affair with Kilgallen to the extent of a sexual relationship, his denial he harmed her is reasonable regarding a woman he certainly cared about. Whether, as noted, Pataky may have been pressured by underworld figures he boasted of knowing to "set up" Kilgallen by leaking information to them and then providing facts about her personal life aiding a killer, or was paid to provide inside information about her (Marc Sinclaire said Kilgallen told him Pataky "didn't have any money at all. She said, 'small newspaper, small job.'"), is perhaps more logical but no concrete facts point to this happening.

There is also no absolute proof that Richard Kollmar, Carlos Marcello, J. Edgar Hoover or others who feared Kilgallen's JFK and Lee Harvey Oswald assassination investigation, had her killed. Based on motive, Marcello is the chief suspect. Sadly, the very evidence to have sealed his fate may have existed in Kilgallen's assassinations file, never recovered.

Any debate as to how Kilgallen died, and how, must include assessment of Marc Sinclaire's 2000 interview statements where he disclosed his personal feelings about his dear friend's death. He said, "Whatever happened, they didn't realize that Dorothy wore a hairpiece. They also didn't realize Dorothy wore false eyelashes. So they were not attuned to that side of it at all. They were really unprepared for how she dressed for the mornings. James [butler] would have known, Evelyn [James' wife] would have known, everyone in that house would have known how she slept and where she slept." He added, "So what is the conspiracy we're talking about? That someone covered it up [her death] for what reason."

Speculating, Sinclaire stated, "Let's say Dorothy didn't die at home. I don't think she did. I think she died somewhere else. So that means you've gotta get her home, get her into the house, and take her upstairs. She didn't die in that bedroom. That's for sure. This is a mystery." Adding to the intrigue, Sinclaire said, was the fact that Kilgallen's regular chauffer

Roosevelt Zanders was sick on the night before and morning of her death. A substitute was on duty, his name never disclosed.

Sinclaire added, "Whether [the mystery] can ever be solved I don't know but it is a mystery. As I said, I don't think she died at home. I think she was brought home." Asked if Ron Pataky was involved, Sinclaire replied, "I think he had the connection but I don't think he'd have enough guts to do something like that."

In an audiotaped interview, Sinclaire addressed the "mystery" of Kilgallen death in a separate manner, stating, "There will be some things about Dorothy's death you'll never be able to find unless you have her [assassination investigation] notes. I don't know whether Richard took those notes or whether they were ever in the house or what but she did have them at the time since I've seen her open them and look at them."

Unfortunately, since November 8, 1965, a black cloud has hovered over Dorothy Kilgallen's death. It began when Dr. James Luke deliberately, it appears from the ME documents, concealed evidence in the ME report and then added "circumstances undetermined" to the mix. Because of the uncertainly, because of the impression that he could not clearly indicate the true cause of death, Kilgallen's reputation was soiled. Some called her a "pill-popper," an "alky" or worse. With no conclusion reached as to her actual cause of death, rumors were the call of the day.

This remarkable woman of strong character, an inspiring and award-winning newspaper columnist, gifted wordsmith, insightful investigative reporter, author and revered television personality, and a true trailblazer in the fight for equal rights for women, deserves better. To the millions of fans, including the thousands of people who attended her showing and funeral service, she was a true hero, one who, as noted, broke the so-called "glass ceiling" long before the term became popular.

An apt description of Kilgallen, who never earned a college degree, confirms she was the type of person worthy of admiration. Her own *Journal-American* portrayed the elegant woman, a true lady, as:

> ...a woman of alabaster complexion, china blue eyes and extreme sensibilities, [one] who dresses with stylist perfection, wears snow white kids

gloves and picturesque hats, neither smokes or swears, drinks to moderation, and attends mass unfailingly each Sunday, she was romantic and sentimental, she weeps and blushes easily…she was warm and kind to her relatives and generous to her friends, loving to her children.

On the day of her funeral, the headline in the *Journal-American* was "They Came to Say Goodbye to Dorothy Kilgallen: People Came by the Thousands to Pay Last Respect." The accompanied text read, "They came to say goodbye to Dorothy. From Washington Heights, from Flatbush, weaving mink hats or slightly shabby cloth coats, some frankly tearful, others solemn." One mourner had flown to New York City from Gary, Indiana and another, Rita Swobodsin, called Kilgallen a hero of near superpower status, stating, "She brought my baby out of a burning building…the building I lived in caught on fire. Miss Kilgallen was across the street and she heard the sirens. She went into the building in her beautiful white and sequined dress and she took my little baby, wet diapers and all, and carried him out of the building."

Even those who crossed hairs with Kilgallen, those with a grudge to bear, those who referred to her as "Dorothy Spillgarbage," respected her courage. They also respected her dogged determination in search of the truth. William Randolph Hearst Jr., the second son of his legendary father, said of Kilgallen, "She was as good a reporter as ever came down the line," adding, "Dorothy had three trademarks: a keen mind, a tailored exterior, and a steel rod as a backbone. [She] was life and death. She reached into the precipices of people's emotions, in both her writings and her personal confrontations with her own existence. She was enthusiastic, open, full of life."

What's My Line? panelist and *Murder One* publisher Bennett Cerf commented on his friend during the November 14, 1965 tribute program shortly after Kilgallen died. After extolling her virtues as "a very tough game player; others knew her as a tough newspaper woman," he then added, "But we got to know her as a human being, and a more loveable, softer, loyal person never lived, and we're going to miss her terribly." Guest panelist Steve Allen said of Kilgallen, "She was a brilliant woman, quick-minded intelligent." This program is preserved at www.youtube.com/watch?v=aMT_KFb1THA.

In his videotaped interview, Marc Sinclaire applauded Kilgallen. He stated, "She was very smart. And she didn't appear tough. She didn't come on like gangbusters but she was very brazen. She would write things that would shock people. She was a very good reporter, with the Sam Sheppard case, Profumo, with all that and remember it was a conservative time so what you might think as not startling today was startling then…She was the real thing." In a separate audiotaped interview, Sinclaire added, "Someone said Dorothy was the first feminist, making money in a man's world when women couldn't do that."

In a taped television interview with talk show host Joe Franklin, Johnnie Ray professed his admiration for Kilgallen. "People who did not know her totally misunderstood her. They thought she was a cold-hearted newspaper woman who would stop at nothing. That was cynical—attack, attack, attack. But Dorothy wasn't any of these things; She was the softest, tenderest, most thoughtful, most loveable woman I have ever known."

Ray added:

The relationship got to the point where I was always having to defend her. Every place we went, people knew we were close and they'd say, "What is she really like?" Unfortunately, she got that tough image from *What's My Line?* She took that show very seriously. She took the game very seriously. She played it to win. She was a real game player. At P. J. Clarke's at two or three in the morning we'd play games. [On the show], she'd forget there was a camera, forget there was an audience. So she had animage with the public of being aggressive and tough and she was none of those things.

Ray's interviews, in four segments, are posted at www.youtube.com /watch?v=lbobzDRDYRc.

To highlight Kilgallen's life, the *Journal-American* devoted seven pages to Kilgallen's life and times. Acclaimed lawyer Louis Nizer told a reporter Kilgallen had "keen insight, vivid and concise descriptive powers and an evaluating intelligence." Producer David Merrick added, "Dorothy Kilgallen was one of the great reporters of our time. Her coverage of trials were journalistic masterpieces. She was a star and gave glamour and glitter to the world of journalism." Sammy Davis, Jr. said, "Broadway won't be the same without her." Actress Joan Crawford lauded her close friend as "one of the greatest women who ever lived."

A *Journal-American* editorial following Kilgallen's death celebrated her life:

> In a profession that is exacting in appraisal of its members, and cautious of excessive praise, Dorothy Kilgallen was recognized everywhere as an all-time great in the history of journalism. She was extraordinarily percept in getting inside events and the people who made them, whether they concerned the coronation of a queen or a murder trial.
>
> She was continuously brilliant in putting down those perceptson paper, so clear and so meticulously attentive to selective details that readers were transported to the scene. Dorothy Kilgallen's readers were not merely informed of happenings—they lived them.
>
> Dorothy was courageous both in her disregard for physical safety, which at times she risked, and in her determination to let no one and nothing stand in her way of getting to the heart of a story.

Bill Slocum, a fellow reporter at the *Journal-American*, wrote, "[Dorothy] was never one of the boys. She was always very much a dame. She could be quite grand when the mood or the necessity was on her. Or she could sit down with the boys and drink a little whisky…she did her job on this earth and, by God, whatever she had to do she did as well as anybody ever did." Famed journalist Dominick Dunne wrote, "…she projected an aura of glamour with her magnificent evening dresses and jewels…She had wit, power, and a mean streak…Everybody read her, and a lot of people were afraid of her."

Plaudits aside regarding Kilgallen's reputation as a top journalist, the legacy of the famed newspaperwoman must focus on her quest for justice. She had an undeniable urge to reveal the truth that was strong at age 17 when she first became a reporter and was even stronger during the days leading up to her murder. It was her father Jim who influenced her to pursue the truth, but somewhere along the line Kilgallen decided to speak for those who were denied justice, for those whose constitutional rights were violated.

To understand how powerful Kilgallen's fight was to demand justice for others, one only has to recall how she stood up and shouted to the world when questioning whether injustice or prejudice reared its ugly head. Examples include her outrage at the anti-Communist book, *Red Channels,* defending Johnnie Ray when he was arrested, questioning Marilyn Monroe's death, testifying for Lenny Bruce at trial, condemning the Dr. Sam Sheppard jury verdict, and her quest to discover whether Jack Ruby was denied a fair trial.

As Kilgallen's insightful analysis of the famous trials in *Murder One* indicates, she was a competent professional with the wisdom of a trial lawyer and her dedication to investigate unmatched when she smelled something "fishy" as she did with the Ruby case. Sadly, Kilgallen, in all likelihood, was slain for writing a book, an affront to every journalist and author before, or since, her senseless death.

CHAPTER 37

To the end, Dorothy Kilgallen did not stop. She never gave up her search for the truth; she never gave up the demand for justice while investigating the JFK assassination. As she wrote after the Jack Ruby trial, "The point to be remembered in this historic case is that the whole truth has not been told. Neither the state of Texas nor the defense put on all of its evidence before the jury. Perhaps it was not necessary, but it would have been desirable from the viewpoint of all of the American people." For historical accuracy, Kilgallen was right.

Sadly, the same justice Kilgallen advocated for others was not provided her when she died. Kilgallen suffered when those in charge swept her death under the rug with absolutely no investigation of any sort.

Instead of a rush to judgment, there was a rush to injustice. The police never searched for fingerprints, nor did they comb the townhouse for other clues as to Kilgallen's death. Neither Detectives Green nor Doyle conducted interviews of potential neighborhood witnesses who may have seen anyone coming and going from the townhouse during the hours before her death. In addition, there were:

- No police interviews of anyone at *What's My Line?*
- No police interviews of patrons at P. J. Clarke's.
- No police interviews of any of those who saw her at the Regency Hotel Bar or its employees.
- No police interview of Western Union manager Dave Spiegel.

- No police interview of Katherine Stone.
- No police interviews of Bob or Jean Bach.

In addition, neither Marc Sinclaire nor Charles Simpson was interviewed. No substantial interviews at the Kilgallen townhouse with the maid, Marie Eichler, the butler, James Clement, or any of Kilgallen's children were conducted. There was also no interview of the tutor and family companion Ibne Hassan, and apparently only one brief interview with Richard Kollmar at the townhouse that was tainted, according to other accounts.

Perhaps most sadly, there was no police interview of Ron Pataky, despite his claims to the contrary. There was not one interview of anyone at his Ohio newspaper, including Jane Horricks. There were no interviews of football player Jim Otis or Anna Maria Alberghetti, both of whom had witnessed a violent side of Pataky. There was no police interview of the substitute limousine driver.

At fault, besides the police, were Kilgallen's journalistic colleagues. They did not follow up on evasive statements made by Dr. Luke including his use of the quizzical words "circumstances undetermined" regarding cause of death. When he told the media he would not comment on "the form" in which Kilgallen had taken the barbiturates, that he would "leave that up in the air," saying "we don't want to give that out—well, just because," these were red flags, just cause for further inquiry.

If a skilled reporter like Kilgallen had read Dr. Luke's shady remarks, he or she would have been on alert that something was amiss. This would have caused them immediately to pound on his door, demanding answers. However, her journalistic colleagues were apparently paying little attention, since no one followed up on the curious comments. They let Dr. Luke get away with unprofessional conduct across the board.

Without doubt, this caused the first potential for the investigation to fail. From the medical examiner documents prepared by Dr. Luke, it is clear that his startling discovery that Tuinal was present in Kilgallen's system—unaccounted for due to the lack of a prescription—should have triggered him to pass this information along to the police or the District

Dorothy Kilgallen in all her glory.

Attorney. They, in turn, could then have launched an investigation—one that would have included questioning the witnesses mentioned who had firsthand knowledge of Kilgallen's personal life, personal habits, drug and drinking habits, and her conduct during the night and the early morning hours before her death on November 8. For instance, if they had spoken to Bob Bach regarding Kilgallen's never leaving P. J. Clarke's until after midnight, or Western Union office manager David Spiegel, who spoke to Kilgallen at 2:20 a.m., they would have known Richard was lying about Kilgallen having retired to bed before midnight.

This investigation would have, it is logical to believe, turned up new evidence that something was amiss regarding her death; that it was not the certain case of accidental death. However, Dr. Luke's actions prohibited any possibility of an investigation. Instead, Kilgallen was mistakenly perceived as a druggie and a drunk who caused her own demise. Friends who loved her, and apparently family members to this day also took Dr. Luke's decision at face value, none fighting like Kilgallen would have fought to uncover the truth when so many questions existed about how she died. They all let her down, walked away, and left poor Dorothy with a tarnished reputation that overshadowed the career of one of the most remarkable media figures in history.

Three years following her death, in 1968, Dr. Charles Umberger and John Broich had the second chance to right the wrong done to Kilgallen. They had proof, through the fresh toxicological tests, confirming the presence of the three dangerous barbiturates in her system, and they could have notified their superiors and/or police authorities of the new evidence. They did not do so, with Broich admitting that he kept the information "under his hat" as instructed by Dr. Umberger.

A decade later, two investigations failed to provide Kilgallen with the justice she deserved. Author Lee Israel first attempted to do so via her *Kilgallen* biography. To her credit, her research of the famous reporter and television star's private and business lives was admirable. Also, toward the end of the book, she attempted to provide several possibilities as to how Kilgallen died. However, for whatever reason, Israel's investigation was incomplete, since she never researched in depth the NYC ME's documents by which she would have discovered the "smoking gun" presence of Tuinal in Kilgallen's system noted in the autopsy report. This is true, unless that portion of the documentation was somehow deleted from any reports the author viewed.

Regardless, Israel's research did not cause any governmental agency such as the Manhattan District Attorney's office to re-open the case. Simultaneously, the House Select Committee on Assassinations' interest in Kilgallen's death, based on the ME documents it requested, was "not substantial," even though, G. Robert Blakey told this author that the Committee thought the death was "fishy." Another dead end resulted as no thorough investigation ensued meaning Kilgallen's best chance to reverse the accidental death conclusion passed by. This is because the HSCA had access to the Medical Examiner's page attached to the autopsy report designating Tuinal in Kilgallen's blood stream. If the Committee had launched an investigation, it appears likely they may have discovered facts that would have challenged Kilgallen's officially-stated cause of death.

A third chance to challenge the conclusion that Kilgallen died by accidental means occurred in 2007 when the *Midwest Today* article written by Sara and published by Larry Jordan appeared. Unfortunately, despite the new evidence offered, especially with regard to statements made by eyewitnesses concerning the events surrounding Kilgallen's death—including Marc Sinclaire, Charles Simpson, Katherine Stone, and, most important, John Broich—law enforcement officials gave no notice to the excellent exposé.

One indication of how the truth about Kilgallen's life and times has been distorted through the years emerged in late 2015 when a group of San Diego residents, led by Gene Bryan, a retired school district landscaper with no experience as either a researcher or investigator, propounded baseless facts and conclusions about the revered media icon. Shockingly, the *San Diego Union-Tribune*, via writer Peter Rowe, quoted Mr. Bryan in an article entitled, "Keeping Conspiracy Alive..." The article, which spread through the internet, abounded with unfounded internet conspiracy theories, and it included Mr. Bryan's comment about Kilgallen having been killed by those close to the Warren Commission without any substantiation for that theory. Mr. Bryan admitted he had no proof, but that disclosure did not deter publication of the wild accusations. Efforts by this author to protect Kilgallen's reputation by persuading Mr. Bryan and Mr. Rowe to inform readers of my investigation, of another side of the story featuring credible facts about Kilgallen and her death, fell on deaf ears. So much for responsible journalism in today's world of sensationalism.

At each juncture where a so-called fresh investigation could have permitted Kilgallen's day in court, so to speak, since there is no statute of limitations for murder, no one carefully examined credible sources, least of all the NYC medical examiner documents. Thus no one became as alarmed as Dr. Luke must have been when he learned what drugs were present in Kilgallen's system. All along the way, others who viewed the ME documents, apparently including Dr. Baden and Dr. Hoffman, either did not seize the opportunity to question the official cause of death, or, more likely viewed only documents devoid of the Tuinal mention.

This said, Dr. Hoffman's declaration to this author that he never saw the proper documents, triggers a plausible explanation, *revealed here for the first time*, as to how Kilgallen suffered the worst possible injustice among so many when she died. Probing why this happened sheds light on the various theories proposed in this book as to why and how Kilgallen was indeed the reporter who knew too much and was silenced for it.

That the ME's report was scattershot indicates exactly the type of behavior John Broich described in his audiotape interview. Recall that he said things in the office were "kinda screwed up...pretty unreliable. I wouldn't trust anything, you know what I mean? I was paranoid as hell when I was there. You never knew what was going to happen from one day to the next."

Before Broich conducted new toxicological tests in 1968, he said Dr. Charles Umberger believed Kilgallen had been murdered. Arguably, the most important clue, besides the discovery of the three barbiturates in her system, was a startling fact: traces of Nembutal were found on one glass discovered on the nightstand in the bedroom where Kilgallen died. As mentioned, this would have been due to sodium, the salt content, in the Nembutal that could leave a telltale sign.

Dr. Umberger concluded the Nembutal residue was present in the glass that Kilgallen drank from (perhaps there was a lipstick stain). When asked what the significance of discovering Nembutal traces on one glass that had been filled with an alcoholic beverage was, Dr. Donald Hoffman told this author in late 2015, "It's a big deal."

Yes, it was. The presence of Nembutal on the glass cannot be over-emphasized. Both Broich and Dr. Umberger had to have known this was undisputed physical evidence, another smoking gun in addition to the discovery of Tuinal in her system. The Nembutal had been discovered in Kilgallen's blood stream and this fact was now substantiated by traces of the drug being present on the glass. No guesswork or speculation was required for these men of science. They knew a dangerous drug Kilgallen would have never taken on purpose had indeed been the "murder weapon" along with the Tuinal and the Seconal combination with the effect accelerated by alcohol.

Why, because it is logical to infer that in order for the Nembutal residue to be present on the glass either in the bottom or on the rim (no clarity was provided), Kilgallen must have ingested *powder*, not the capsules, while sipping her drink, likely vodka and tonic. Otherwise, no residue would have been noticeable had she had ingested the powerful drug in capsule form.

That Kilgallen ingested powdered barbiturates rather than in capsule form may explain why Dr. Luke was quoted in the November 16, 1965 *New York Herald-Tribune* as stating, it may be recalled, "Dr. Luke would not speculate about the form in which Miss Kilgallen had taken the barbiturates. 'We'd rather leave that up in the air, he said. 'We don't want to give that out—well, just because...'" with the "because" due to his inability to fit this fact, the powdered barbiturates, to the accidental death conclusion he wanted to reach. Adding "circumstances undetermined" to the cause of death also masked the truth as he knew it to be.

Important to recall is that Nembutal's effects in high doses have led to its use in executions. As a Schedule II Controlled Substance, the drug is now subject to the strictest rules of government regulators. Physicians and pharmacists have to track every pill.

Broich and Dr. Umberger also knew it was illogical to assume anyone as smart as Kilgallen would break open the capsules before ingesting them. With these facts in mind, the two men must have concluded foul play had been responsible for Kilgallen's death, and that the famous journalist had been murdered at the townhouse where she had ingested the lethal dose of barbiturates. Recall Broich told wife Eileen that Kilgallen had been "bumped off."

If this *is* what the two men concluded, then their silence, the cover-up in 1968, is inexcusable and unethical, and it borders on the illegal. They withheld evidence. They had a chance to show the world Kilgallen did not take her own life, or die by accident, since 1) three barbiturates were in her system, including Tuinal and Nembutal; 2) traces of the Nembutal were on one glass; and most importantly, 3) since there were *two* glasses present on the bedside table, this apparently meant someone was in the bedroom with

Kilgallen when she died. Suicide was thus not a viable cause of her death, the two men must have realized, and accidental death could be ruled out.[1]

Based on these observations, and those of Marc Sinclaire, Charles Simpson and other eyewitnesses to the events surrounding Kilgallen's death, hopefully her children, those still alive who knew her well, and millions of fans across the globe, will take solace in realizing that she was killed for what she knew, instead of having been instrumental in her own death. This brave woman's reputation should be restored once and for all so that she is remembered for a body of work rivaling any journalist or investigative reporter, man or woman, in history.

* * * * *

To be certain, John Broich and Dr. Umberger, who blamed toxic office politics as the reason for not disclosing conclusive evidence Kilgallen had not committed suicide or died accidentally, failed her and those who loved her. However, based on fresh evidence uncovered by this author, there may have been a worthy explanation for doing so as well as why there was no future investigation of Kilgallen's death. The explanation for this happening is connected to threats against certain members of the ME's office during those years. This, in turn, solidifies the finger being pointed at underworld figures being responsible for Kilgallen's death, either by their own hand or potentially through an operatives' cooperation.

During interviews with this author in 2015, Broich's widow Eileen and his son Chris, an ex-policeman, revealed being approached in 2011 by Stephen Goldner, a forensic toxicologist in the NYC medical examiner's office and a close, personal friend of the Broich family. According to Chris Broich, Goldner explained that he was writing a book about "how the Mafia controlled the NYC ME's office." During the conversation, Goldner told Chris, "Your dad was one of the heroes, because he wouldn't alter toxicology reports like others did in the ME's office."

---

[1] There appears no way to prove how the two glasses were transported to the Medical Examiner's Office and whether Dr. Luke ever knew of their existence. How they ended up in Dr. Umberger's hands is also a mystery.

Eileen Broich told this author that John "was forced to leave" the ME's office, confirming what Goldner said to Chris. She added, "John had to leave. He admitted Mafia presence in the office. They were intimidating. He called one time from the city and was terrified. He was strong-willed. He wouldn't be bought. There was pressure to fudge results. I said, 'Why don't you go to the police?' John said, 'They can't help me.'"

Eileen Broich recalled the family "moving several times, even to Pennsylvania because John believed we were being followed." She added, "the ME office was investigated. A lot of shenanigans were going on with corpses, necrophilia and such." Chris Broich said his father had been "blacklisted," causing problems with alternative employment in his field.

In late 2015, during his interview with this author, Steve Goldner, the supervising forensic toxicologist at the ME's office from 1970-1974, confirmed Eileen Broich's account regarding Mafia "control" of the ME's office in the early-to-mid-1960s. Goldner—also an attorney who, to date, is responsible for more than 230 FDA-approved drugs and medical devices—said, "his understanding was that the same paranoia, paranoia being rampant, existing then [1970s] had existed in the mid-to-late 1960s because of the Mafia influence." Asked to be specific, Goldner said, "The Mafia had taken control of a large part of the analyses [being done]." He agreed that he, Broich and other toxicologists were expected "to cooperate" and sign-off on reports even if they doubted the accuracy.

This atmosphere, Goldner admitted, related to "cases where the reports didn't add up, didn't tell the whole story." He recalled, "Well, it wasn't as if Joe Bonnano[2] or a guy from Brooklyn walked in and said 'I own you guys,' but we knew what was going on. But on a day-to-day basis, it was pretty clear what was happening." Goldner then added:

> For instance, one-half to two-thirds of the people employed in the laboratories were Sicilian, related to each other, pretty much from the same couple of towns in Sicily. And anyone who was supposed to have a college

---

[2] Bonanno ("Joe Bananas"), born in Castellammare del Golfo, Sicily, rose to the status of Don in New York City at age 26. He ruled the Bonanno crime family after the murder of Salvatore Maranzano during the four-year bloody "Castelammare Wars." Curiously, Melvin Belli's private investigator Jim Licavoli told this author that his boss' bookkeeper "had ties to the Bonanno crime family."

degree somehow those records were lost, supposedly since they got their degrees in Sicily....On the third day I got there, I asked a guy who supposedly had a PhD about a particular chemical I wanted to order....I drew the chemical structure for him. He asked his lieutenant and came back and said, "I don't think we can get this. It's very rare." The structure was a simple one, for Benzene, commonly used. That made me know he was not actually a chemist.

Asked about the fudging of toxicology reports, Goldner confirmed he had witnessed this happening. He added that certain cases, like Kilgallen's in the 1960s, "peaked interest and were never solved." Goldner added, "There was a pattern to these cases, you could infer things that didn't add up."

Goldner consistently recalled that he and John Broich "worked to stop the Mafia influence, stop this inappropriate influence." That was "costly for John, costly for me," Goldner said, adding, "Investigations went nowhere, and yes, I was scared because of the pressure. [They made it clear] that it isn't going to work if you go to the cops." Asked if Eileen Broich's statement that John told her he was "terrified" and could not call the police because "they can't help" was valid, Goldner said the statement had the ring of truth, based on his discussions with Broich.

Goldner then related the final incident that led to his and Broich's being "forced to leave" the office: "There was an analysis work done by a person not competent to do so, not trained, and it ended up in an official toxicology report. John and I were told to sign off, and we refused to do so. We knew we were being set up but had to sign or else. It was like, listen, 'the Sicilians are running the place and you better sign.' When we didn't, we were escorted out of the office and that was it."

Dr. Donald Hoffman confirmed Steve Goldner's assessment of the ME office to this author, adding the caveat, "I don't honestly believe it was quite that sinister." He then stated, "[But] there were some serious issues concerning the quality of the work that came out of that lab at that time." Regarding John Broich's fear of repercussion if he exposed the 1968 tests that pointed to foul play that caused Kilgallen's death, Dr. Hoffman said, "It's perfectly plausible."

Dr. Hoffman also confirmed that some Sicilians worked at the ME office, but he would admit to no knowledge of their potential links to the underworld. Regarding Steven Goldner's assertions that he was forced out of the office, Dr. Hoffman told this author Goldner "was a bright guy who had issues with the administration." Dr. Hoffman recalled, "There was something Steve was asked to do, to sign a report, and he refused to do so. I believe he was told that if he didn't sign it, 'we'll have no choice but to terminate you,' and they did."

Following up on Goldner's assertions of Mafia control of the ME's office, a source who demanded anonymity due to safety concerns, when asked about why Brooklyn Deputy medical examiner Dominick DiMaio was connected to the Kilgallen case (signed Certificate of Death) instead of the Manhattan deputy ME, told this author, "That's very unusual. I don't know of any high-profile cases like this one where a deputy from another bureau was involved in signing a death certificate in a different bureau. Why didn't Dr. Luke just sign it or someone from his bureau?" He then added, "But, it was known, or perhaps rumored is a better word, that DiMaio was known to take care of things for the Mafia."[3]

In a December 1995 interview with an associate of Kathryn Fauble's, Dr. DiMaio, asked about why he signed Kilgallen's the Certificate, replied, "I wasn't stationed in Manhattan [at the time of her death]. I was stationed

---

[3] Confirmation of Goldner's allegation that DiMaio may have "taken care of things for the Mafia" have not been fruitful. In his book, *Morgue: A Life in Death* written with Ron Franscell, DiMaio's son Vincent extols the virtues of his father, writing that he coveted his "father's energy, his sense of justice, his fascination with mystery…and his ability to corral his emotions." Ironically, on October 4, 1981, Vincent conducted a private autopsy of the remains of Lee Harvey Oswald, whose body was exhumed to make certain it truly was Oswald in his grave. It was.

in Brooklyn for 15 years. And she died in Manhattan. Are you sure I signed it?" Assured he had done so based on the interviewer possessing a certified copy, DiMaio stated, "The only way I could have signed it…occasionally what happens is that you are temporarily assigned to an area if someone is not available then you will sign it. I never did the autopsy. I don't know why the hell I signed it. I knew nothing about the case. I had very little contact with [Dr.] Luke. Still can't understand why I signed it unless I was compelled to do so."

No follow-up question was asked regarding DiMaio's "compelled to do so" answer. Recall that John Broich also weighed in on DiMaio's involvement in Kilgallen's death, stating in his audiotaped interview, "Regarding the Certificate of Death, it was most unusual for DiMaio to sign it for Dr. Luke, since DiMaio was deputy chief for Brooklyn, and Kilgallen died in Manhattan."

If there was underworld influence blunting any investigation before it began, did Mafioso Frank Costello, at the behest of Carlos Marcello, use his power to influence the signing of Kilgallen's Certificate of Death by a Junior medical examiner who was stationed in another ME Office bureau and had no connection to her case. Was this done to prevent any follow-up by the ME's office— controlled by the Mafia as John Broich and Stephen Goldner alleged—into the mysterious circumstances surrounding the famous columnist's death?

Most importantly, was this possible scenario complete with DiMaio's signing of the Certificate of Death, essentially closing Kilgallen's case, simply a continuation of the mob operation Kilgallen believed had occurred to assassinate JFK and Lee Harvey Oswald? Had Marcello and the Mafia's control of the events following the assassinations stretched not only to the very day Kilgallen died two years later but even to the official documents erroneously pinpointing her time of death as "12 Noon" on November 8, 1965, a complete impossibility.

Worse, Dr. DiMaio had signed a document "For James Luke,' beneath the following printed words: "I hereby certify that in accordance with the provisions of law, I took charge of the dead body. I further certify from the investigation and post mortem examination with autopsy that in my opinion, death occurred on the date and at the hour stated above." Filed November 10, 1965, two days after Kilgallen died, DiMaio's untruthful statements marked yet another injustice inflicted on the courageous woman who fought for justice her entire life.

CHAPTER 38

Perhaps Dorothy Kilgallen's tombstone should be etched with words she wrote within days after Jack Ruby shot Lee Harvey Oswald. Questioning the assassinations investigations, Kilgallen wrote something important for the ages: "Justice is a big rug. When you pull it out from under one person, a lot of others fall, too." This strong statement is as true today as it was five decades ago. If, one day in the future, Kilgallen's thick file on the JFK assassination investigation is recovered, her search for justice in the death of her beloved president may be completed.

Instead, Kilgallen is currently the forgotten woman in any discussion of the JFK assassination, despite her having launched an investigation second to none, and one far superior especially with regard to objectivity to that of the Warren Commission or, arguably, the House Select Committee on Assassinations. Sadly, for history's sake, her being erased from the map means than none of Kilgallen's insightful *Journal-American* columns, ones based on credible evidence by an eyewitness to the events in Dallas questioning the "Oswald Alone" theory ("The Oswald File Must Not Close," "DA to Link Ruby to Oswald," etc.) has ever surfaced in print until now.

In the so-called leading books on the subject—*Cased Closed*, by Gerald Posner; *Legacy of Secrecy*, by Lamar Waldron and Thom Hartmann; *Killing Kennedy*, by Bill O'Reilly; and *The Kennedy Half-Century*, by Larry J. Sabato—Kilgallen is not even mentioned, or is mentioned solely in passing, on only one page.

Although former Charles Manson prosecutor Vincent Bugliosi wrote of Kilgallen's investigations in his book *Reclaiming History*, he severely distorted her coverage of the assassinations by completely misrepresenting the facts, ignoring her columns and disregarding Kilgallen having exposed Ruby's Warren Commission testimony before its release date. Bugliosi also discounted (actually made fun of) any notion that Kilgallen had interviewed Jack Ruby during his trial. He apparently never interviewed Ruby's co-counsel, Joe Tonahill or read newspaper accounts or Judge Joe Brown's book confirming the interviews. Like many others, including J. Edgar Hoover, promoting the "Oswald Alone" theory, past and present, Bugliosi fit certain facts to the conclusions he wanted to reach and dismissed credible facts in opposition to those conclusions. This accounts for his unfair treatment of Kilgallen and her pursuit of the truth.

The bottom line is that whoever silenced Kilgallen successfully accomplished the ultimate goal: her voice was never heard again. She was never able to dismiss all the crazy talk of "Oswald Alone" and instead proclaim that, based on her research, what happened in Dallas in November, 1963, was a plain and simple mob operation, start to finish. If Kilgallen had lived, as mentioned, the course of history would have been altered.

Hopefully, when confronted with the fresh facts presented in this book, the Manhattan District Attorney's office will decide to re-open the investigation into her death. Several witnesses to what happened in the days, months and years surrounding Kilgallen's death are still alive. They include Ron Pataky, Dr. Donald Hoffman, Dr. Michael Baden, Dr. Steve Goldner, John Mahan, Phyllis McGuire, Jim Lehrer, Barbara Walters, Larry King, Dr. Ibne Hassan, Alan Eichler, Johnny Whiteside, Eileen Broich and her son Chris, and most importantly, "Dickie," Jill and Kerry Kollmar. Questioning them about their recollections of what happened 50 years ago is important for history's sake.[1]

---

[1] Also of interest to the D.A.'s office and the general public are the plethora of photograph, documents and other memorabilia about Kilgallen's life and times available at the Billy Rose Theatre Division of the New York Public Library.

Regardless, it seems entirely appropriate to imagine what may have happened if Kilgallen made her planned trip to New Orleans in November, 1965:

Returning to New York City from New Orleans with her new evidence connecting Marcello, Oswald and Ruby, Kilgallen completed her JFK and Oswald assassinations investigation. She exposed the evidence in a series of Journal-American articles, or perhaps more likely, organized the material into manuscript form so that Bennett Cerf could have rushed her book into publication at Random House. Either way, Kilgallen's conclusion that the JFK and Oswald assassinations were simply part of a very successful mob operation, it appears certain, would have shone through.

Soon after, the shocking evidence Kilgallen revealed triggered a full-scale grand jury investigation of the twin assassinations. With Kilgallen as the star witness, and her evidence having triggered a full-scale investigation including subpoenaing of relevant witnesses, the Grand Jury issued an indictment charging Carlos Marcello and his Dallas underlings with conspiracy to murder JFK and Oswald.

Based on the same evidence Kilgallen produced, J. Edgar Hoover was indicted. The charge was obstruction of justice by deliberately preventing any investigation of the twin assassinations. He resigned pending the outcome of the court proceedings.

Through Kilgallen's disclosures, disbarment proceedings were filed against Melvin Belli for having compromised Jack Ruby's constitutional rights to adequate representation. Ruby's new attorney was working on a plea agreement with the Dallas prosecutors that would save his life.

Instead of being forgotten through the years Kilgallen's findings were included in any and all discussions and debates about the JFK assassination. As a result of her relentless search for what really occurred in Dallas in November 1963, Kilgallen's theories became part of the historical record. For her tireless dedication to truth and justice, Dorothy Kilgallen earned the Pulitzer Prize for Journalism. In the audience, husband Richard and children Dickie, Jill and Kerry loudly applauded their wife and mother, a true beacon of inspiration whose work acumen serve as a role model to men and women alike.

To be certain, Dorothy Kilgallen balanced motherhood with a far-reaching professional career—one that entailed larger-than-life achievements—in a manner that overwhelms those of modern-day female media personalities. Today these achievements go unrecognized, her name is not even listed among the finest reporters in history, man or woman. There are no awards in her name, no tributes, most people remember her for being a *What's My Line?* game show celebrity instead of for her accomplishments as a gifted wordsmith, superb columnist, and one of the finest investigative reporters who ever covered a high-profile trial.

In the days and years ahead, it is hoped that Kilgallen will receive the recognition she deserves but instead of being memorialized by the remarks of colleagues, friends or celebrities, perhaps this inspiring woman should be remembered best by a comment made by one of her loyal "Voice of Broadway" readers as noted in the *New York Post Daily Magazine*:

> During her 30-plus years on the newspaper scene, marriages have floundered, murderers have gone to their reward, kings have fallen, queens have been installed, and Dorothy Kilgallen has brought to all of these events a dash of color, a pinch of moral indignation, a soupçon of understanding and two tablespoons of malice. She was the very best at what she did.

EPILOGUE

Through the years, this author has become known for exposing the truth about important matters of historical importance in my 20+ published books. Each one has been controversial and each time heavy criticism has come my way.

In *Down for the Count*, my denouncing the verdict in the Mike Tyson rape trial was condemned. In *Miscarriage of Justice*, my questioning whether the life sentence imposed on spy Jonathan Pollard was proper ignited a backlash by those who believed he should have been executed.

When I wrote *Beneath the Mask of Holiness: Thomas Merton and the Forbidden Love Affair that Set Him Free*, those who love Merton chastised me for having the audacity to reveal Merton's human side. My book, *The Poison Patriarch: How the Betrayals of Joseph P. Kennedy Caused the Assassination of JFK* was rejected by folks who worship the Kennedys despite their being, arguably, the worst political family in history.

This time, the intention is to give Dorothy Kilgallen her "day in court," so to speak, albeit 50 years after she died. Critics, and perhaps her family members, will criticize me for failing to let her rest in peace but as Thomas Merton once said, "If you want to help others, you have got to make up your mind to write things that some will condemn." Despite objections, hopefully what I have written will help clear Kilgallen's reputation because this amazing woman certainly deserves it.

This book was born of eight words: "They've killed Dorothy; now they'll go after Ruby."

They were uttered, as noted, by Jack Ruby's attorney Melvin Belli whom I knew personally during the 1980s. He said them to friend Dr. Martin Schorr shortly after Kilgallen's death.

Dr. Schorr's revelation happened while I was researching a biography of Belli, published as *Melvin Belli: King of the Courtroom* in 2007. I then used the information gathered about Belli's representation of Ruby as the foundation for *The Poison Patriarch*. Published in 2013, it is the only book written by a criminal defense trial lawyer and network legal analyst based on motive and why Bobby Kennedy was not killed in 1963 instead of why JFK was. For more information about that book, check my website, www. markshawbooks.com.

Despite considerable evidence to the contrary based on common sense and logic, especially with regard to any plausible motive for Oswald alone to have assassinated the president, this true distortion of history has prevailed. Many simply just do not want to believe there was a conspiracy to kill JFK, and these people continue to be in denial. But in recent years, polls have shown that most Americans, especially intelligent young people, have discarded the myths and decided that yes, JFK's murder was orchestrated by more than one person.

Throughout the writing process for *The Poison Patriarch*, Belli's words about Kilgallen's death haunted me and I knew I had to investigate her mysterious death, a cold case if there ever was one. I began by researching every account written by journalists, authors, and those circulating on the internet including both the incredible and the outlandish. As the research progressed, I was saddened by the amount of false information spread about Kilgallen, the first true media icon.

When I read the words "circumstances unknown" describing Kilgallen's death imbedded in the New York City medical examiner's report, my curiosity was peaked. What I hope this book accomplishes is to turn "circumstances unknown" into circumstances *known*. However, doing so proved most difficult due to the complexities of dealing with a cold case five decades old. Most of the eyewitnesses to what happened have long since passed and retrieving physical evidence was impossible. I thus concentrated first on the most credible aspects of Lee Israel's *Kilgallen* biography and

Jonny Whiteside's Johnnie Ray biography *Cry*. I was also most fortunate to read the superb investigative article "Who Killed Dorothy Kilgallen?" written by Sara Jordan in *Midwest Today* and published by her father Larry who also contributed.

It was at this point in time that a true blessing happened when I learned of superb researcher Kathryn Fauble whose passion for discovering the truth about how Kilgallen died, and why, was matched by an associate who apparently did much of the legwork. Amazingly enough, I was told there existed several videotaped and audiotaped interviews available with those who knew Kilgallen best, including hairdressers Marc Sinclaire and Charles Simpson. Kathryn was kind enough to permit me to use the preserved interviews as well as other information she provided about Kilgallen's life and times as the foundation for discovering what really occurred before, during and after the famous journalist and TV star's death.

As time progressed, I continued the research by reading as many Kilgallen columns and investigative articles as possible. The documents provided insight into her personality and amazing work acumen. I grew to respect her more and more as the days passed. Many times I said to myself, *Dorothy, I'm going to give you the investigation you deserved many years ago. And I'm going to make sure the true story of your life and times is told.* Several times, I felt as if the Holy Spirit was guiding me along, that Dorothy was actually speaking to me from the hereafter, guiding me to clues and fresh evidence critical to solving the mystery as to why she died and how. Along the way, I kept reminding myself that I was fighting for Dorothy, that I was her defender, her paladin harking back to the days when I was a public defender in the criminal courts. She was truly a remarkable woman. Dorothy may have been a college dropout but she was smart, in fact, smarter than anyone who has ever investigated the case she cared most about, the JFK assassination. And through the years, no one had fought for Dorothy, not her friends, her journalistic colleagues, and not her children. Only the latter know why and one regret I have is that Kilgallen's two sons, Dickie and Kerry, and daughter Jill would not speak to me about their mother. I posted messages for both Dickie and Kerry on Facebook but neither responded. On two different occasions, I spoke to Jill for a short time explaining my intentions in the book and the desire to secure her side of the story.

During a trip to Los Angeles, I left two voice messages for her suggesting we meet. And later a long message informing Jill that I had completed my research, intended to publish the book, and intended to persuade the Manhattan D.A. to re-open her mother's case. I pointed out that if she or one of her brothers wanted to read my manuscript, they were welcome to do so with the promise to consider never publishing the book if they objected. Again, no response was received from Jill.

To provide a context for the years, months and days before and after Kilgallen died, I stitched her story together with those most impacting her life. She was indeed, with all due respect to Martha Gelhorn and others who were journalistic pioneers, the first true female media icon, a woman who stood tall while competing in a man's world.

Regarding Kilgallen's investigation of the JFK and Oswald assassinations, unlike those who have written about it as self-proclaimed experts, Kilgallen was present, front and center, from the day the president was shot through the Jack Ruby trial, with a front row seat as an eyewitness to history. What she heard and saw provide credibility for what she wrote as the lone wolf screaming about the absurdity of the "Oswald Alone" theories propounded by J. Edgar Hoover. I have no doubt that if she had not been eliminated, the course of history, as noted, would have been altered since Kilgallen had the power to trigger a full-scale grand jury investigation based on the evidence she had uncovered. Hopefully, what she said will be taken seriously with the end result not only a re-examination of her death by the Manhattan District Attorney's office since Ron Pataky, a main suspect, is still alive, but Congress deciding to re-open the investigation of the JFK assassination to permit the evidence accumulated through her columns, articles, and statements to friends and colleagues and that of reputable researchers to be heard loud and clear. If this happens, I have no doubt the ludicrous "Oswald Alone" theory will be erased from the history books so that young people can understand the truth about what happened, that the death of JFK was in fact simply part of, as Kilgallen discovered, a mob operation based on revenge, as noted in this book. When this happens, it should be recalled that it was JFK himself who said, "The great enemy of truth is often not the lie—deliberate, contrived, and dishonest—but the myth—persistent, persuasive, and unrealistic. Belief in myths allows the comfort of opinion without the discomfort of thought."

Ironically, in my opinion, Kilgallen's tragic death marks her as "collateral damage" due to Joseph P. Kennedy's double cross of the Mafia by ordering JFK to appoint Robert Kennedy attorney general when he had to know RFK would target the underworld figures. When Bobby did, JFK was a dead man, and Kilgallen was killed trying to prove why and by whom.

Most importantly, I believe my research has lain to rest notions Kilgallen either committed suicide or died by an accidental overdose of barbiturates combined with too much alcohol. For too long, speculation of these two causes of death has cast doubt over her career. This despite all the evidence pointing to the only plausible explanation: Kilgallen was murdered to silence the reporter who knew too much about the JFK and Oswald assassinations.

Of all of the words spoken about Dorothy Kilgallen through the years, those propounded by her *What's My Line?* fellow panel member Bennett Cerf, impact me the most. He said of his friend, "A lot of people knew Dorothy as a very tough game player; others knew her as tough newspaper woman.... But we got to know her as a human being, and a more loveable, softer, loyal person never lived, and we're going to miss her terribly."

Bless you Dorothy. You were a champion in every sense of the word.

ACKNOWLEDGMENTS

While my name appears on the cover of this book as author, what I have written is due in part, to the incredible cooperation provided me by many people who assisted with the story I wanted to tell.

These people include Sara and Larry Jordan of *Midwest Today* magazine, two gifted journalists whose 2007 article, "Who Killed Dorothy Kilgallen?" was a masterpiece. The investigation they launched was first rate and I thank them for sharing the information they gathered with me. Also to be thanked is gifted researcher Kathryn Fauble, a tireless researcher who has sought the truth about Kilgallen's death for many years, and her associates who assisted the effort.

I wish to thank Lauren Mandell, Online Marketing Associate, *NY Post,* and Marcia Morgan, FBI Records Management Division, Washington, D.C. Thanks also to Vanessa St. Oegger-Menn for her assistance with transcription of a Richard Kollmer interview.

Carol Lind and Joyce Revilla are thanked for their thoughts about Melvin Belli crucial to understanding his role in the Jack Ruby case and his relationship with Dorothy Kilgallen during the Ruby trial.

I thank Mike Horii, Dave Foley, Earle Peterson, Randy and Karen Baker, Jim Whitesell, Randy Boris, Arielle Neal, June Cardinale, Jonna MacDougall, and Marcia Bauma for their feedback after reading various manuscript drafts. Each provided comments and suggestions most helpful. Also my friend Randy Boris for his help with regard to certain toxilogical questions that arose during my research.

Special thanks to Greg Desilet, who provided expert editing skills and book suggestions all around. And to Marcia Bauman, whose editing assistance improved the text considerably as the book neared its printing.

Also thanks to Hien Nguyen, who provided expert research at the National Archives. Her contribution to the worthiness of the final product is substantial. James Wong at Circle Video in Burlingame, California, is thanked for editing nearly a hundred clips from the videotaped and audiotaped interviews noted in the book and posted on the book's website. Special thanks to Gael Chandler, Jay Scherberth and Marcia Bauman for their superb creative abilities with the book trailer. Great people.

To publisher Anthony Ziccardi and his colleagues at Post Hill Press, I'm honored to be one of your authors. To my crack agent, Frank Weimann of Folio Literary Management, thanks for your belief in our book and for your hard work in securing a top-flight publisher. You are the best at what you do, a tireless agent whose reputation is unmatched in the literary world.

My wife Wen-ying Lu, my true love, is thanked for her support and superb editing skills. Her confidence in me and belief in this book helped me through the rough times when I wanted to give up the fight. To my dearly departed canine friend Black Sox, you are always with me in my heart and soul.

Certainly, the Holy Spirit guiding me every day is responsible for any effort on my part to publish books that make people stop and think about the truth. My spiritual guru, Thomas Merton, is thanked for his wisdom; for helping me be the best spiritual person I can be.

To Dorothy Kilgallen, I trust this book is one you would favor. Your career was truly remarkable. I hope my effort to chronicle your life and times lives up to the high journalism standards you set for yourself.

Mark Shaw

PHOTOGRAPH
SOURCES

Cover: Kilgallen at typewriter, Corbis Images

Page 6: Kilgallen wearing her favorite wide-brimmed hat, Corbis Images

Page 8: Dorothy and Sister Eleanor, Corbis Images

Page 9: Kilgallen, Ekins, and Kieran entering "The Race Around the World," Author Collection, photo purchased from Tribune Photo Archives

Page 14: Richard Kollmar, Author Collection, photo purchased from Tribune Photo Archives

Page 20: *What's My Line?* Stars: Dorothy Kilgallen, Steve Allen, Arlene Francis, Bennett Cerf, and Moderator John Charles Daly, Getty Images

Page 26: Kilgallen at Dr. Sam Sheppard Trial – 1954, Corbis Images

Page 28: Dorothy Kilgallen and Johnnie Ray with unidentified friend, Corbis Images

Page 36: Dorothy Kilgallen and youngest son Kerry at townhouse, Author Collection, photo purchased from Tribune Photo Archives

Page 42: Kilgallen and Ernest Hemingway at the Stork Club circa early 1961. Credit: Billy Rose Theatre Division: The New York Public Library for the Performing Arts, Astor, Lenox and Tilden Foundations

Page 66: Kilgallen and Belli at Ruby trial, Author Collection, courtesy of Videotape Owner

Page 71: Kilgallen whispering in Tonahill's ear, Author Collection, courtesy of Videotape Owner

Page 92: Kilgallen's confidant and hairdresser Marc Sinclair, Author Collection, courtesy of Videotape Owner

Page 94: Kilgallen at time of death, Author Collection, photo purchased from Tribune Photo Archives

Page 117: John and Eileen Broich photograph, Author Collection, courtesy of Broich family

Page 123: *Murder One* cover, Author Collection

Page 143: Sinclaire pointing at J/A Article re: Mae/Richard funeral confrontation, Author Collection

Page 167: Charles Simpson, Author Collection, courtesy of Videotape Owner

Page 182: Marcello being deported to Guatemala, Corbis Images

Page 214: Mafia Don Frank Costello, Corbis Images

Page 219: Katherine Stone points to Regency Hotel bar booth where Kilgallen sat with "Mystery Man" hours before she died, Author Collection, courtesy of Videotape Owner

Page 235: Kilgallen and Pataky, Author Collection, courtesy of Videotape Owner

Page 256: Ron Pataky in Ohio, Author Collection, courtesy of Videotape Owner

Page 276: Kilgallen in all her glory, Author Collection, photo purchased from Tribune Photo Archives

REFERENCE NOTES

The content of this book is the result of accessing as many credible print sources as possible and while interviewing those who have firsthand information about the life and times of Dorothy Kilgallen and others mentioned in the book.

Regarding print sources, only well-researched books, newspapers, magazines, and credible internet sites were considered. When possible, quotes used were confirmed through a second source.

Concerning the information focusing on the JFK and Lee Harvey Oswald assassinations, interviews conducted during the author's 10-year-plus research for his two books, *Melvin Belli: King of the Courtroom* and *The Poison Patriarch: How the Betrayals of Joseph P. Kennedy Caused the Assassination of JFK* were utilized when necessary. Nearly 100 individuals with firsthand accounts were woven into the text for those books and this one. Each was an eyewitness to history; each had a different perspective of what occurred before, during, and after the Dallas killings 50 year ago.

Secondary sources regarding the assassinations were only included when other information corroborated whatever facts were discovered. Certainly all information collected from FBI and CIA files was accurate based on the author having secured the files through the Freedom of Information Act. Kilgallen's autopsy report, exposed here for the first time, was authenticated through the National Archives.

Readers are welcome to dispute the author's sources and any, and all, facts and theories proposed in this book. Based on feedback, the author will revise future editions based on suggestions and corrections.

Quotes

Kilgallen's fame from *New York Post Daily Magazine* series, "The Dorothy Kilgallen Story," April, 1960. "Justice is a big rug..." from Kilgallen *Journal-American* article.

Introduction

Information about Kilgallen funeral and additional facts about her from the *New York Journal-American*, United Press International accounts and *Kilgallen: A Biography* by Lee Israel, 1979. Details about Kilgallen's death were from the NYC medical examiner's report, November 1965. Marlon Swing quote from *Cry: The Johnnie Ray Story* by Johnny Whiteside, 1994. Bennett Cerf quote on Kilgallen from Kathryn Fauble collection.

Chapter 1

Kilgallen background from *Kilgallen: A Biography* by Lee Israel, 1979. Kilgallen information about wanting to be a reporter and mother's disagreement from *TV Radio Mirror* interview, August 1960. Quote re: Jim Kilgallen's editor, text on Kilgallen fame prediction her early writing and interest in crime reporting, her college days, her first published writing quote, and promotional material from *New York Evening-Journal* archives.

Chapter 2

Facts about Kilgallen's coverage of Antonio murder case from *Journal-American* archives. Information about Kilgallen's coverage of the Bruno Hauptman trial, her flight around the world, her Hollywood experiences, her trip to the Queen's coronation, and her "Voice of Broadway" column are based on *Kilgallen, A Biography* by Lee Israel, 1979. Kilgallen quote re: Nellie Bly from *Journal-American* archives and footnote information about Bly from *Eighty Days: Nellie and Elizabeth Bisland's History Making Trip Around the World* by Matthew Goodman, 2014. Further information

301

about Kilgallen's around the world adventure from her book, *Girl Around the World*, 1936. Information about Kilgallen arriving to board the Hindenburg from *New York Post Daily Magazine*, April 1960. Details about *The Sinner Takes All* from www.imdb.com/title/tt0029573/. Sobel quotes re: Kilgallen from *Journal-American* archives. Hearst newspaper chain Kilgallen announcement from *Journal-American* archives. Kilgallen column mentioning Kollmar from *Journal-American* archives.

Chapter 3

Kilgallen mention of Kollmar in column from Kathryn Fauble collection. Text about Dorothy Kilgallen's wedding, the sandwich being named after her, the birth of her second child, the Lonergan trial coverage, the *Breakfast with Dorothy and Dick* program, *Dorothy's Diary*, *Leave it to the Girls*, and her stand against those named in the *Counterattack* based on *Kilgallen: A Biography* by Lee Israel, 1979. Kilgallen FBI notation from FBI files.

Jean Bach's comment about the Dorothy and Dick radio program from E! Network's *Mysteries and Scandals*, 1998. Footnote quote from Bobby Short re: Kilgallen column from *TV Radio Mirror*.

Chapter 4

Information about Kilgallen and Kollmer radio program from *Broadcasting: The Weekly Magazine*, April 1945. Kilgallen titles and second radio program based on *Kilgallen* by Lee Israel, 1979. *Leave it to the Girls* details from Israel biography. *What's My Line?* details from Israel biography and other sources. Gil Fates' comment re: origin of *WML?* from *What's My Line, TV's Most Famous Panel Show*, 1978. Kilgallen's comments about the show from *TV Radio Mirror*, August 1960.

Steve Allen's comments about Kilgallen and *What's My Line?* from E! Network's *Mysteries and Scandals*, 1998. Marlon Swing quotes re: Kilgallen and *What's My Line?* from E! Network's *Mysteries and Scandals*, 1998. Comment re: Kilgallen prowess on show from *New York Post Daily Magazine* series, 1960. Kilgallen objection to Communist publication and Bach escort details from Israel biography. Kilgallen and CIA standoff re: sources from CIA documents.

Johnnie Ray information from *Cry* by Jonny Whiteside, 1994. Ray at Copacabana from *Cry*. Kilgallen coverage of Queen Elizabeth coronation from Israel book. Kilgallen's "look" from *New York Post Daily Magazine*, April 1960.

Chapter 5

Birth of Kerry from *Kilgallen* by Lee Israel, 1979. Kilgallen column on mothers from *Journal-American* archives. Dr. Sam Sheppard trial coverage by Kilgallen and Bob Considine comments on Kilgallen's star power from Hearst Syndicate article. Johnnie Ray Kilgallen column from *Journal-American* archives. Information on Edward R. Murrow Kollmar family interviews from *Person to Person* archives.

Monaco wedding and *What's My Line?* details from Israel biography. Kilgallen description quote by *New York Post Daily Magazine*. Description of Kilgallen and Ray romance from *Cry* by Jonny Whiteside, 1994. Kilgallen columns on politics and Hepburn, etc. from Kathryn Fauble collection. Bill Slocum's description of Kilgallen's celebrity status from Kathryn Fauble collection.

Chapter 6

Kilgallen Sinatra series from Heart Syndicate article and Kilgallen/Sinatra feud from *His Way: The Unauthorized Biography of Frank Sinatra* by Kitty Kelley, 1986. Bobby Short encounter based on Israel biography. Kilgallen townhouse description and party information from the *New York Post Daily Magazine* series. Steve Allen quote about Kilgallen parties from E! Network's *Mysteries and Scandals*, 1998. Liz Smith quote from Whiteside book. Johnnie Ray quotes re: Ray and Kilgallen from episode of *Mysteries and Scandals* appearing on the E! Network, 1998. Ray's comments about Kilgallen based on Whiteside book. Wesinger quotes from Whiteside book.

Chapter 7

Sinatra "Voice of Broadway" column from Hearst Syndicate articles. Information on Kilgallen and rules from Whiteside book. Information on Kilgallen and Milton Berle show from Israel book. Kilgallen columns from Hearst Syndicate articles. Information about "63rd Street Parties" and Ray/Kilgallen romance from Whiteside book. Kilgallen criticism of Jack Parr, anti-Castro column, and info re: Kilgallen's "Cloop" office based on Israel book. Kilgallen's comments on Nina Khrushchev and quote in footnote by Louis Sobel from Hearst Syndicate article. Anonymous comment on Kilgallen becoming "notorious" from Jonny Whiteside book.

Chapter 8

Quotes re: Johnnie Ray Detroit trial and Marlon Swing comments re: Kilgallen from Jonny Whiteside book. Finch trial information based on Israel book. Quote re: Kilgallen celebrity status at Finch trial from *Time Magazine*. Information about and quotes by Kilgallen from *TV Radio Mirror*, 1960. Kilgallen Random House publishing deal from Israel book.

Kilgallen 1960 presidential election prediction from Hearst Syndicate archives. Jean Bach comment about Kilgallen marriage from E! Network's *Mysteries and Scandals*, 1998. Election information from *The Poison Patriarch*. Kilgallen quote on Kennedy's from Israel book. Kilgallen comments re: *NY Post Daily Magazine* articles from *Journal-American* archives. Kilgallen inauguration information from Israel book. Kilgallen/Sinatra feud facts from Hearst Syndicate archives. Kilgallen and Ray information re: nightlife from Whiteside book.

Hemingway's comments from *New York Post Daily Magazine* Kilgallen series. Kilgallen comments re: Hemingway from Hearst Syndicate archives. Alan Eichler's comments from author interview. Tad Mann quote from his book, *Beyond the Marquee*, 2006. Kilgallen/Johnnie Ray information from Whiteside book. Kilgallen comments on PT-109 film from *Journal-American* archives. Kilgallen mention of White House visit with Kerry meeting JFK from Whiteside book.

Chapter 9

Kilgallen's knowledge of JFK and Marilyn Monroe affair and her column about Monroe death from Hearst Syndicate archives. Kilgallen mention of Ruark book column from *Journal-American* archives. Ruark comments re: Sinatra from Scripps-Howard Newspaper Alliance archives. Mortimer being attacked by Sinatra from Kitty Kelly book, *My Way*, 2010. Profumo trial coverage by Kilgallen from Hearst Syndicate article. Kennedy visiting Dallas from *Dallas Morning News* archives. Kilgallen/Shepard case from Israel book. Costello quote from *Contract on America* by David E. Scheim, 1988.

Chapter 10

Kilgallen earnings based on Israel book. Kilgallen column from *Journal-American* archives. Kilgallen and Richard quarrel over Johnnie Ray from Whiteside book. Kilgallen column on "big business figure" from Hearst Syndicate column. Account of JFK assassination from various newspaper accounts. Hoover call to RFK from Gentry book. Kilgallen column on JFK death from Hearst Syndicate article. Oswald statement based on *Dallas Morning News* stories. RFK statement to Guthman from *RFK* by C. David Heymann, 1998. Kilgallen column on JFK assassination from Hearst Syndicate.

Chapter 11

Description of Ruby shooting Oswald from various newspaper accounts. Kilgallen contacting sources at Dallas Police Department based on Israel book. Ruby shooting from *Contract on America* by David E. Scheim, 1988. Kilgallen reaction based on various sources including Israel book.

Belli statement from author interview of J. Kelly Farris. Kilgallen contacting sources at DPD from *Dallas Morning News*. Ruby statement to Archer from British documentary, *Viewpoint 88: The Men Who Killed Kennedy*. Hoover proclamations based on *The Poison Patriarch*, 2013.

Kilgallen watching JFK funeral and her observations based on Israel book. Kilgallen column on Kennedys from Hearst Syndicate article. RFK reactions from *The Poison Patriarch*. Hoover press release from *Washington Post*.

Chapter 12

Kilgallen column on JFK death from *Journal-American* archives. Bill Alexander observations from author interview. Kilgallen reaction to Belli as Ruby's lawyer from *The Poison Patriarch* by Mark Shaw, 2013. Belli footnote re: conflicting versions as to representation of Ruby from Belli's books, *Dallas Justice* and *My Life on Trial*. Belli arrival in Dallas from *My Life on Trial* by Melvin Belli, 1976. Kilgallen's "The Oswald File Must Not Close" column from *Journal-American* archives.

Chapter 13

Belli communication with Kilgallen based on *My Life On Trial* book. Ruby/Belli conversation from *The Poison Patriarch* by Mark Shaw, 2013. Kilgallen research on Belli based on *Melvin Belli: King of the Courtroom* by Mark Shaw, 2007. Hoover text based on *J. Edgar Hoover: The Man and his Secrets* by Curt Gentry, 1991. LBJ and RFK meeting from David Talbot's book, *Brothers: The Hidden History of the Kennedy Years* (2007). Jeff Shesol's footnote comments from *Mutual Contempt: Lyndon Johnson, Robert Kennedy, and the Feud that Defined a Decade*. New York: 1997.

John Connolly' quote from PBS documentary. Kilgallen column on assassination from *Journal-American* archives. Kuhn speech from *The Poison Patriarch* by Mark Shaw, 2013.

Belli trial strategy from *My Life On Trial* by Melvin Belli, 1976. McCone and O'Donnell's quotes from David Talbot's book, *Brothers: The Hidden History of the Kennedy Years* (2007). Ruby/Belli jail visit from *My Life On Trial*.

Chapter 14

Belli announcement of insanity defense from *My Life On Trial.* Belli/Kilgallen interaction from *The Poison Patriarch* and Kilgallen later actions. Ruby's brother interaction based on *The Poison Patriarch.* Quotes re: Ruby trial from *Life Magazine,* Feb. 29, 1964. Kilgallen access to defense letter to WC and Kilgallen column on government refusal to give Ruby defense documents from *Journal-American* archives.

Tonahill and others criticism of Belli insanity defense from *The Poison Patriarch.* Belli and Kilgallen interaction based on author interview with Joyce Revilla, Belli secretary, 2014. RFK actions and Ethel Kennedy comments from David Talbot's book, *Brothers: The Hidden History of the Kennedy Years,* 2007. Kilgallen's comments about Ruby and Oswald being acquainted from Hearst Syndicate. Bob Considine's quotes re: Kilgallen from *Dallas Morning News.* Kilgallen's comment to Jim Lehrer based on Israel book.

Chapter 15

Kilgallen visiting Dealey Plaza from *Dallas Morning News* archives. Ruby/Belli discussions from *The Poison Patriarch.* Hoover/Tolson dialogue from Gentry Book. Belli inner thoughts from *King of the Courtroom.* Kilgallen interview with Jack Ruby from Joe Tonahill DVD interview by associate of investigative reporter Kathryn Fauble. Kilgallen column from *Journal-American* archives. Ruby trial information based on Ruby trial transcripts. Belli/Kilgallen interaction from *The Poison Patriarch.* Kilgallen column from Hearst Syndicate archives. Justice Department lack of cooperation from *House Select Committee on Assassinations Report,* 1979.

Belli/Ruby interaction from *The Poison Patriarch.* Kilgallen second interview with Ruby from *My Life On Trial* by Melvin Belli, 1976. Ruby trial testimony from court records. Tonahill comments re: Ruby interview from audiotaped interview. Kilgallen calling Ruby a "gangster" from Ruby account during medical evaluation (JFK microfilm, vol.5, p D24.) and from several sources including *Legacy of Secrecy* by Lamar Waldron,

2008 and *Dallas Justice* by Melvin Belli, 1964. Wise comments based on *The Poison Patriarch*. RFK impressions including Salinger comments from *Robert Kennedy: His Life* by Evan Thomas, 2000.

Belli's mistaking Ruby for Oswald during trial based on *Dallas and the Jack Ruby Trial: Memoir of Judge Joe B. Brown, Sr.* by Diane Holloway Ph.D., 2001. Belli comment to Milton Hunt from author interview with Hunt. Ruby wanting to testify from *The Poison Patriarch*. *The Jack Ruby Trial Revisited: The Diary of Jury Foreman Max Causey* by Max Causey and John Mark Dempsey, 2000.

Chapter 16

Alexander's comments based on author interviews with Alexander. Belli final argument from *The Poison Patriarch*. Kilgallen comment re: Belli argument from *Journal-American* archives. Alexander comments from *The Poison Patriarch*. Ruby trial verdict from *My Life On Trial*. Belli comments re: verdict and his firing from *Dallas Morning News*. Kilgallen's column from Hearst Syndicate. Lane comment from Israel book and other sources. Kilgallen footnote comments about Mark Lane from Jim Bohannon Show (date unknown).

Chapter 17

Kilgallen meeting with F. Lee Bailey based on Israel book and trial transcript notes. RFK's comments based on *Robert Kennedy: His Life* by Evan Thomas, 2000. Kilgallen and Lenny Bruce case from Israel book. Kilgallen's Ruby Warren Commission information from *Journal-American* and *Associated Press* archives. FBI investigation of Kilgallen and her continuing research in Dallas based on Israel book. Sabato footnote quote from *The Kennedy Half-Century* by Larry J. Sabato, 2013.

Kilgallen columns on FBI investigation and Ruby Warren Commission testimony from *Journal-American* archives. FBI reaction to Kilgallen disclosures and her defiant stand from FBI files. Belli comments from *Boston Herald*. Ruby comments from Warren Commission report.

Kilgallen receiving police log based on Israel book. Kilgallen comments on Curry reaction to JFK death based on *Journal-American* archives. Kilgallen appearance on *Nightlife* from Israel book. Earl Ruby comments to Seth Kantor from *Who Was Jack Ruby?*, 1978.

Chapter 18

Hoover handwriting on Kilgallen column text from FBI files. Re-creation of a JFK assassination scenario based on Israel book. Kilgallen's warning to Mark Lane and code names based on Israel book. Kilgallen "Thank you" column from *Journal-American* archives. Kilgallen calling report "laughable" and the Clemons interview column from Hearst Syndicate. Jack Ruby suicide attempts from *Who Was Jack Ruby?* by Seth Kantor, 1978. Ruby's statement from the *Dallas Morning News* archives. Multiple declarations there was an assassination conspiracy to Marlon Swing and others based on Israel book. Kilgallen column re: Mark Lane from Hearst Syndicate.

Kilgallen trip to Europe, her comments on *Murder One*, and Ray's comments from *Cry* by Jonny Whiteside. Kilgallen's appearance on *Nightlife* based on Israel book. Ruby's trial declaration from Federal Court trial transcripts. Kilgallen columns on Marina Oswald and on continuing investigation of JFK and Oswald assassinations from *Journal-American* archives. Kilgallen's appearance on *Hot Line* based on Israel book. Jean Bach's footnote comments re: Kilgallen JFK assassination file from E! Network's *Mysteries and Scandals*, 1998. Details re: the Kilgallen New Orleans trip with Marc Sinclaire from videotaped interview. Kilgallen's declarations to Gebbias and Simpson based on Israel book. Footnote re: Sinclaire prominence from Hearst Syndicate.

Wade's comments from *Associated Press* article. Sinclaire's statement re: speaking with Kilgallen on Nov. 6 from videotaped interview. Kilgallen visiting Latin Quarter nightclub from researcher Kathryn Fauble. Kilgallen's movements after the *What's My Line?* program based on Israel book. Kilgallen's reported death based on *Journal-American* archives.

Chapter 19

Announcement of Kilgallen death and Sobel quotes from Hearst Syndicate. Considine quotes from Hearst Headline Service. Kilgallen autopsy report and accompanying documents from National Archives Record Number 180-10071-10433, Agency File number 007250 from the House Select Committee on Assassinations.

Chapter 20

Conflicting details about Kilgallen's death from *Journal-American* archives. Police report information from NYC police department records. Maid finding Kilgallen body and further details re: Kilgallen death from Hearst Syndicate archives. Report of Dr. Luke's conclusions from *New York Times* archives. Quotes re: Kilgallen death from *Journal-American* and *New York Post. New York Times* account from *NYT* archives. *New York Herald-Tribune* report from archives.

Israel quotes from Dr. Luke based on Israel book. Israel quotes re: "unidentified chemist" from Israel book. Identity of John Broich from *Midwest Today* article "Who Killed Dorothy Kilgallen?" by Sara Jordan, 2007 as provided by Kathryn Fauble. John Broich audiotaped interview courtesy of Kathryn Fauble. Dr. Baden and Hoffman comments based on Israel book. Dr. Hoffman interview by author, winter 2015. Eileen Broich interview by author, winter 2015.

Chapter 21

Comments re: Kilgallen and Ray drunk based Israel book. Joe Tonahill comments from interview by Kathryn Fauble associate in the 1990s. Comments on Kilgallen financial status from Marc Sinclaire videotaped interview. Quotes re: Kilgallen being paid a $10,000 advance by Random House in 1961 from Gil Fate's book, *What's My Line? The Inside History of TV's Most Famous Panel Show,* 1978. Information on whether Kilgallen wrote *Murder One* from 1978 letter from Mrs. Phyllis Wagner to author Lee Israel.

Levine information based on Israel book. Quote re: Kilgallen manuscript from *Murder One*. Bailey comment from Hearst Syndicate. Jim Kilgallen and Bennett Cerf quotes from *Journal-American* archives. The book cover text and book flap text from *Murder One*. Kilgallen footnote quote re: independence from *Variety* comment as related in *New York Post Daily Magazine* article, April, 1960. Kilgallen quotes re: Sheppard case from *Journal-American* archives. Kilgallen description of Marilyn Sheppard from *New York Post Daily Magazine*, April 1960.

Kilgallen meeting with Bailey and her comments from *New York Post Daily Magazine* article.

Chapter 22

Text about Kilgallen trip to Las Vegas with Johnnie Ray from *Cry* by Jonny Whiteside. John Daly comment re: Kilgallen from *Journal-American* archives. Kilgallen appearance on *WML?* from (www.youtube.com/watch?v=6gn6jS1UK78).

Sinclaire comments from videotaped interview. Dave Spiegel's text from Bob Considine article, November 10, 1965. Dee Anthony information based on Israel book. Ian Anderson's comments re: Anthony from Anthony Dee from www.independent.co.uk/news/obituaries/dee-anthony-manager -who-helped-joe-cocker-peter-frampton-and-jethro-tull-break-into-the -american-market-1877890.html. Eicher comment re: Johnnie Ray and Mafia based on author interview. Text from *Murder One* Preface from book by Kilgallen. Ibne Hassan quotes from author interview winter 2015. Sinclaire comments re: Kilgallen suicide from videotaped interview. Detective Doyle quotes and footnote information based on Israel book. Footnote quote from Sobel from *Journal-American* archives. G. Robert Blakey information based on email exchange with this author, April 5, 2015.

Chapter 23

Marc Sinclaire comments re: Mrs. Henry Ford II from Sinclaire DVD interview by Kathryn Fauble colleague. Frank Sinatra information from Kitty Kelley book *His Way*, 2010 and Israel books. Sinatra comments about Kilgallen from Israel book and www.thisamericanlife.org/radio-archives /episode/54/transcript and *Sinatra: The Chairman* by James Kaplan, 2015. Kilgallen's harsh words about Sinatra from the Kaplan book. Presley comment re Sinatra from *Rhapsody In Black* by John Kruth, 2013. Footnote re: Sinatra links to Mafia from Kaplan book. Footnote comments by Winchell and Sobel from *Journal-American* archives. Sinatra quote re: Kilgallen's death and Dolly Sinatra comment about her son excerpted from "Frank Sinatra Had A Cold" on the official website of acclaimed writer Gay Talese. Sinatra Mafia connections and providing money to Cohen upon prison release from *The Poison Patriarch*.

Sinatra connection to Bugsy Siegel, Cohen and Costello from *The Poison Patriarch*. Lawford quote re: Sinatra based on Kelly book.

Quotes re: Kollmar being an alcoholic and philanderer and Manson's comments based on Israel book. Hatfield information based on Israel book. Kilgallen comment regarding not seeing Richard and his neighborhood wanderings and hobbies from Whiteside book. Mae Kilgallen's accusation, "You killed my Daughter" to Richard Kollmar from Marc Sinclaire's video-taped interview, 2000.

Kilgallen love affair with Ray from Israel book. Joan Bach comments from Israel book. Alan Eicher statement from author interview. Ray/Kollmar fight from Israel book and *Cry* by Whiteside. Kilgallen meeting Ray from Whiteside book.

Sinclaire comments re: Kerry Kollmar threats, buying a gun, Kerry kidnapping potential, Kilgallen changing her will, Switzerland trip, etc. from Sinclaire videotaped interview. Details re: Kerry potentially being fathered by Johnnie Ray from Sinclaire interview. Eichler re: Ray never divulging his being Kerry's birth father and letter from Elma from researcher Kathryn Fauble's assistant.

Information on Kilgallen will from Israel book and *NY Times* and Sinclaire audiotaped interview by researcher Kathryn Fauble associate. Fogerty info from Sinclaire videotaped interview. Kerry blog statements from kerryslifeblog.blogspot.com/2009/04/sweet-jane.html. Sinclaire comments re: Kollmar's mental state from Sinclaire videotaped interview. Kilgallen and Kollmar "headed in separate directions" based on Israel book. George Hopkins account of Kilgallen and Ray meeting in 1952 from researcher Kathryn Fauble. Kollmar not performing his "husbandly duties" from *Cry*. Sinclaire's comments re: Kilgallen married life from audiotaped interview by Kathryn Fauble associate.

Kollmar suicide details from Israel book. Evans re: Kollmar barbs from Israel book. Kerry comment re: Kollmar and Tuinal from Israel book. Bauer and Verne comments from Israel book. Clement nervousness from Sinclaire video. Cerf and Kollmar drunk comment from Israel book. Kollmar lies based on Israel book and Kollmar statement to ME Dr. Luke from official documents. Kollmar statement to Bob and Jean Bach from Israel book. Kollmar statement to Mark Lane from Israel book. Kollmar refusal to permit Kilgallen autopsy from *Cry* by Jonny Whiteside. Kollmar radio interview from Long John Nebel program, aired November 21, 1967.

Israel comments re: Kollmar involvement in Kilgallen death from Israel book. Sinclaire's view re: Kollmar link to Kilgallen death from his videotape interview. Israel comment re: who may have killed Kilgallen from her book.

Chapter 24

Johnson reference re: Kilgallen *Journal-American* column. Kilgallen and son Kerry visit to White House from Israel book. Kilgallen's column re: recollection from Hearst Syndicate. Swing recollection of Kilgallen/Kennedy encounter from *Cry* by Jonny Whiteside. Bob Bach account of JFK/Kilgallen meeting at Stork Club from Israel book.

Kilgallen covering the Ruby trial and Lehrer account from *My Life on Trial, Dallas Justice*, and *The Poison Patriarch*. Belli/Kilgallen interaction from interview with Joyce Rivella, Belli's secretary, and *The Poison Patriarch*. Footnote quote re: Cohen and Belli from *The New York Times* archives.

Ruby testimony based on Warren Commission report. Belli's mention of Kilgallen in *Dallas Justice* and *My Life on Trial*. Television footage of Kilgallen and Belli from NBC footage. Russell comments re: Belli not discussing Ruby trial from *The Poison Patriarch*. Swing's comments from *Cry* by Jonny Whiteside. Ruby statement from *Dallas Morning News* and Warren Commission report.

Chapter 25

Quotes from Liz Smith's syndicated column from *Spokane Daily Chronicle*, December 25, 1976. House Select Committee on Assassinations report text from the Warren Commission report. CIA information re: Kilgallen from government documents. Simpson and Sinclaire interview information from videotaped interviews in 2000 by Kathryn Fauble associate. Marlon Swing comments about Kilgallen from E! Network television special.

Belli comment to Dr. Martin Schorr and Lind and Ellison comments about Belli's disclosures from author interviews with Dr. Schorr, Lind and Ellison. Statements by Kilgallen to Gebbia re: JFK assassination based on Israel book.

Chapter 26

J. Edgar Hoover information based on various sources including Gentry book, *The Poison Patriarch* and FBI files received under the Freedom of Information Act. Hoover directives from Gentry book. Kilgallen column, "Oswald File Must Not Close" from Hearst Syndicate. September 1964 and September 1959 memos from FBI files secured under Freedom of Information Act. "Dickie" Kollmar being contacted by FBI based on Israel book.

Summary of information about Carlos Marcello from *The Poison Patriarch*. Footnote re: Cohen from FBI files secured under the Freedom of Information Act. Giancana/RFK exchange from McClellan Hearings record. RFK comments re: gangster from his book, *The Enemy Within*.

Tina Sinatra's comments from *Sixty Minutes* interview and Sinatra family website at www.sinatrafamily.com. Joe Kennedy soliciting Sam

Giancana's help re: 1960 election from *The Poison Patriarch* and *Sinatra: The Chairman* by James Kaplan, 2015. Paul Anka quotes re: Giancana from *My Way* by Paul Anka, 2013. Ebbins' quotes re: Campbell, JFK and Lawford from *Sinatra: The Chairman* by James Kaplan, 2015. Evelyn Lincoln quote from *The Poison Patriarch*.

Seigenthaler quotes from author interview. Footnote re Joe Kennedy and the president attempting to stop RFK from pursuing the Mafia, etc. from *The Poison Patriarch*. Quote about Marcello from HSCA report. Information re: Marcello being deported from *The Poison Patriarch*. Ragano footnote quotes re: Giancana from Ragano's book, *Mob Lawyer*, 1995. Pileggi quote from author interview, winter, 2015. Quote re: "rabbit punch" to Giancana from *Mafia Princess*, 1984. Marcello desperation and Joe Kennedy being warned from *The Poison Patriarch*. Nancy Ragano quotes from author interview. Marcello trial account from *The Poison Patriarch*.

Robert F. Kennedy Jr. comments to Charlie Rose from 2013 Dallas interview. RFK's comments from O'Donnell based on *Robert Kennedy: His Life* by Evan Thomas, 2000. Footnote quote from Robert F. Kennedy re: Marcello and Civello from *Chicago Tribune*, 1963. Footnote quotes re: Ruby friendships with Campisi from *Contract on America: The Mafia Murder of President John F. Kennedy*, by David Scheim, 1988. Revilla footnote quote from author interview.

O'Connor and Ellison comments about Belli from *The Poison Patriarch*, Hunt quote from Belli from *The Poison Patriarch* and Nancy Ragano quotes from *The Poison Patriarch*. Farris quotes re Belli and Oswald from author interview. HSCA comment re: Marcello from HSCA report. Tonahill quotes re: Kilgallen/Jack Ruby interview from Tonahill videotaped interviews by Kathryn Fauble associate. Pelosi footnote comment from *The Kennedy Half Century* by Larry J. Sabato, 2014. Blakey and Billing's comments re: Marcello empire from *The Plot To Kill the President*, 1981. Vaccara quote regarding Marcello based on, *Carlos Marcello: The Man Behind the JFK Assassination*, 2014. Allegations against Marcello from HSCA report.

Chapter 27

Lee Israel comments re: Kilgallen tracing Ruby's mob ties from September 30, 1995 audiotaped interview with researcher Kathryn Fauble's associate. Whiteside comments about Kilgallen JFK assassination from Whiteside book, *Cry* and 1998 episode of E! Network's *Mysteries and Scandals*. Kilgallen quotes re: DA Wade and links between Oswald and Ruby from her *Journal-American* column.

Pelosi footnote comment from *The Kennedy Half-Century* by Larry J. Sabato, 2013. Details re: Kilgallen New Orleans trips from Marc Sinclaire interview. Kilgallen comment re: Ruby from *Journal-American* archives. Ruby/Marcello/Pecora connection from HSCA report. Jack Anderson column footnote quote from *Washington Post* archives, September 7, 1956.

Henry Wade's comments re: Ruby sentence from *Journal-American* archives. Information regarding Ruby trial reversal from court records. Information regarding Ruby death from author interviews with Joe Tonahill and Bill Alexander and from *Chicago Tribune*, January 1967.

Maggie McNelli's quote from *NY Post Daily Magazine* article, April 1960. Jean Bach quote about Kilgallen being the "apple of Jim's eye" from E! Network's *Mysteries and Scandals* program, 1998. Mark Lane's quote about Kilgallen based on Israel book. Kilgallen quote from Hearst Syndicate.

Chapter 28

Information on peculiar circumstances at death scene from Marc Sinclaire videotaped and audiotaped interviews by Kathryn Fauble associate. Kilgallen quote re: Marilyn Monroe death from Hearst Syndicate. Quote re: Kilgallen wearing earrings from Israel book. Hassan quotes re: servants and James Clement from author interview November 1, 2015. Simpson quotes from videotaped interview.

Sinclaire quotes re: Kilgallen's actions prior to final *What's My Line?* appearance from his videotaped interview. Heller's comment from Kathryn Fauble associate. Daly's comment re: Kilgallen appearance at final *What's My Line?* program from Israel book. Account of Kilgallen and Bob Bach at P. J. Clarke's from Israel book. Jean Bach footnote account of Bob Bach and Kilgallen from E! Network's *Mysteries and Scandals*, 1998. Information about Kilgallen's townhouse from Cry by Jonny Ray and a blog posting titled "Testing the Waters: A Place to share some stories, air some laundry, and hear some feedback" by Kerry Kollmar on April 6, 2009 (kerryslifeblog .blogspot.com/2009_12_01_archive.html) viewed August 26, 2015. Spiegel's quotes from Bob Considine column, Hearst Syndicates.

Sinclaire's footnote quotes re: Kilgallen "liking" the Regency Hotel Bar due to multiple entrances from his videotaped interview by Kathryn Fauble associate. Ellen O'Hara quote from Kerry Kollmar blog.

Chapter 29

Bill Franklin and Johnnie Ray's quote about Kilgallen and JFK assassination research and missing assassination file from *Cry* by Jonny Whiteside, 1994. Eichler's comments about Ray from author interview, 2015. Rossi comment from www.retrokimmer.com/2013/10/the-mysterious-death-of-dorothy .html. Liz Smith comment from same website. Jean Bach's comment about Kilgallen and "violent action" from E! Network's *Mysteries and Scandals*, 1998.

Earl Ruby comment about Kilgallen's death being "suspicious" from Sept. 30, 1995 audiotaped interview with researcher Kathryn Fauble's associate. Phyllis McGuire's statement about Kilgallen's death from author Lee Israel audiotaped interview September 30, 1995.

Richard Kollmar's comment re: Kilgallen file from Israel book. Whiteside's comments from his book, *Cry*. Information about Frank Costello being friends with Kilgallen from *New York Post Daily Magazine*, April 28, 1960. Sinclaire's comments re: Kilgallen/Costello friendship from his videotaped interview. Footnote re: Costello and Hoover friendship from *J. Edgar Hoover: The Man and his Secrets* by Curt Gentry. Paul Anka information about Costello from Anka's book *My Way*.

Footnote quote re: Marie Eichler from Lee Israel from her book *Can You Ever Forgive Me?*, 2008. Quote about Kilgallen/Costello friendship from *New York Post Daily Magazine* article, April 1960. Quotes about Hoover/Costello friendship from *J. Edgar Hoover: The Man and the Secrets* by Curt Gentry, 1991.

Information about Frank Costello from *Mafia Kingfish* by John H. Davis, 1989 and *Five Families* by Selwyn Raab, 2005. Pileggi quote from author interview, November 2015. Costello being a "silent partner in the Copacabana" from "Frank Sinatra Had A Cold" on the official website of acclaimed writer Gay Talese (www.randomhouse.com/kvpa/talese/). Mark Lane quote from Liz Smith column titled "The Kilgallen Mystery" from *Spokane Daily Chronicle*, December 25, 1976. Swing quote from *Cry* by Jonny Whiteside. Sinclaire quotes from videotaped interviews by researcher Kathryn Fauble's associate. Liz Smith column from nationally syndicated articles. Simpson quote from videotaped interview by Kathryn Fauble associate.

Chapter 30

Katherine Stone account from videotaped interview by Kathryn Fauble associate. Harvey Daniels comment from Israel book. Information about the mix of a "Mickey Finn" and chloral hydrate from the Palo Alto (CA) Medical Foundation and www.drugaddictiontreatment.com/types-of-addiction /prescription-drug-addiction/chloral-hydrate-addiction/.

Information about barbiturates from Physicians' Desk Reference Book (www.pdr.net/. Randall Boris comments from author interview 2015. Kilgallen blood alcohol level from Israel book. Medical information re: Kilgallen liver, etc. from NYC medical examiner's report. Sinclaire comments re: Kilgallen and pills from his videotaped interview by Kathryn Fauble associate. Dr. Hoffman quotes from author interview Feb. 2 and November 1, 2015.

Information regarding Regency Hotel management's refusal to permit Lee Israel to interview employees from Israel book. Drs. Baden and Hoffman information from Israel book.

Chapter 31

Marc Sinclaire's statement re: Kilgallen's loneliness from his videotaped interview with Kathryn Fauble associate. Kilgallen meeting Ron Pataky from her *Journal-American* column 1964. Account of European trip from Box Office and Louis Sobel account from *Journal-American* archives. Israel account of Pataky meeting Kilgallen from Israel book. Pataky version of meeting from Larry Jordan *Midwest Today* interview, 2007. Marc Sinclaire's differing account re: Pataky statements from Sinclaire 1995 video interview. Jill Kollmar comments re: author interview, 2014 and 2015. Conflicting accounts by Pataky to the mid-2000 interviews from Israel book. Israel comments from letter to researcher Kathryn Fauble, April 7, 1992. Additional information about Ron Pataky based on *Cry* by Jonny Whiteside, 1994.

Pataky comments to Larry Jordan from *Midwest Today* article. Sinclaire re: valentines from Pataky to Kilgallen from videotaped interview. Swing comments re: Pataky and Kilgallen from Israel book. Larry Jordan comments re: Pataky from author interview. Pataky letters from Kathryn Fauble collection.

Pataky re: whereabouts on day Kilgallen died from author interview with Larry Jordan. Horricks conflicting story from researcher Kathryn Fauble letter files. Pataky comments to Larry Jordan based on author interview with Jordan. Bob Bach comments from Israel book. Kilgallen letter to Pataky from researcher Kathryn Fauble files. Pataky admitting telephone conversation with Kilgallen from Israel. Pataky about learning of Kilgallen death from Kathryn Fauble interview.

Pataky quotes re: Kilgallen not being suicidal and re: his knowing Sam Giancana from Larry Jordan interview. Footnote quote from Paul Anka about Giancana and Phyllis McGuire from Anka book, *My Way*. CIA mention of Roselli, McGuire and Kilgallen from CIA files. Footnote quote re: Pataky future after leaving Columbus newspaper from his Facebook page.

Pataky comments about Giancana and mobsters, police contacting him, and not visiting Kilgallen's townhouse from Larry Jordan interview. Footnote re: Pataky column on Phyllis McGuire play from *Columbus Citizen-Journal*. CIA quote re: Roselli sitting at table with Kilgallen at Copacabana from CIA files.

Chapter 32

Pataky comments from Larry Jordan interview. Confusion about Regency Hotel keys from Sinclaire videotaped interview. Pataky conflicting stories re: attending *WML?* show from Larry Jordan interview. Sinclaire comments re: "Beau" from videotaped interview. Pataky footnote comments re: *WML?* viewing on Sundays from interview by Kathryn Fauble associate.

Sinclaire and Simpson comments from videotaped interviews. Pataky denials from Larry Jordan interview. Sinclaire quotes re: Pataky from videotaped interview. Quote about Pataky's character from anonymous source. Footnote re: Kilgallen's column not mentioning Pataky from *Journal-American* archives. Marlon Swing's comment from E! Network's *Mysteries and Scandals*, 1998. Lane, Gebbia and Whiteside comments from sources noted above

Headlines and information about Pataky violent behavior with actress Anna Maria Alberghetti from *Columbus Dispatch* and Israel book. Footnote quote from Israel re: Alberghetti from letter to researcher Kathryn Fauble, April 7, 1992. Details regarding Pataky/Otis confrontation from *Columbus Dispatch*, April 1971.

Chapter 33

Ron Pataky comments based on interview with this author on October 22, 2014. Marc Sinclaire's comments re: Pataky quotes from his videotaped interview. Dee Anthony's comment about Pataky from Kathryn Fauble associate audio interview.

Chapter 34

Sinclaire's comments re: Pataky involvement in Kilgallen's death from his videotaped interview. Earl Wilson column from *Milwaukee Sentinel*, November 22, 1965. Pataky police officer information from *Columbus Dispatch* April 14, 1971. Pataky "Arthur" column from *Columbus Citizen Journal*, November 17, 1965.

Pataky inconsistent statements based on various Pataky interviews – Lee Israel, Larry Jordan and this author. Pataky poems from Larry Jordan and from Pataky website. Source: www.seeyouhome.com/ron/worlds-p-r-n-f /DOOR3.pdf (viewed August 16, 2014).

Chapter 35

Pataky quotes from author interview October 22, 2014. Author comments based on previous text. Footnote comments by Pataky from Larry Jordan interview.

Chapter 36

Pataky statements from author interview September 11, 2015 and February 19, 2016 emails. Sinclaire quotes re: Kilgallen "mystery" and Zander footnote from videotaped and audiotaped interviews 2000. Information re: article describing Kilgallen from *Journal-American* archives. Description of Kilgallen and reference to Kilgallen being called "Dorothy Spillgarbage" from *New York Post Daily Magazine* article, April 1960. Funeral information and account of Kilgallen bravery in saving baby in fire from *Journal-American*, November 11, 1965. Hearst Jr. quotes from *New York Post Daily Magazine* article and The Hearsts by Hearst, Jr. and Jack Casserly, 1991., April 1969. Bennett Cerf and Steve Allen quotes on Kilgallen from www.youtube.com/watch?v=aMT_KFb1THA. Sinclaire comments from videotaped interview 2000 and audiotaped interview 1997. Johnny Ray comments re: Kilgallen from Joe Franklin program: (www.youtube.com /watch?v=lbobzDRDYRc)

Nizer, Merrick, Davis and Crawford quotes about Kilgallen from Hearst Syndicate, November 1965. Editorial about Kilgallen and Slocum column from *Journal-American* archives, November 1965. Dominick Dunne comment re: Kilgallen from *Vanity Fair*, August 2000. Information on *Counterattack* release, Bobby Short Plaza Hotel incident, Marilyn Monroe column, Lenny Bruce information based on Israel book. Defending Johnnie Ray on Detroit criminal charges based on *Ray* by Jonny

Whiteside, 1994. Sam Sheppard case information from Supreme Court file and *Murder One* by Dorothy Kilgallen, 1967.

Chapter 37

Column about JFK assassination from *Journal-American* archives. Facts about Kilgallen death from NY Post NY Journal-American and NYC medical examiner report. Information regarding Bryan article by Rowe based on *Union-Tribune* and several author emails to both. Blakey quotes from author interview. Broich comments from *Midwest Today* interview.

John Broich quotes from Kathryn Fauble's associate's interview. Eileen Broich, Chris Broich and Steve Goldner quotes based on author interviews 2015. Joe Bonnano footnote information from his own book, *A Man of Honor*, 2003. Hoffman comments on ME office and Goldner quotes from author interview, November 1, 2015.

Chapter 38

Coo and Sheppard case information from *Murder One*. Kilgallen column on justice from *Journal-American* archives. Quote from *Journal-American* reader re: Kilgallen from *New York Post Daily Magazine*, April 1960.

Epilogue

Dr. Martin Schorr quote from author interview. Cerf comment from *Journal-American* archives. Information about JFK assassination from *The Poison Patriarch* by Mark Shaw, 2013.

Index

ABOUT THE
AUTHOR

A California attorney and the author of over 20 books including *The Poison Patriarch*, *Miscarriage of Justice*, *Beneath the Mask of Holiness*, and *Down for the Count*. Mark Shaw was a legal analyst for *USA Today* and CNN during the Mike Tyson, O.J. Simpson and Kobe Bryant trials. His articles have been featured in *Huffington Post*, *USA Today*, and the *Aspen Daily News*, among others. More about Mr. Shaw may be found at markshawbooks.com.